Krishan Chopra M.D., Fellow of the Royal College of Physicians, Edinburgh, was attached to the Cardiac Department of London Hospital and the National Heart Hospital, London in the capacity of a visiting physician for the year 1954. Formerly Professor of Medicine and Chief of Cardiology at A.F. Medical College, Pune, Dr. Chopra has been Head of the Department of Medicine and Cardiology at the prestigious Mool Chand Khairati Ram Hospital, New Delhi for the last twenty-five years. He lectures widely and is on the faculty of the Centre for Professional Development in Higher Education at the University of Delhi. He is also Chairman of the Heart Care Foundation of India.

Dr. Chopra is the author of *Save Your Heart* and has contributed chapters to many other books. He has published over 300 articles and is Consultant Editor of the *Indian Journal of Clinical Practice, Medinews* and *Indian Cardiothoracic Journal.*

Krishan Chopra M.D.
Foreword by Deepak Chopra M.D.

YOUR LIFE IS IN YOUR HANDS

THE PATH TO LASTING HEALTH AND HAPPINESS

ELEMENT

Shaftesbury, Dorset • Boston, Massachusetts • Melbourne, Victoria

© Element Books Limited 1999
Text © Krishan Chopra 1997
Foreword © Deepak Chopra 1997

First published in India in 1997 by Penguin Books India (P) Ltd.

This edition first published in the USA in 1999 by
Element Books, Inc.
160 North Washington Street
Boston, MA 02114

Published in the UK in 1999 by
Element Books Limited
Shaftesbury, Dorset SP7 8BP

Published in Australia in 1999 by
Element Books and distributed
by Penguin Australia Ltd
487 Maroondah Highway, Ringwood,
Victoria 3134

Cover design by Slatter-Anderson
Design by Mark Slader
Typeset by Footnote Graphics, Warminster, Wilts
Printed and bound in the USA by Courier Westford

British Library Cataloguing in Publication
data available

Library of Congress Cataloging in Publication
data available

ISBN 1-86204-500-3

This book gives non-specific, general advice and should
not be relied on as a substitute for proper medical consultation.
The author and publisher cannot accept responsibility for illness
arising out of the failure to seek medical advice from
a doctor.

For my wife, Pushpa
and my children
Deepak, Sanjiv, Rita, Amita
and grandchildren
Priya, Mallika, Gautam, Kanika and Bharat

Contents

Foreword

By
Deepak Chopra M.D.

One of my earliest memories of my father is watching him sail away on an ocean liner from the docks of Bombay into the sunset on his way to England. My brother, Sanjiv, who was then three years old, and I, six years old, clutched our toys as we watched the ship disappear over the horizon. Daddy was going to England to learn to be a cardiologist. If he passed his exams Daddy would come back in eight months, and bring us many more toys. We were excited at the prospect and couldn't understand why our mother was crying. Daddy had received a scholarship to go to England for advanced studies but it was only enough to pay for his passage. Mother, Sanjiv, and I were to stay behind in India, and pray every day to God that Daddy would be successful in his studies, so we could soon be united as a family again.

Many months later we received a telegram from England saying that my father had passed his exams and had been made a member of the Royal College of Physicians in Edinburgh. The evening on which we received the telegram was an occasion of great celebration. My grandfather (Daddy's father) took out his old army rifle and shot a few rounds into the sky. We cut a cake and then my grandfather took us to see a movie that had just been released in Bombay, *Ali Baba and the Forty Thieves*.

We came back late from the movie and went to bed very excited. At about 2 a.m., we woke up to the sound of crying and wailing. Grandfather had died in his sleep. He was cremated the next day and his ashes were brought home in a small earthen jar. Daddy returned three weeks later on the ship from Southampton, England. (It took three weeks in those days to travel from England to India.)

He came home on a Saturday morning. I remember him entering the house, going up to my grandmother, holding her in his arms, sobbing and weeping loudly. Several minutes later, he turned to us with teary eyes and said, "Come to the other room, I have some wonderful toys for you." Indeed they were wonderful—an electrical train with tracks and tunnels, a plastic clown that made funny faces, a cricket bat, and many other marvelous things—but we were no longer interested in our toys. We wanted to know why Grandfather, who had taken us to the movies a few days ago, had disappeared and why, when we asked where he was, my grandmother would point to a small earthen jar whose ashes would soon be immersed in the Ganges River.

These incidents sparked a lifelong search in me for the meaning of life and death and also laid the foundation for my future insights into the mind-body connection. As I later learned, Grandfather had a severe heart condition and had already outlived all his doctor's predictions. He had been waiting for Daddy to pass his exams, to receive that telegram from England, to shoot some rifle rounds into the sky, cut a cake, and take his grandchildren to see *Ali Baba and the Forty Thieves*. He wanted to do all that before he undertook his next karmic journey.

My father always encouraged us to ask questions, but never answered them directly. He would tell us stories and leave us to figure out the answers. My dad is the greatest storyteller in the world and since childhood my life had been graced by dramatic, romantic tales of his encounters with people and patients. Stories from World War II, when he was part of the British Army under siege by the Japanese in Burma, stories of Lord Mountbatten and having dinner with the Queen of England. Stories of miraculous lives and recoveries, stories of joy and suffering, ignorance and enlightenment. Oh, they were so good—and his stories created for us a magical world of mystery, adventure, wonderment, and enchantment.

This book contains a lot of the wisdom he imparted to us as my brother and I grew up and as my father learned through his own experiences of life. I believe this book also touches on the more universal aspects of my father's life. Its wisdom will transform the lives of all those who read it so that as they metabolize the insights contained here they will develop the ability to literally take responsibility for their well-being and begin to understand what it means to hold your life in your own hands. This book is in many ways the essence of his life. As I go through its pages, a phrase here, a sentence there, will trigger a chain of memories that evoke the deeply felt karmic bond that I shared and continue to share with my father. Today, I know that the person I call "me" is actually a bundle of memories and desires, dreams and wishes cultivated so tenderly by this man, Krishan Chopra. More than anything else I feel deep gratitude and love for him and my mother who so effortlessly and spontaneously and magically shared their love with Sanjiv and me and nurtured us from tender beginnings to who we are today.

Preface

The wisdom of thousands of years of mystical experience is walking hand in hand with the emerging knowledge of our science.

—FRED ALAN WOLF

This is a wonderful time to be on earth. A new and positive vision of life and health is emerging, based on the latest findings of modern science combined with some of the most ancient wisdom on the planet. This new knowledge offers the key to a long, healthy, and productive life to anyone who wants to take advantage of it.

Very few people know what positive health is. The majority of us are busy abusing our bodies and slowly killing ourselves, primarily because our lives are not in harmony with the laws of nature. A huge proportion of our serious illnesses today, including cancer and heart disease, are largely due to our lifestyles, and are fully preventable.

Six persons die every minute around the globe due to smoking. Many others die of alcohol abuse, or because they overeat or eat the wrong foods. Most of us don't get enough exercise even though it is medically indisputable that exercise is necessary for good health and a feeling of vitality. Most of us are attacking our own minds and bodies with negative thoughts of jealousy, greed, or anger.

The affluent and upper middle class suffer from over-consumptive malnutrition. They eat too much, though studies have shown that persons who eat less live longer, and they eat unhealthy, heavy, fatty foods that have definitely been correlated with increased heart disease and cancer.

Each morsel of food I eat or juice I drink, each breath of air that I inhale, each thought and feeling that I have gets metabolized; it goes to each of the fifty trillion cells in my body and becomes me. What we eat thus matters a lot, but what is eating us matters much more.

It has now been scientifically verified that our thoughts and mental attitudes are the most crucial determinant of our physical state of health, our well-being, happiness, efficiency, creativity, and productivity. Our thoughts of love and fear, pleasure and pain, compassion and hate, anger or jealousy are not ephemeral, transient abstractions but bioelectrical medical events that determine our health or disease, happiness or unhappiness.

With this knowledge so clearly laid out before us, we now have a very clear choice: to participate in actively creating good health by developing good habits, or to lower our immunity and weaken our bodies by wrong, unhealthy lifestyle choices.

Good sound sleep, not too little or too much; the right amount of nourishing food; regular exercise and participation in sports; listening to soothing music; laughter; playing with children and being childlike yourself; not falling victim to addictions; having regard for basic human values and the laws of nature; doing useful, enjoyable work; and using the ancient wisdom of yoga, meditation, and prayer for spiritual development—these are some of the keys to health and happiness. If we want to have a long and useful life, it is of the utmost importance that we take advantage of this knowledge. That is what this book is all about.

As you go along in your reading, I hope you will observe that the theme and spirit of this book, in the words of Paramahansa Yogananda, is to "eat right, act right, and above all think right." With these three powerful principles we can pave the way to healthy, happy, and productive living.

Ancient wisdom tells us that the origin of love is at the cosmic level, and offers guidance to help us tap that love. With love in our hearts, we can have the best that life has to offer. We can work vigorously, and yet rise above selfish limitations. Then our work and achievements will be useful not only to us, but also to the community and the world. Through ancient practices such as meditation and yoga, we can overcome stress, petty jealousies, anger, and hostility and gain inner harmony, joy, peace, and contentment.

Stress has been with us since we lived in caves a couple of million years ago. We have survived it through the ages because of the development of the human intellect and the faculty of discrimination, basic human values, and spirituality.

Ironically, despite all our modern advances, we are victims of stress more often in these modern times than ever before. The present age is full of fear, suspicion, conflicts, and struggles. Our way of life has been eroded. We are constantly drifting toward self-aggrandizement, selfishness, aimless living, hatred, lack of contentment, and ultimately self-destruction. All this is happening because there is scant regard for human values. Far more importance has been given to the race for material wealth and the quest for transient worldly pleasures than to spiritual development and basic human goodness.

It is here that ancient wisdom can come to our aid. The knowledge is there. Meditation, pranayama, asanas, the knowledge of Dharma, the precious teachings about Self-realization— the knowledge has been around for thousands of years, and scientific research is every day verifying its truth. We just need to make use of it.

As an Indian, I am proud that many of these great teachings come from the rich heritage of my tradition. As a physician, I am proud that much of the new knowledge about longevity and health is emerging from medical research. As a father, I am proud that one of the world's guiding lights in the synthesis of East and West, ancient wisdom and modern science, is my son, Deepak Chopra.

I have had a very good innings in life, and ultimately got the best reward anyone could ever wish for. Both my sons, Deepak and Sanjiv, were gifted children, and since they matured into manhood, have made their mark as outstanding authors and teachers and done their parents proud in every way. There could be no better honor for me.

Let me make it clear that I take no credit for it. On the contrary, my children and grandchildren have been and continue to be my best teachers. I know well that there is no reason whatsoever for parents to take any credit for the success of their children in life. According to the theory of karma, which I elaborate in the early parts of the book, we bring our own accumulated knowledge and tendencies with us into our present life. As parents, the best we can do is provide the conditions for our children to unfold the potential they already carry within their minds and hearts.

I have written this book in my late seventies. I have been practicing medicine for over fifty years, and continue to work full time today, often twelve to fifteen hours per day. I work in the hospital as a consulting cardiologist and engage in various academic activities, conferences, and continuing medical education programs for doctors. I also devote a lot of time to public awareness programs, teaching prevention of heart disease. I enjoy my work, and I am sure it keeps me young.

The book contains no fiction, only real-life incidents, encounters, and experiences that concerned me, my patients, and my family, including my parents, my wife and children, and my grandchildren. I include them only because they have been instructive for me and have enriched my life, and I believe they might be of some value and interest to you. Like many doctors, I have had the privilege of being in the confidence of my patients and have shared their secrets and been a part of some very difficult times in their lives. I am grateful for this privilege and for the love it enabled us to share. The names of patients and others whose cases have been cited in the book have been changed to protect their identities.

Doctors have no geographical or religious boundaries. Our aim is, and should be, to share the responsibility not only to prolong individual lives, but also to improve the quality of life in the whole of society and throughout the world. We all have to get together, aim at the creation of a disease-free society in which all remain healthy physically, psychologically, and spiritually, and work together to achieve it.

Acknowledgments

This book is dedicated to my late mother whose adherence to the path of Dharma was an example to everyone around her. She firmly believed that anything gained in this world, whether spiritual knowledge or material wealth, while negotiating one's duty, is futile.

To Pushpa, my wife, for the silent lessons in spirituality over the five decades of our married life. She has been the spirit behind all decisions in my life, including the idea of writing this book.

To my children, Deepak, Sanjiv, Rita, and Amita, and to our grandchildren, Priya, Mallika, Gautam, Kanika, and Bharat. As you go through this book you will agree that I started learning from all of them right from their early childhood, and the process of learning is continuing.

To all my patients, whose secrets I shared.

To my colleagues Dr. K.K. Aggarwal and Dr. H.K. Chopra, consultant cardiologists, who have been with me through thick and thin. They have been constantly engaged in the battle against death and the crusade for prevention of disease, and have worked hard to spread the message of health and hope contained in this book.

My grateful thanks are due to Lynn Franklin for her critical literary comments and guidance in the preparation of the final manuscript and publication of this book, and for introducing me to Jack Forem, a brilliant editor. I am indebted to Jack and deeply appreciate his contribution and patience. My special thanks go to David Davidar, of Penguin Books, for his valuable suggestions on the preparation of the final manuscript and for the title of the book, and to Krishan Chopra, also at Penguin, for his constructive editorial input. My thanks to Julia McCutchen and Susan Lascelles of Element Books for their enthusiasm and involvement in the publishing and editing of this revised edition.

I owe my gratitude to Ms. Annie Durai and Mr. Brij Mohan Tiwari for typing the script, always smilingly.

Copyright permission to use excerpts is gratefully acknowledged from the following:

Timelife Syndication, New York for *Time* magazine article, "Can Science Slow the Aging Clock," in the issue dated January 20, 1997; the Sharma Mai Self-Realization Fellowship International, Los Angeles for "The Way of Salvation," by Sri Daya Mata in *Self-Realization*, Summer 1996; the *Hindu* and Dr. M. Srinivasan, author of "Occult Chemistry Re-evaluated," published on October 30, and November 6, 1994; Frank Bracho for "Food Habits of the Pre-Columbian Peoples," a personal communication subsequently published in the *Journal of Alternative and Complementary Medicine*, Washington D.C.; Sri Ramakrishna Math, Madras for *Patanjali's Yoga Sutras* by Swami Prabhavananda and Christopher Isherwood; Swami Parthasarthy, author of *The Symbolism of Hindu Gods and Rituals* (Vedanta Life Institute, Bombay); and the State University of New York Press for *The Concise Yoga Vasistha* by Swami Ventakesananda.

God made the rivers flow,
They cease not from flowing,
They feel no weariness,
They fly swiftly like birds in the air
May the stream of my life
Flow into the river of righteousness
Loosen the bonds of fear if any that bind me
Let not the thread of my Song of Love and Happiness
Be cut while I sing and let
Not my work end before its fulfillment

—RIG VEDA, 11:28

PART ONE

YOUR LIFE IS IN YOUR HANDS

1

The Global Epidemic of Stress

Health is the foundation of well-being virtue, prosperity, wealth, happiness, and salvation.

—CHARAKA SAMHITA

I first met Savita fifteen years ago when she came to my office with her father-in-law, who was suffering from a heart ailment. She was a young bride then, and her husband, Pradeep, a bright young man, was working in marketing. They seemed to be a happy couple.

I didn't see them again until two years ago, when Pradeep brought Savita to my office complaining of pains in her chest. The pains had been going on for several weeks, but for the last two or three days they had been occurring at the slightest exertion and were accompanied by shortness of breath and some sweating.

The ECG and other tests confirmed that Savita had angina. She was only thirty-four—rather young for coronary heart disease. We kept her in the hospital for a few days till her pains stabilized. When her condition improved, I talked to her and Pradeep in depth. It seems that Savita had been suffering from depression and insomnia for nearly a year. As we spoke, the reasons came out.

Savita told me that she was very proud of Pradeep. "He is a

wonderful husband and doing so well," she said. Indeed, Pradeep was an achiever. A very ambitious, hard-working person, he went up the ladder quickly in the company he was working for when I first met them, and now had his own chain of companies. He was doing extremely well financially. But there were problems.

"He has no time for breakfast," Savita told me. "He hastily gobbles toast or something before he rushes to his office. At work there are tensions, anxieties, and the rush to beat each deadline before the next one comes up. We have no regular meals. When he finally reaches home—late, of course—he has a sandwich in one hand and a pen in the other. And he has a phone and a fax machine in the car."

"I can't help it," Pradeep broke in, somewhat defensively. "I have to work in the car. What else can I do? It takes a long time commuting to and from the office. You know how bad the traffic is. I can't afford to waste all that valuable time."

Savita picked up where she had left off. "In the office there are endless cups of tea and coffee, and overflowing ashtrays. At home, we have a fax machine in the bedroom, and there are phone calls all the time. When it is supposed to be our sleeping time, it is office time in New York and Pradeep has to talk business over the phone.

"Often he comes home so late, because of an important meeting, that I'm already asleep. This leads to arguments between us.

"Occasionally he may be home a little earlier than usual, but then he might ask me to get ready in just a few minutes as he has invited some friends for cocktails. Over drinks, the discussions on business matters with his clients from abroad may go on for hours, and we reach home very late.

"I thought that if I did some work in his office, that would keep me busy and I would see more of him. But in the office, I would hear discussions about the intricacies of business, and that was an extra strain on me."

Clearly, Savita's problems with her heart stemmed to a great extent from the stressful lifestyle she and Pradeep were leading.

Indeed, the effects of stress on the heart have been known since time immemorial. Five thousand years ago, according to the story recorded in the ancient Indian epic the Ramayana, King Dasharatha, in order to honor a boon he had long ago promised to his young queen Kaikeyi, had to send his beloved son Rama, heir to the throne, to the forest for fourteen years. The extreme agitation he felt resulted in his dying of cardiac arrest.

As the English physician William Harvey wrote in the early seventeenth century, "Every affection of the mind is attended by either pain or pleasure, hope or fear, and is the cause of agitation whose influence extends to the heart."

We gave Savita a balloon angioplasty treatment for her angina, and she felt much better. I didn't wish to upset her, but I had to inform her that in more than 33 percent of patients who undergo this treatment, restenosis (obstruction) recurs at the same or another site within only about three months, and the procedure has to be repeated. She needed to do something about the stress in her life.

Women and Heart Disease: Victims of Our Modern Lifestyle?

If you are thinking that it is unusual to use a woman as an example of a cardiac patient, until quite recently you would have been completely right. I used to teach my students in the medical college that women *never* have angina or heart attacks before the onset of menopause. The reason? Female hormones are protective against atherosclerosis, the hardening of the arteries caused by fatty deposits on the inner lining of the blood vessels, and atherosclerosis of the coronary arteries is a cause of heart attacks.

The situation has changed dramatically in recent years. Now more than one third of heart attack and angina patients worldwide are young women between the ages of thirty and forty-five. Apparently the protective effect of female sex hormones has been neutralized by women's newly acquired lifestyle.

The majority of heart disease patients still are men, but more than one third are now women. The rate is higher in urban areas and is rising steeply everywhere.

The strongest predictor of death from heart disease in women is diabetes, which carries a 4.5-fold increased risk. There are over ten million diabetics in India, the majority of them women. There are over fifteen million diabetics in the USA and nearly 1.5 million in the UK.

Another major risk factor, for both men and women, is high cholesterol levels in the blood. The body makes more cholesterol when you are emotionally stressed, and women are under greater emotional pressure than ever before. Women's average levels of both total cholesterol and the "bad" LDL cholesterol (low density lipoprotein) are high, while levels of the "good" protective cholesterol (high density lipoprotein, or HDL) are low.

Triglycerides, another risk factor for heart disease, appear in the blood after you eat a meal containing a lot of fat. Triglyceride levels are high among Indian women.

Yet another risk factor, especially when it occurs along with other risks, is obesity, or being significantly overweight. This too is increasingly common among women.

The increased incidence of obesity, diabetes, high cholesterol, and coronary heart disease can be attributed in large part to two main factors:

— poor diet, containing too many sweets, fatty foods, and deep-fried foods which have a lot of hidden fat, and
— insufficient physical activity, a condition common among middle-class and affluent urban women.

In addition, more and more women throughout the world are consuming tobacco, clearly shown to be a major risk factor for heart disease. Tobacco companies have proven adept at using advertising to successfully promote smoking as a sign of women's increasing independence and equality. Tragically, it will also be a cause of women's increasing suffering and death from lung cancer and heart disease.

Savita's life could hardly have been a more perfect example of these risk factors. She never undertook any exercise, was fond of chocolates and sweets, was overweight, and smoked. As the story of her life with Pradeep revealed, she had a lot of mental stress as well. And stress is one of the most powerful causative factors in heart disease. Savita, like her husband, was becoming a time-stacker, juggling with two or more tasks at a time without doing justice to any of them, and living life in the fast lane. She had no time to look at a beautiful sunset and relax; she had no time for traditional yoga and meditation. This adoption of a modern Western lifestyle by Indian women would seem to have brought about some negative effects on their health and happiness. More and more women work outside the home these days. This puts a heavy load on them as they often take primary responsibility for the children and the household in addition to working at their jobs.

Some Stress Has Its Place

Before we go any further, it is important to say that stress is an unavoidable fact of life that has been with us since the beginning of time, and will always be part of human life. Responding creatively to it has been responsible for our continued survival on this planet.

Some stress makes life interesting and meaningful. It keeps you on your toes. If you are driving in chaotic city traffic, it will help keep you alert about your safety and the safety of others around you. But too much stress and tension are cause for concern, as they will almost inevitably interfere with your daily activities and have a negative impact on your health and happiness.

Everybody has ups and downs, and surely life would be dull without them. The stresses and tensions of daily living cannot and should not be completely avoided or eliminated, otherwise life would become a mere passive existence, rather than active, creative living. But if it is not properly managed, stress can become a source of unhappiness and disease.

The Dangers of Stress

Let us first understand what stress can actually do to us; then we will be motivated to find ways to avoid letting it get us down.

Whenever we are faced with a threat, challenge, or danger, our body reacts with what is called the "fight or flight" response. The hypothalamus, a small portion of the brain that controls all the automatic functions of the body, activates the nervous system and hormonal system. What follows is an instantaneous and almost miraculous mobilization of all the body's forces, helping us to tackle the situation and protect ourselves, either by fighting or running away.

Chemicals such as adrenaline and noradrenaline are released into the bloodstream, producing a surge of energy along with faster heart rate (120–200 beats per minute), increased blood pressure, and faster breathing, in order to take in more oxygen. Blood flow to the brain and muscles increases, making us stronger and more alert. The pupils of the eyes dilate to increase visual ability, and hearing power is likewise heightened. Arteries in the limbs constrict and the blood clots more easily, to prevent blood loss in case of injury in the anticipated fight.

When the threatening situation has either been met or diverted, the nervous system allows the muscles to relax, and the heart rate and breathing return to normal. The body is, however, left with a residue of fatigue that can be quite considerable.

This response pattern served well when the primitive ape-man had to face a wild animal, and there are occasional events in life when it is an extremely helpful protective mechanism. But the manifestations are exactly the same when we need to face the boss or rush to meet a deadline, and that is the cause of many health problems.

If we live our life with so much anxiety and tension that everyday events feel like tigers about to pounce, we will be continually gearing ourselves up for battle, and the body's powerful fight or flight response will recur day after day. This will be exhausting, and the resulting build-up of stress on body and mind may end up making us miserable, worried, sleepless, depressed, and ill. And if, like Savita, we allow it to build up week after week, month after month for fifteen years or more, it can also lead to serious heart problems.

Stress can also induce or aggravate other diseases, such as bronchial asthma, colitis, and neurodermatitis. But the brunt of it (especially in the elderly) generally falls on the heart. If there is already high blood pressure, stressors such as extremes of weather as well as anxiety, anger, and frustration may precipitate exaggerated levels of harmful chemicals in the body, which can then aggravate heart disease or trigger a heart attack.

Experiments have been conducted in which a person is asked to do mental arithmetic, solving difficult problems in a short time while a stern examiner repeatedly reproaches him for "incorrect" answers. The result of this stressful experience is a marked rise in both systolic and diastolic blood pressure both in people who have high blood pressure and (to a lesser extent) in those with normal pressure. The heart's rhythms may also become quite irregular.

Stress in the modern world comes from every direction. Many of us are busy killing ourselves slowly by indulging in smoking, alcohol abuse, greed, jealousy, and the race to acquire wealth at all costs, by means fair or foul. Other psychological pressures, such as anxiety, a fit of anger, or having sex with someone other than one's marital partner, have been known to bring on heart attacks.

Repeated exposure to stress induces changes in the nervous system that can provoke the heart to miss beats. Cumulative stress can cause potentially dangerous irregularities of the heart-beat and decreased flow through the coronary arteries.

So far, I have been focusing on Savita because she was the patient who came to me with the actual heart problem. But if you look at Pradeep's life, you can see that he has been under even more stress than his wife for many years, and it is clear that he is headed for trouble.

Pradeep told me that sometimes he feels completely exhausted but does not know what he can do about it. He feels that he has to continue doing what he is doing. "Why should I slow down?" he asked me, without expecting a convincing answer. "Each little bit of effort means another step up the ladder"—in his case to heights of glory in the business world. And why should he stop smoking and consuming alcohol? Both help him to relax. After all, he said, he has no symptoms of disease.

The fact is that Pradeep doesn't realize what he is heading for. Probably his sense of achievement is protective to some extent, and perhaps he has been genetically blessed with a strong constitution, but how long can he keep going? Even now he can't sleep without a tranquilizer. Scotch whisky helps him to relax, but its effect is over in a few hours. He admits he has been more irritable lately, and gets angry with his staff over minor matters.

Although he has no specific disease symptoms, Pradeep certainly cannot be considered a healthy man. Many diseases, including heart disease, may remain in the formative stages for years. During this time the person has no obvious symptoms except perhaps a general feeling of not being quite up to the mark.

Besides, a positive state of health and happiness is much more than the absence of disease.

Symptoms of Stress

Typical symptoms of excess stress include nervousness, heart palpitations, loss of appetite, and difficulty sleeping. These are all symptoms of anxiety. Some anxiety is a natural part of life, but prolonged anxiety can lead to serious conditions such as stomach ulcers, high blood pressure, angina, heart disease, and cancer.

Stress can also bring on depression. Again, a certain amount of depression may be considered normal in human beings and may occur, for example, when we fall short of what we expect or hope for. But prolonged depression can result in deep fatigue, inability to concentrate and to cope with one's responsibilities, sleeplessness, loss of appetite, feelings of worthlessness and hopelessness, and a lack of interest in family, sex, and life in general.

Prolonged or repeated episodes of stress can exacerbate the disease process and accelerate aging. This is illustrated by a rather heartless biology experiment performed a number of years ago, in which young rats were thrown time and again into a tank of water. Rats are not adept swimmers, so the animal will flail about trying in vain to climb out of the tank, only to repeatedly slip back down from the glass wall into the water.

After a few minutes the rat is totally exhausted and on the verge of drowning. The experimenter pulls it out and allows it to rest. The procedure is repeated over the following days. Within a short period, usually less than three weeks, the rat undergoes dramatic changes. The pressure of so much daily stress ages its tissues enormously. If the experiment is continued, the rat will die of "old age" in a matter of a month. On dissection, its heart, liver, lungs, and other organs will be as dark, tough, and fibrous as those of a rat that lived a normal lifespan of two or three years.

This same abnormal acceleration of aging can happen to us, if we allow ourselves to live under prolonged stress. However, unlike the rats, we can use our intellect and sense of discrimination to manage stress to our advantage, and thus avoid premature aging and falling victim to disease. Use your physical and mental abilities to the full, but don't be on the run all the time, or you will be separated from your loved ones much earlier than you should be. Wise men hasten slowly in life.

Causes of Stress

Medical science has identified many causes of stress:

— the death of a spouse, family member, or friend
— a sudden difficult or painful event, such as a major illness, an accident, or loss of a job

— divorce or separation from a spouse
— financial problems, such as reduced income or mounting debts
— a new job
— moving to a new location
— increased family responsibilities, such as a new child
— retirement, with its enforced leisure and reduced income.

Even without these unusual events, the ordinary events of daily life are often stressful enough to bring on serious medical problems. Serum cholesterol, one of the risk factors for heart disease, can be greatly elevated by chronic work stress. One study, for example, found that cholesterol levels went up in certified public accountants in the USA during their tax preparation season.

Increased sickness and higher death rates due to heart attacks are more common in people who lack close family and community ties, and particularly among bereaved men. Heart disease is also more common in people who have financial problems or interpersonal conflicts, and among those who are overachievers or have very aggressive personalities.

Strong emotions, or situations that are emotionally trying, frequently have an adverse affect upon the heart. One of my patients, who was in the hospital for angina, underwent ventricular tachycardia (irregular heartbeat) and showed other changes on his ECG whenever his business partner visited him. Another patient suffered from spasms of the arteries supplying the heart when his estranged wife came for a visit.

Cumulative stress can affect the already functionally compromised hearts of elderly people much more adversely than those of younger people, and then an emotional upheaval can lead to a heart catastrophe. In a study published in the *American Journal of Cardiology* in 1993, patients with a history of angina were asked to recall a recent event that had made them angry. As they thought about the upsetting situation, significant narrowing of the coronary arteries was observed, along with symptoms of angina.

This astonishing fact—that even the *thought* or *memory* of anger can unfavorably affect the heart—gives us an important clue regarding how we can manage stress to create better health. It suggests that our ability to handle stress depends to a large extent on our minds, and on the quality of our thoughts. We will look in depth at this crucial insight in Chapter 2.

Savita's balloon angioplasty treatment completely eliminated her angina symptoms. She was feeling much relieved a few days later, when I had a long talk with her and tried to impress on her that this was not the end of the story.

"You know, you have the same heart as before the treatment," I told her. "The arteries of your heart are not normal, and in one or two places the narrowing is critical. We have dealt with this for the moment, and you are fine. But to remain fine, without those horrible chest pains, and to avoid bypass surgery or the possibility of a heart attack, you need to change your lifestyle. Surgery is not the way to keep healthy. If you continue with the same life you had before the treatment, you are inviting recurrences."

It took me several sittings with Pradeep and Savita to convince them they needed to change their way of living in order to lead a truly happy, healthy life. Once they became convinced, they acted immediately on their new understanding. We had sessions together on diet and on exercise. I sent them to classes to learn yoga asanas, pranayama (breathing exercises), and meditation. It is two years now since both of them began to meditate regularly and took up a low-fat vegetarian diet. Self-destructive habits, including smoking and excess alcohol use, have dropped off spontaneously.

They are far more relaxed, happy, contented, and healthy, and are really enjoying life after many years of suffering. They find more time to play with their children. They are working together now; harmony and peace prevail at home and in the office.

Once Pradeep realized how much stress he was carrying, and how very much better he could feel without drinking, smoking, and pushing himself beyond a reasonable limit, I think he would have accepted some decrease in his business success as a fair price to pay for increased happiness and better health. But the fact is that his business is flourishing even better than before.

You cannot avoid stress in your life, but you can learn to manage it. I have used this chapter to paint a rather dark portrait of the problems of stress and ill health facing us as individuals and as a society. But in the story of Pradeep and Savita I have also given a glimpse of where the solutions lie. In the rest of the book I will introduce you to many effective ways to combat stress and improve your health and well-being using simple, entirely natural means.

Although I have come to recognize and appreciate these strategies over fifty years of medical practice, they are not my private discoveries. Rather, they are the fruit of modern scientific research and time-tested ancient wisdom. In an age of ever-increasing stress, they are vital secrets to good health. And according to the great Indian physician Charaka, "Health is the foundation of well-being, virtue, prosperity, happiness, and salvation."

2

Your Life is in Your Hands

Everything we are is a result of our thoughts.

—BUDDHA, DHAMMAPADA

The birds of worry and care flying over your head you may not be able to change. But you don't have to let them build nests in your hair.

—CHINESE PROVERB

Everything that seems to happen to me I asked for.

—DEEPAK CHOPRA

Trilok Nath was admitted to our hospital with severe chest pain one evening. He was thirty-eight years old, tall and handsome. He never smoked, and consumed alcohol only occasionally and in strict moderation. He had a history of high blood pressure but no heart disease in his family. Nevertheless, the pain was typical of a coronary event and both the ECG and echocardiograph showed definite evidence of a mild heart attack.

His wife Pritima, a good-looking young woman, was the only person who accompanied him to the hospital, and she continued to look after him after he was shifted from the intensive care unit to his room.

Trilok Nath made an uneventful recovery with no complications and no residual damage to the heart. We scheduled
him to come for a checkup two weeks following his discharge.
Instead, he landed in the hospital after only a week, with chest
pains lasting longer than the previous time, along with a fall in
blood pressure, excessive sweating, and his ECG showing marked
changes with a significant missing of beats. This time he took
longer to recover from the attack, and seemed very anxious and
depressed when he was shifted to the intermediate care room.

As I entered his room the next day on my rounds, I saw a
woman with two young children. She was introduced to me as
Geeta, the wife of Mr Trilok Nath! Pritima, the woman who had
been with him before, was not present, though I had seen her
that morning as well as during the four or five days he had been
in intensive care.

On subsequent days, I noticed that even during visiting
hours, only one of the two women would be present in his room
at a time. I didn't know whether they organized it that way or it
was coincidental.

I soon discovered that indeed our patient was suffering
from "Two Wives Syndrome." He was in a state of constant
depression in the presence of either of the "wives," and when
neither one was with him.

I knew that any anxiety or grief lurking in his mind was not
good for him and could be very damaging to his chances of a full
recovery, so one day when he was alone in his room, I asked him
if he knew what was causing his depression. After a little
hesitation, he broke down and told me the story.

"I married Geeta fifteen years ago," he said, "and I had two
fine children from her, the boy and girl you saw with her this
week. She was a simple, good housewife, a good mother, and she
loved me quite devotedly. We lived in Punjabi Bagh [an exclusive
suburb in west Delhi].

"Not long after we were married, I became friendly with
Geeta's younger sister Pritima. She was a lecturer in a college in
south Delhi and lived in an apartment there, all by herself. At

first we were just friends. But in due course the intimacy developed further, and we began living together as husband and wife.

"In the morning, I would leave my house early and spend some time with Pritima on my way to work. Then I would stop and spend part of the evening with her before returning home. After some time, I started staying some nights in her apartment. I would tell Geeta that I had to go out of Delhi on business."

For thirteen long years, Trilok Nath successfully fooled his wife and lived with both sisters. Gradually his attention to his wife dwindled to a minimum. Then, one evening, when he was supposed to be away in Bombay on business, Geeta paid a surprise visit to her sister and found them together. From that moment onward, Geeta knew that her husband had no concept of loyalty to her.

Though Trilok Nath now lived almost entirely with Pritima, he never really thought of getting a divorce from Geeta and re-marrying. "I was never sure I really loved Pritima, or if it was only sensual pleasure," he admitted. I asked him if he was happy living with her. Again, he wasn't sure.

Happiness is not in the object, it is in the mind. A dog chews a dry bone until he hurts his gums and blood comes out. He licks the blood and thinks he is chewing on some juicy meat. Trilok Nath was licking that juicy blood, knowing in his heart of hearts that he was not doing the right thing. How could he really be happy?

It is a legal offence in India to marry a second wife, although some people do it anyhow when they realize that the first wife is too timid to move the court. Geeta was not very educated and Trilok Nath knew she would not confide in her relatives, not even her parents. They wouldn't be able to support her if her husband left her in the lurch, and she was worried about the future of her two children.

None of the three persons involved was at peace, but the worst sufferer was Trilok Nath. "All along I felt guilty underneath, but ever since things have been out in the open, I've realized that I've followed a wrong path by living with my sister-in-law. I've cheated my wife and neglected my children, and the feelings of guilt are with me all the time, day in and day out."

I had noticed earlier that whenever his wife Geeta visited him, he felt his heart missing heats, and the bedside monitor too showed a missing of heartbeats and ECG changes indicating lack of blood supply. The feeling of bearing a heavy weight on his chest sometimes got so bad that he felt as if an elephant was sitting on him.

I knew now that his feelings of guilt were eating him up, and that this was the cause of his two heart attacks. Unfortunately, we didn't yet know the solution; he appeared to be caught in a web of circumstances, a web that he had created.

Coronary angiography revealed that there was a 70 percent narrowing of one of the three major coronary arteries. Apparently stress caused a spasm in the blocked part of the artery, causing further narrowing; this reduced the blood supply to a portion of the heart and precipitated the attacks. The situation warranted dilation of the artery by balloon angioplasty, and we decided to go ahead with it. Trilok Nath wanted to go home for three days to sort out some affairs. He was sent home on medication and was asked to return to the hospital on the fourth day for the procedure.

In those three days, a lot of problems arose for Trilok Nath. Pritima demanded that he marry her immediately, so that in case something happened to him during the operation she would inherit part of his property. She brought her lawyer to demonstrate the urgency of her position. The lawyer told Trilok Nath that if his first wife went to court after he married for a second time, nothing would happen.

"But the law says the husband can go to prison for seven to ten years for bigamy," Trilok Nath protested. "How can you say nothing will happen?"

"Most of the judgeships in India are still held by men, not women," the lawyer explained. "Therefore the courts behave in a lenient manner and arrange things so the husband gets out of the mess lightly. Some sort of compromise is always worked out."

Geeta didn't want to be a party to any discussion. She knew that as things stood, if anything happened to her husband she was the legal heir to the property, and she was not interested in making any changes to her status.

Then Pritima's lawyer suggested a way out. All Trilok Nath would have to do was convert to Islam, since a Muslim in India is permitted to have more than one wife. Then he could legally marry Pritima.

With great reluctance, Trilok Nath succumbed to the pressure and agreed to the proposal.

The day before he was due to go to the hospital, but before either the ceremony of conversion to Islam or the marriage to Pritima took place, Trilok Nath suffered a severe heart attack and died on the way to the hospital. His already heavy burden of guilt had increased, as he did not feel it was morally right for him to convert to another faith simply to circumvent the law of the country and work his way out of his personal dilemma, rather than out of belief. But he didn't have the courage to tell Pritima he would not do it. The only way he found to escape his overwhelming guilt was to have a heart attack and die. He was his own judge, he was the jury, and he alone condemned himself to the punishment.

The Power of Choice

As the story of Trilok Nath so clearly illustrates, our thoughts and feelings can lead either to happiness or unhappiness, sickness or health. Our thoughts determine whether we are marching in the direction of misery or heading for health and happiness.

It's no secret that thoughts and feelings influence behavior. Self-doubt, guilt, hopelessness—thoughts like the ones that must have gone through Trilok Nath's mind in his final hours, "There is no solution to my problem, no way out, I don't even deserve to find an answer because of what I have done"—such thoughts lead to disaster.

Researchers say that if a person devalues himself or sees

himself as a failure, that is how it will be. Visualize and anticipate failure, and you will almost certainly fail. This is called a "self-fulfilling prophecy"—if we don't believe we will succeed, if we don't believe we can be truly happy, we don't really try; thus we prove ourselves correct.

On the other hand, positive thoughts, self-confidence, faith in life and in God, a belief that we *can* discover or create a way to fulfill our needs or desires—such thoughts fuel us with energy for creative action. So our thoughts determine our direction and our likelihood of success.

There is also a direct link between our thoughts and our health. Until recently, the Western scientific model of the connection between mind and body was rather vague. Descartes and other famous philosophers of the seventeenth century helped build walls between the body and mind. They asserted that the two are segregated, divided into separate realms, one abstract, one material, with nothing connecting them. Over the years this became the accepted dogma of science.

But many people before and since did not entirely agree. Aristotle, nearly 3,000 years ago, was among the first to suggest a connection between our mental state and our health. He said that "soul and body react sympathetically to each other." Charles Darwin believed the mind-body connection was important. And Sir William Osler, one of the founders of modern medicine, declared about one hundred years ago that our mind has a lot to do with recovery or failure to recover from disease. People everywhere intuitively sense the truth behind statements like "There is no physician like cheerful thought for dissipating the ills of the body."

However, it is only in the last ten to fifteen years that medical scientists have started seriously rethinking this question. A series of discoveries has demonstrated that three aspects of the body

— the central nervous system, which is the seat of thoughts, ideas, perceptions, emotions, and memories;

— the immune system, which defends the body from infection; and

— the endocrine system, which secretes powerful hormones

are not separate from each other as hitherto believed, but are intimately linked and interconnected. Professor Howard Friedman at the University of California at Riverside analyzed one hundred scientific papers that studied the relationship between people's state of mind and their physical health. He found that certain states of mind are very dangerous: If you are depressed, anxious, chronically pessimistic, angry, or irritable, your chances of getting a major illness are *doubled*. The stress hormones and other brain chemicals generated by these negative states of mind flood the body and reduce the ability of the immune system to fight disease.

Because of such findings, leading scientists such as Candace Pert, formerly of the US National Institute of Mental Health, believe that the walls erected between mind and body by materialistic science are crumbling. Pert asserts that there is no strong distinction between mind (the abstract thinking center), and the material, physical brain. Rather, there is "mind" or intelligence in every cell of the body. Even immune cells are "thinking" cells.

The quantum physicist David Bohm is of the opinion that the word "psychosomatic" should not be used any longer, as it perpetuates the concept that mind and body are different. Health and disease are never entirely physical or entirely psychological. A number of writers today are using the term "bodymind" to demonstrate this new understanding.

Important clues to confirm this view have come from recent advances in brain imaging techniques. Using these methods, scientists can now map and photograph the brain, revealing the workings of your mind, your thoughts and feelings.

Brain-scanning devices exploit the fact that when the brain goes to work performing the tasks that create our subjective world of thoughts and awareness, it consumes energy. The fifty billion or so neurons in the brain are metabolically so active that while the brain accounts for just 2 percent of our body weight, it demands 15 percent of our blood supply and 25 percent of all the oxygen we breathe. Being conscious may feel effortless, but it is the single most energy-consuming thing we do.

Every thought we have involves the generation of electrical and magnetic fields, due to the firing of nerve cells. Every wave of this activity is accompanied by telltale surges of glucose consumption, local blood flow, and the activity of neurotransmitters. The brain-scanning imaging devices can "see," photograph, and map these microscopic fluctuations in the brain. What they see is that as our thought patterns change, so do the patterns of brain activity.

Thoughts as Events

The significance of this is simple but very profound: thoughts are not merely some kind of transient, purely mental abstraction; they are concrete, physical, electromagnetic events.

In the 1980s the technique of Positron Emission Tomography (PET) was first used to record brain activity during the thought process. Glucose tagged with radioactive isotopes was injected intravenously into volunteers while they were lying in the scanner, carrying out various mental tasks, such as solving a puzzle, recalling a happy event, or remembering a moment of anger. A ring of detector crystals then picked up the emitted gamma rays to create a photographic pattern, showing which parts of the brain were undergoing more and less activity.

As research evolved, it became quite clear that different parts of the brain are involved in different mental processes. When the mind is busy focusing careful attention, for example, a part of the frontal lobes (known as the anterior cingulate) "lights up." What is most important for our concern here is that the pattern made by the recall of anger is completely different from the patterns made by thoughts of compassion and love.

This is borne out by research into neurotransmitters (also

known as neuropeptides). Thus far, more than a hundred of these powerful biochemicals have been discovered. These molecules, sometimes called messenger molecules or "bio-chemical words," communicate to the entire body. At one time it was believed that these molecules just "talked" to the brain and nervous system. Now it is known that not only do they also talk to the immune system and the endocrine system, but *those* systems also produce messenger molecules, which talk to each other and to the nervous system.

The three systems are interlinked, which is why the science growing up around these discoveries is being called "psycho-neuroimmunology." Clusters of receptor cells in the brain, stomach, and intestines, in the kidneys, in the heart, and throughout the body, all send and receive messages and talk to each other.

These messenger molecules don't travel in straight lines down the trunks of neurons; they circulate freely through the body's inner space. As Deepak Chopra points out, brain researchers have found cascades of these biochemicals, but unlike a stream these cascades have no banks; they flow any-where and everywhere. Fearful thoughts produce cascades of fearful chemicals, angry thoughts produce angry chemicals, joyful, loving thoughts produce loving, joyful chemicals.

What this means is that it is harmful to your health to hate someone, to be jealous, or to harbor or foster any negative feelings and thoughts. The person you hate does not suffer. He or she may not even know about it. Not only are the thoughts of hatred or jealousy in you like a cancer, eating you up all the time, but also at the same time, the negative and unhappy thoughts are also being translated into "unhappy" neuropeptides, molecules that immediately signal the body to produce chemicals like adrenalin and noradrenaline, which in turn increase heart rate and blood pressure, raise cholesterol, and lower immunity. These stress the body, increase anxiety, and lead to disease.

Positive, happy thoughts produce neuropeptides that are the precursors of chemicals such as endorphins, which give us a feeling of well-being and happiness. When such "happy" molecules are flowing throughout your system, "talking" to trillions of your cells, you manage stress well, raise your immunity, and thus prevent, retard, and even reverse disease.

Health and the Mind-Body Connection

Research has brought forth many examples to demonstrate how our thoughts profoundly affect and determine our state of health and happiness. One recent study, published in the prestigious *New England Journal of Medicine*, on the ten-year survival of patients of breast cancer, revealed that survival was much longer in patients who had a "fighting spirit."

Patients who give up, or who have low self-regard, tend to succumb more readily than those who remain optimistic. Clearly an individual's self-esteem and "hope factor" play a very important part in one's life. One of my own cancer patients told me, "I have cancer, cancer does not have me. I am confident I can get rid of it." He has been doing very well now for many years.

It is truly amazing how our thoughts—even our sub-conscious attitudes—can influence our lives. One of the more remarkable statistics I have heard is that more heart attacks occur on Monday mornings than at any other time. Apparently there are many people who would rather die, or at least go to the hospital, than go to work. After an enjoyable long weekend, they simply don't want to go back to work, so they "decide" to have a heart attack. Of course other people, perhaps even with latent heart disease or other illnesses, love their work and enjoy it; this attitude generates neurotransmitters that increase their immunity and help keep the underlying disease in check.

Researchers are now trying to clone and synthesize the help-ful, positive neuropeptides. I hope they succeed. But I believe that you can heal yourself more effectively by changing your lifestyle, and by engaging yourself in activities and relationships that raise waves of love, happiness, compassion, and other positive thoughts and emotions. Then, in a natural way, the right

type of molecules will be released in your system at the right time
and in the right amount, without any side effects.

Our Thoughts Can Even Influence Whether We Live or Die

Deepak Chopra tells a moving story that occurred when he was
still a medical student. He had developed a quiet rapport with an
elderly patient, a peasant farmer who was dying of liver disease.
When Deepak was to leave the hospital for the next stage in his
studies, he went to the patient's room to say goodbye. "Now that
you are leaving, I have nothing more to live for, and I shall die,"
the man said. It was probably true, as he had wasted away to
about eighty pounds, but Deepak with all good intentions
blurted out, "Don't be silly. You can't die until I come back to
see you again."

When Deepak returned a month later, he was surprised to
see the patient's name on one of the doors, and rushed in to find
the emaciated man curled on the bed in a fetal position. When
the young doctor gently touched the old man, he turned his
huge eyes toward him. " 'You have come back,' he muttered.
'You said I could not die without seeing you again—now I see
you.' Then he closed his eyes and died."

This remarkable story reveals the power of the mind not
only over sickness and health, but also over life and death itself. I
have witnessed more than a few such instances in my medical
practice over the decades. One of them involved a friend of mine.

Hari Nath was chief pathologist at our hospital. In earlier
years we had been colleagues at the medical college in Pune, and
I knew him well as an excellent pathologist, a conscientious
worker, and a gentleman. He took a lot of interest in academic
activities and got on well with all his colleagues. He was a home
bird and spent all his spare time with his wife and two children, a
boy and a girl.

One evening I was informed that there was an emergency in
my waiting room. Upon opening the door I was shocked to find

Hari Nath lying on the floor, unconscious. I was told that he had been sitting in a chair waiting to talk to me when he suddenly fainted.

In a short while he came around. Apparently he had suffered a "vasovagal faint," which generally occurs either when you have been in a stuffy room for quite some time, or when you hear some very bad news.

When he entered my office, much to my surprise, Hari Nath started crying. He told me that his wife, Suraya, had had a fever and a sore throat for the last few days, so he tested her blood that afternoon to see if she had any bacterial infection. To his shock and horror, he found that she had acute myloid leukemia. Of several types of blood cancer, this is the worst, a type that strikes suddenly and with great force.

"I've just come from the All-India Institute of Medical Sciences," he told me. "I showed the slides to Professor Raman, an expert in blood cancer, and he has confirmed the diagnosis. Now I want you to please take over her treatment."

I was flattered by his faith in me, but I am not an oncologist. "No," I said. "The best thing would be to take her to Tata Memorial Cancer Hospital in Bombay."

He did not agree. He felt that he couldn't leave his two children in Delhi and be away in Bombay for weeks at a time. Instead, he caught the evening flight to Bombay and returned the next day with a protocol of chemotherapy treatment laid out by the expert in blood cancer at the Tata Cancer Hospital.

Normally, blood cells are produced in the bone marrow. In this case, instead of normal cells, cancer cells are manufactured at great speed. The treatment consists of knocking off all the abnormal cells with very potent chemotherapeutic agents. In the process the normal cells also get destroyed, but it is hoped that the bone marrow will then start producing healthy cells instead of cancer cells. In some cases this very drastic form of treatment succeeds; a long remission may occur and the patient may become normal for a varying period of time.

During the procedure, as the few protecting white cells are

destroyed, the patient has to be isolated and the room kept sterilized to prevent the very real possibility of a severe infection. We created such a facility for Suraya, and treatment was started. After the first round of chemotherapy there was some improvement, but after the second round the bone marrow could not regenerate any white cells, and a few days later Suraya died of fulminant septicemia.

Hari Nath was a broken man. Everything had happened so quickly, and it was very difficult for him to believe that his wife was gone. In due course he found courage, or at least showed a lot of it. This helped his children pursue their studies. His son became an engineer and moved to the USA, and within about five years his daughter became a doctor and married a young man who lived in England.

Hari Nath was a lonely man now. He started losing weight, and one day, passing his hand over his abdomen, found that his liver and spleen were enlarged. He examined his blood himself, and found that he was suffering from chronic myloid leukemia: the same type of blood cancer that had taken the life of his dear wife Suraya, but not in the same acute form.

He went to England and visited his daughter for a few days. While there he consulted a top Harley Street specialist, who made some recommendations and advised him to watch his blood count; aggressive treatment did not seem to be called for at this point. Then he proceeded to the USA, visited with his son, and returned to Delhi—all without mentioning anything to anyone about his condition.

A few days later he suddenly became quite ill, and died of acute myloid leukemia. It seems that not only did he carry the disease in his mind for many years, but he also knew that his body was suffering from it for quite some time. But he postponed his death by pure will, harboring the dreaded cancer for years in a milder, chronic form until his children graduated and settled in life; then he paid them a last visit, and let go.

This is not as fantastical as it sounds. According to a study from the University of California at San Diego, mortality rates in

China dropped 35 percent the week before the Moon Festival, one of the most auspicious days in the Chinese calendar. When the festival ended, death rates climbed up again, and by a week later were 34 percent higher than the days before the festival.

Does this suggest that people can postpone their death (at least for some period of time) if they have a compelling reason? It seems so. Then, when the important situation has passed, or they think they have completed their mission in life, as Hari Nath believed, they yield to death willingly.

Faith and Healing

The ancient physician Hippocrates said, "Even though a patient may be aware that his condition is perilous, he may yet recover because he has faith in the goodness of his physician." Faith in the doctor or in the treatment can indeed produce tremendous results for a patient. This has been proven by the administration of "placebos" and "nocebos."

A placebo is a dummy drug, such as a sugar pill, that is given to a patient, who is told that it is a powerful new medicine that will cure his condition. Research has clearly shown that a large percentage of patients respond to the "drug," presumably because the doctor has told them it will work. A nocebo is exactly the reverse: it is a viable, proven drug that is given to a patient, but the patient does not respond because the doctor has signalled that the medication may not help him.

This research shows what many people have realized, that doctors have to be very careful when dealing with their patients. The fear in a doctor's eyes, Deepak Chopra writes in *Quantum Healing*, can be a terrible stroke of condemnation. The impulses from the patient's brain, which may have been telling him that he is definitely going to recover, will now convey that he *may* recover, which is quite a different thing. On the other hand, a doctor's reassuring words make all the difference in his recovery.

Medical statistics appeal to the head, but they can sometimes cause a great deal of trouble. I know of a cancer patient who, after surgery and chemotherapy, had a long period of re-mission and was doing very well until one day his family physician showed surprise. He told the patient he was amazed to see him do so well for six years, because according to the statistics patients like him don't survive for more than two to three years. Within the next two weeks the patient started to feel unwell, and was soon found to have a recurrence of his cancer with widespread metastases.

An apparently healthy, normal man with no symptoms went for a routine checkup. His stress test showed some minor changes, and his doctor suggested a diagnostic coronary angio-gram. Although the angiogram showed a not very significant narrowing of two of the coronary arteries, the cardiologist told him that it would be safer to have bypass surgery than to be on medication, as he could have a heart attack at any time.

That night, the patient couldn't sleep because of the anxiety, and from the next day on, he started having angina. It was real angina, because emotional upsets can cause severe spasm of the coronary artery with even a small underlying narrowing.

Adi Shankara said "we grow old and die because we see other people grow old and die." Once the patient knows he has heart disease or cancer, he becomes worried and anxious, because he has heard of or seen people die of their disease. If, on top of that, doctors start telling him statistics, who knows what can happen? That is why the doctor must be careful to uplift the patient and provide encouragement and love.

Positive Thinking Helps

In addition to faith in the doctor or the treatment, other mental factors seem able to activate the body's healing intelligence, factors such as belief in one's own powers of self-healing or the sheer desire to continue living, perhaps in order to care for one's children. The mental/emotional framework is central to the person's recovery.

One of the main themes underlying Deepak Chopra's

teaching and research is that emotions are not just fleeting events in mental space, they are expressions of the fundamental stuff of life. In all ancient traditions, the breath of life is equated with the spirit, and to raise or lower someone's spirits is correspondingly reflected in the body. The body is capable of producing any biochemical response once the mind has triggered the appropriate suggestion; wherever a thought goes, a chemical goes with it.

What, then, is the link between belief and biology? We have just begun to explore what will surely be one of the great themes of medical research in the upcoming decades. And what could be more important? For each person holds in his hands the unbounded potential for shaping his health and aging process. He only has to free himself from his preconceptions regarding disease and the eventual degeneration of the body, liberate his mind from conditioned concepts. Then he can, as the Rig Veda says, move with the infinite in Nature's power, hold the fire of the soul, and life, and healing.

Zest for Life is Healing

During my more than half a century of medical practice, I have often seen the power of the mind help in healing and recovery. Quite a few patients, after an acute heart attack that could have crushed their spirit and their zest for life, have demonstrated a fervent will to live and gone on to live long and well.

Arun Gupta, thirty-seven years of age, was rushed to our hospital with a massive heart attack. His pulse was thready and irregular, and his blood pressure so low it could not be recorded. He was also in a state of cardiogenic shock, a dangerous condition that more often than not ends in death.

Cardiogenic shock occurs when one of the major coronary arteries is blocked with a clot. A large chunk of the heart muscles is without blood supply and oxygen, and its function is grossly impaired. Because of the clot, not enough blood is thrown into circulation during the heart's contraction. The brain gets insufficient blood, and thinking is impaired. The kidneys also don't receive enough blood supply, so urine output falls and eventually a complete kidney shutdown can occur. The heart itself doesn't receive enough nourishment and oxygen, and unless the jeopardized area is salvaged by restoring its blood supply, the heart may stop working and the patient can die.

Medications were given to Mr. Gupta to relieve his pain and raise his blood pressure, and streptokinase was administered to dissolve the clots in the clogged artery of the heart. But there was no response, no improvement.

After three hours I walked out of the intensive coronary care unit to find his wife and relatives waiting. One of the relations was a doctor. After listening to my report on Mr. Gupta's condition, the doctor said, "I know that once a heart attack patient goes into a state of cardiogenic shock, his chances of recovery are remote. But could you tell me what percentage of such patients recover?"

I told him that according to the statistics available from various studies, 90 percent of this type of patient don't recover.

"Then the outlook seems obvious, chances being almost zero," he said. Listening to the pronouncement made by the wise doctor, Gupta's wife started crying.

I have never been one to be carried away by statistics when faced with a seriously ill patient. He may be one of those ten in a hundred who come out of cardiogenic shock, and if he is, as far as he is concerned, the statistic is 100 percent recovery. I admonished the doctor for pronouncing the prognosis on our behalf, and assured Mrs. Gupta that we never give up and were providing her husband with the best intensive treatment available. I also urged her to invoke God's grace for her husband's recovery.

After another few hours, Mr. Gupta started showing signs of improvement. From the second day onward, although there were episodes of pain and some breathlessness, he was definitely on the road to recovery.

I learned that he was generally in good health but that he

had developed some unwise habits. For two years he had been smoking, and although he was a vegetarian, he consumed a large quantity of deep-fried "junk food" such as samosas and pakoras, as well as sweets. He also never did any exercise and lately had been under great mental stress because his business partner had cheated him.

Before he was discharged, we had a long chat, and I saw that he was one of those people who would readily comply with suggested lifestyle changes. In addition to his own willingness to change his habits for the sake of his health, he had the complete support of his wife, brothers, and friends.

On the basis of our talk, Mr. Gupta started regular morning walks, and leaned heavily toward a sattvic diet, free from fat and sugar, full of fruit and green vegetables. He started regular daily yoga asanas, pranayama, and meditation.

The stress factor in his life was further reduced when his brothers helped him sort out the problem with his business partner. His life was smooth sailing now.

"While I was in the hospital it was like traveling in a dark tunnel, with no light in sight. Now it is sunshine all over," he remarked a few weeks after his heart attack. I wanted to do a treadmill test on him, so that we could plan his further management and treatment. I thought a coronary angiogram, and then a balloon angioplasty or bypass surgery might well be in order.

"Give me at least three months to consolidate my gains and then you can do any tests you want on me," he said. "I am sure you'll find that I won't require any surgery."

We tested him three months later. Just before his discharge from the hospital, a color Doppler echo had shown a clot lying inside the heart. A repeat of the test now showed no clot at all. And his treadmill test was only mildly positive. He had been correct: surgery was indeed unnecessary, and I congratulated him on his achievement.

Mr. Gupta persisted in his changed lifestyle, and a year later repeated the treadmill test, which this time was completely negative. Now, nine years later, he continues to enjoy his routine of exercise, meditation, and simple sattvic food. He has been off medications of every kind for the last six years.

Mainstream medicine's official position is that a sick artery follows its own course of degeneration. No matter what you might believe, think, or do—so goes the official gospel—such arteries relentlessly pursue their grim course, worsening a little every day, eventually becoming blocked and strangulating the heart muscle.

But Dean Ornish (author of *Dr. Dean Ornish's Program for Reversing Heart Disease*) had his patients use simple yoga exercises, a daily walk, meditation, and a low-fat diet and proved scientifically that heart disease *can* be reversed. A deposit of cholesterol plaque looks solid, but like everything in the body, it is alive and changing. New molecules drift in and old ones drift out; new capillaries may develop to bring oxygen and nourishment to the heart muscle. Purification and healing can take place.

Mr. Gupta has been entirely successful in reversing the state of his heart arteries by effecting some simple changes in his lifestyle. You can do it too.

Your Life is in Your Hands

Every year, half a million Americans, 180,000 Britons and three million Indians die from heart attacks as a result of atherosclerosis, in which the coronary arteries that carry blood to the heart are progressively clogged with fatty deposits until insufficient blood reaches the heart, and the person has a heart attack. The only widely accepted "cure" for this dangerous situation today is to increase the flow of blood through the arteries either by balloon angioplasty or bypass surgery.

For years now, I have been prescribing lifestyle changes to my patients, trying to impress upon them that if they adopt the regimen outlined in Dean Ornish's book, they stand a good chance of avoiding bypass surgery. Some give the program a try, adhere to it well, and benefit tremendously. One sixty-five-year-old man with triple vessel disease who would not agree to have bypass surgery is doing very well on this regimen, showing steady improvement over two years. He and other patients have understood how lifestyle changes can benefit their heart and their overall health, and are acting on their understanding.

There are, of course, patients who argue that these lifestyle changes are all right in theory, but not in practice. Some complain that the regimen is too drastic, a charge made by many "mainstream" physicians attached to the high-tech (and well-paying) surgical methods. Replying to an interviewer who brought up this issue, Dean Ornish replied, "I don't understand why asking people to eat a well-balanced vegetarian diet is considered too drastic, but it is medically conservative to cut people open."

These natural recommendations—a lighter, purer diet, some meditation, regular exercise, and simple yoga stretches—are gentle and noninvasive. Compared to surgery or even to the side effects of cholesterol-reducing drugs, these practices are safe, natural, and simple. But they do require that the patient do something more than pop a pill or lie down on a table and surrender to the surgeon's knife.

Many patients, conditioned to swallowing pills, continue to want a quick fix. Some simply won't agree to change their lifestyle. They don't want to learn the art of meditation, or alter their familiar diet even though it has given them heart disease; they don't want to take the trouble to walk for half an hour every day. They want "a pill for every ill."

Those who willingly adopt a healthier new routine usually start enjoying not only how they feel, but also the program itself, and they soon begin to benefit from it. It is clear to me that this program, especially meditation, can prevent, retard, or even reverse heart disease.

As I mentioned, plaque in the coronary arteries may look solid, but it is actually alive and changing. When "negative" molecules are replaced by "happy" molecules through yoga asanas and meditation, the body's biochemistry changes and you can begin to unbuild the blocks previously built in the arteries of your heart.

The low-fat vegetarian diet may well be a major factor in the success of Dean Ornish's program. But I believe that what you eat matters, but what is eating you up matters much more. From that perspective, the main role in reversal of heart disease is played by a quiet mind, attained and maintained by regular meditation, which puts you in touch with the finer levels of consciousness and opens the channels of healing.

Your health, as with so much in life, happens the way you want it, the way you set it up. The choice is yours. Your life is in your hands.

PART TWO

FOUNDATIONS OF A HAPPY, HEALTHY LIFE

3

Dharma: The Ancient Path of Righteous Living

Each one of us will one day be judged by our standard of life, not by our standard of living; by our measure of giving, not by our measure of wealth; by our simple goodness, not by our seeming greatness.

—WILLIAM ARTHUR WARD

Righteous people eat the remains of sacrifice and are thereby freed from sin.

—BHAGAVAD GITA, 3:13

When I was in primary school, my mother told me a story about three men who, after they died, were interviewed at the gates of heaven and hell by Yama, the god of death. They all had to give an accounting of their lives, reporting the actions they had performed during their allotted time on earth.

The first man told Yama that he built a number of temples and installed images of God in them. He offered prayers, decorated the temples, tolled the bells in God's name. Hundreds and thousands of people thronged to the temples and offered their prayers.

The second man then gave his accounting, enumerating the

good actions he had built up to his credit. He had constructed several schools and two hospitals, and all these institutions were named after him. With these works, he said, he had contributed to the education and well-being of the whole population.

Lord Yama knew that these two men had earned all their money by dishonest and corrupt means, fleecing thousands of innocent men and women. Even the so-called religious and philanthropic institutions they had built, which brought them name and fame, were being used for profit. Parents had to pay large sums of money to get their wards admitted to the schools, and huge profits were being taken in by the hospitals. They offered prayers for personal benefits, with their hearts full of greed, jealousy, and discontent.

Lord Yama knew all that, and directed that the two men be taken to hell for their nefarious activities while they were on earth.

The third man was a farmer. After he heard the two men speak and saw the judgment of Lord Yama about their destinies, he hung his head and silently began to follow them. Lord Yama shouted after him, "Stop! Where are you going? I have yet to hear you speak."

The poor man turned back and said quietly, "Sire, these two gentlemen did such good things. They built temples, hospitals, and schools, and sang God's glory, and that wasn't considered good enough for them to enter the gates of heaven. And I, who did nothing of the sort, how can I deserve to go to heaven?

"For all the days of my life I woke up very early and went to the fields to plow the land. I brought up my children with great difficulty, as the plot of land I had was small and the soil was rocky. We never had any reserves of wheat or rice, but my neighbor was kind, and we helped each other in times of difficulty. Lord, I had no time to offer prayers or to remember God. I did not know much about Him anyway.

"My sons have grown up. I managed to send them to the village school, and they were doing quite well when I left. That is all I have to say."

Yama replied to the man, "You have used your allotted time on earth well. You worked hard, did your duty, cared for your family. You never told lies, never cheated anyone or harmed anyone. Whatever small opportunity you had to be kind and to help your neighbor, you didn't hesitate." And he pointed the man toward the gates of heaven.

After completing the story my mother said, "Whether there is a heaven somewhere or not, I hope you now know what I understand by Dharma, your duty to yourself, to your family, and to your fellow beings. That should be our prayer and our religion. Just going to temple is not enough. It's not even necessary. Anything gained in this world, whether material wealth or even spiritual knowledge, while neglecting one's Dharma, is futile."

Growing up with Dharma

To me, my mother was an embodiment of Dharma. Her work and all her actions were free from desires and selfish motives. She only did what ought to be done. She sought no personal gain, had no obsession to be rewarded for her work. She had no love for money or jewelry. It seemed to me that all her work was undertaken with a perfect sense of non-attachment. She worked with a spirit of renunciation in action—but not *of* action—as she was constantly engaged in caring for the household and the children. Her aim in life was to serve and work for work's sake, and she was in complete harmony with herself and with everyone around, her mind at rest.

Mother had a heart full of love, and her actions expressed the feeling that loving is giving oneself totally, without wanting anything in return. Her work for her children was all in love. There in the small kitchen of our modest house I saw love being poured out in abundance. The food she cooked for us had the fragrance of unlimited love that overflowed into whatever she did.

Even her reprimands were made with love. She was never upset or angry with anyone at any time, but when she observed someone doing something wrong she "scolded" him or her in her own special way. In a voice soft but firm, the tone expressing disapproval, she spoke the following sentence in Punjabi (she never completed school, but she could read and write Hindi and Gurmukhi): "Tera kadi kakh na jaye." Translated into English this would read, "May you never lose anything, even a piece of straw, any time in your life." The person concerned got a blessing instead of a curse for doing something obviously wrong.

She recited verses from Guru Granth Sahib and the Bhagavad Gita, and taught us that the ancient wisdom contained in our scriptures tells every individual to speak the truth, not to hurt anyone by word or deed, to respect elders and teachers, and to follow the path of righteousness in every sphere of activity in our lives. One should hate no one, nor be jealous of anyone. We should strive to see God in all beings, as He alone dwells in the heart of all. I am certain that she herself saw the Lord in everyone.

And I always saw the presence of God in her. The reverence and respect I had for her was unbounded.

All my life I have cherished the unbounded love she showered on all her children, our friends, and, indeed, on everyone around. No visitor to our house, whether our school friends or a relative of our cleaning woman, could leave our house without being served with tea snacks or a meal. The hospitality accorded by her to all her visitors and guests was traditionally Indian, and left a deep impact on us children. She was a perfect example of the attitude of service, of doing one's duty without expecting anything in return.

The Rewards of Selflessness

This principle of sacrifice and service, of working with no expectation of reward, is deep in the Indian tradition. A. Parthasarthy says that the Hindu worship of the cow and the bull symbolizes esteem for this noble principle, and helps imbibe it into day-to-day living in India.

The bull toils all day in the hot sun, cultivating the fields of

India. In return for his hard labor, he gets some dry grass and water. The bull embodies the principle of maximum work, no grumbling: no ego or craving for the fruits of its "action." Likewise, the cow gives milk freely. Both the bull and the cow live for the benefit of others.

Lord Krishna refers to Arjuna in the Bhagavad Gita as a "bull among the Bharatas," perhaps because his life was dedicated to others. Unlike many people in modern times, who seem to believe in doing as little as possible with maximum gain, one who believes in maximum work with minimum personal gain is a bull in society, living the lofty principles of life exemplified by the bull.

Mother conveyed to me time and again that what everyone seeks in life is happiness and peace. But if you look around, what most of us are actually doing is acting in this world for the fulfillment of our own wants, according to our own likes and dislikes. Man can never be successful in attaining peace this way. When he learns to act according to his duty and abides by the basic values of life, only then is he following the path of Dharma, the path of righteousness; then he will be as happy as a lark.

There are obvious disparities in the lives of human beings. Each one of us takes birth according to the actions we have performed in previous births. We have to adopt the path of Dharma and live a righteous life according to how we have been placed. We have to perform our duty for its own sake, because it's the right thing to do, not because it brings name and fame.

Mother would recite the story of the Ramayana and point out to us that Ravana led a life of sensuality, while Rama was an embodiment of Dharma. Ravana was a great and powerful king, who had all the comforts of life, but he did not have happiness. He may have conquered the three worlds, but he did not conquer himself. He was doing wrong—notably the abduction of Sita—and like everyone who does something wrong, he knew it and lived in fear. Rama, on the other hand, had no comforts while living in the forest, but he was in peace because he had conquered his mind and was living according to Dharma.

The epic of Ramayana portrays the character of people with contrasting values. For thousands of years it has shown millions of readers and listeners that there is a clear distinction between paths in life, and that we have the freedom to exercise choice as to which path we follow. By observing the characters and their choices, we can see that only the righteous way of life—Dharma —results in happiness.

What is Dharma?

R. S. Nathan of the Chinmaya Mission throws light on the word Dharma. He says (in *The Progress of Indian Philosophical Thought*) that the word Dharma has acquired such an all-comprehensive and complex significance that it is now almost impossible to bring it within the compass of a precise definition. Nor is it possible to find an exact equivalent for this word in other languages.

The word Dharma is derived from the Sanskrit root, *dhri*, to uphold or sustain. It stands for that which holds up or supports the existence of a thing. It can be said to be the "law of being," the essential property or characteristic of something. It is the luminosity of the sun, the heat of fire, the wetness of water, the sweetness of sugar, the whiteness of milk. It is also the divine spark of existence in man.

Dharma is on two levels. It has an individual level and a cosmic, universal level. At the individual level, one is an artist, a musician, a physician, a farmer. That is one's *swadharma* or individual, personal tendency. At the same time, it indicates the path and duties required to live up to, or completely unfold, that individual nature.

At the cosmic level, Dharma is common to all individuals at all times. It comprises the ideals, purposes, and right ways of life that should be followed both as an individual and as a member of society. It is the law of right living, the observance of which secures the double object of happiness in life and liberation from all bondage.

The essential nature of man is the power of realizing the divine. That distinguishes man from all other beings. This power is therefore *manava dharma*, man's dharma. Divinity is already within us, deep within our being. "Everything in creation is essentially divine," sing the Upanishads again and again. It is given only to human beings to fully manifest the divinity within us, and become divine. Once we do so, we enjoy unbounded freedom, bliss, and wisdom.

So long as our impure, agitated mind stands in the way, we do not perceive the divine nature, just as light cannot be seen through the smoke-coated chimney of an oil lamp. If we want light, we have to cleanse the chimney. If we want to bring out the divinity in us, we have to cleanse our mind. Lust, greed, anger, hatred, pride, all obscure the divinity and have to be dropped off once and for all. "The measure of human life is man transcending himself," says Chaturvedi Badrinath. "This is ultimate Dharma."

The Mahabharata emphatically states that nobody has ever violated the principles of Dharma without courting disaster. Adharma (not following the path of Dharma) might carry a man to the heights of power and prosperity for a while, but it is all temporary. Heights gained through adharma, through wrong or unrighteous actions, will surely be a prelude to a certain fall. That which sustains is Dharma.

If you uphold the basic values of life, the code of conduct sacred to all societies, with perseverance and dedication, all stumbling blocks will turn into stepping stones to the attainment of peace and happiness, in this life and the life hereafter.

How important is it to live in accord with Dharma. Swami Vivekananda said, "Let people praise you or blame you; let fortune smile or frown upon you. Let your body fall today or after a yuga. But see that you do not deviate from the path of Dharma."

The Right Path of Life

As I have emphasized throughout this book, man is endowed with the faculty of discrimination, which gives us freedom of choice. Since choice is available, we can and should choose the right action, in the right direction. It is our duty; that much, everyone is expected to do.

We can better perform the right action if we appreciate our role in the scheme of things. The whole universe is orderly. Stars, galaxies, rivers, plants, forests, animals—all follow the laws of nature. They cannot and do not violate these laws, and

Dharma and the Gita

There is no profession, no Dharma, which is demeaning in any way, provided you perform your work diligently, with devotion and dedication. Lord Krishna was a prince and represented divinity. Yet he offered himself for the job as Arjuna's charioteer for the duration of the Mahabharata war.

The job of a chariot driver was not considered dignified in those days, even though it required considerable skill to handle the reins of the chariot's many horses at the same time. The direction in which the vehicle should turn or go was usually indicated by the master of the chariot, sitting at a higher level than the charioteer, not by an oral command but by his toes touching the charioteer's shoulder.

Lord Krishna took the assignment of being charioteer to Arjuna voluntarily, thus showing the eagerness of the Divine to be of service to his devotees. He declared and demonstrated that every action performed, every work undertaken in the right spirit is dignified. As part of his duty, Krishna, the Lord of the universe, scrubbed the back of his horses every evening after the battle and fed them with his own hands.

In his childhood Krishna demonstrated the power of divine love. Later he guided his friend and disciple Arjuna to victory in a war between good and evil, Dharma and adharma, and guided all mankind for all time by showing them the path of true victory and bliss in this life.

harmony prevails. Only man has choice over his actions. When his mind is calm, he is able to see the order and intelligence in the cosmos, the harmony of creation, and he will cultivate a proper attitude toward life and duty.

Strict discipline is initially required for observance of Dharma, but in course of time it becomes second nature. No intelligent person will allow himself to slip back into the ruts of his previous lifestyle after beginning to follow the path of Dharma.

We human beings are drawn both to good actions, which result in happiness, and to evil actions, which lead to suffering. We can attain happiness only if we choose virtuous living and follow the path of Dharma.

Man is an embodied soul, pure consciousness, the experiencer underlying all experiences. This essential nature of all of us is happiness and bliss, pure joy, residing deep within at the quantum level in pure form. It bubbles to the surface only under the right conditions. All real happiness arises when we follow the path of Dharma, ultimately leading to Self-realization: directly knowing that pure joy.

In modern society money, physical beauty, and worldly success are equated with happiness. These transient pleasures cannot be compared with pure inner joy. But to be a man or woman of realization and be in a state of unbroken bliss and absolute freedom from all bondage and all worldly objects is not for everyone. It is open to all, but you have to recognize it as a worthwhile goal, and you have to persevere to achieve it.

Dharma and Religion

Although Dharma is often used to denote "religion," it has a much wider and deeper meaning. I always thought my mother was very religious; now when I recollect the various incidents in her life, I realize she walked the path of Dharma, the right way of living. That is why she lived such a happy, stress-free life and radiated such love and peace.

The code of such a life is inherently and instinctively present within our soul or consciousness. It is universally present in the heart of all human beings, whether they reside on a remote, isolated island, or in the so-called civilized, "advanced" countries. We need only look inside ourselves to rediscover the universal basic human values of life and Dharma.

Whether we follow one religion or another, or don't follow one at all, doesn't really matter. Swami Vivekananda said over a hundred years ago that he was ready to go to the mosque and say his prayers to Allah alongside a Muslim, enter the church of a Christian and kneel before the crucifix, enter a Buddhist temple or pagoda, or go to the forest and meditate with the Hindu, because he knew that the same light enlightens the heart of every human being.

Swami Vivekananda's master, Sri Ramakrishna Paramahansa, said it is like climbing a mountain: there are many paths, and you can reach the top by any of the paths, provided you walk up with dedication, faith, and perseverance, and don't hold the impression that the path you are following is the only one and the best one.

Swami Vivekananda clarified this teaching of Ramakrishna by reminding people of all religions, at the World Parliament of Religions in Chicago over one hundred years ago, that the human spirit is singular, regardless of the faith or religion of various men and women. The spirit, pure consciousness, is one, and if one follows the dictates of consciousness, the spiritual harmony of all mankind can be achieved. I feel that this is Dharma. And it is the lesson I learned as a young boy at the feet of my mother.

Everything I received from her, through the stories she told us or the manner in which she cooked and served our family and our visitors, became indelible and unalterable and has stayed with me all my life. Her life was like a breeze of fresh air, a breeze of purity, sincerity, and goodness.

She had many ways of teaching us. When I was a boy, we seldom discussed things with our father. He would simply decide the course of action for everyone. Everything had to be done his way, otherwise he would get annoyed and reprimand us. And then there would be mother, taking our side and shielding us.

But not if we were wrong! When I was in high school, I wasn't allowed to step outside the house for a late-night movie with a friend, as my father was against our seeing movies, except when a religious film came to town. Then he would take the whole family, whether we were interested or not. I had made a new friend at school who was very fond of movies, and I started going out with him. I would leave the house after everyone was asleep, around 9:30 p.m., leaving the front door unlocked.

My mother somehow or other knew everything I did. She would lock the door from the inside and keep awake until midnight, and was at the door just at the right time. When I came home I would find the door locked, but I wouldn't knock or ring the bell, lest my father find out. I just waited silently, and very soon she opened the door and let me in.

This happened three times. Each time, she told me that what I was doing was not right. I was afraid that if my father found out, I would get hell! The fourth time, she warned me that the way things were going, she was afraid I might go astray with my new friend; if I went on like this and didn't listen to her, she would tell my father. And she did! I had to face his wrath in front of all the members of the family. I loved her all the more for that.

From then onward, whenever I could not make up my mind about something, I sat with her and sought her guidance. When the time came for me to go to medical college to become a doctor, my mind was in great conflict. Did I really want to do this?

Mother wanted me to be a doctor. "It will be a satisfying profession for you, I am sure," she told me. When she saw I was still undecided, she was not annoyed with me. Rather, she said, "Somehow or other I had suspected that you would not like to do it; the course is long, and one has to work hard to become a doctor." These words had a magical effect. In her subtle way she challenged me, and I took up medicine and have never regretted it.

During the last few months of her life, my mother went to the home of my eldest brother in Lucknow. She had a special weakness and love for him. She loved all her children, but always lavished more care and affection on whichever one of us was not doing as well as the others, at school or later on in life. She firmly believed that if there was any vital force in the world it was unconditional love.

Pushpa and I were in Pune at that time. We got the news that my mother was in the hospital after sustaining a head injury in an accident. Her arms were paralyzed, and she had fallen into a coma. We rushed to Lucknow and, when we reached her room, the neurosurgeon and other attending physicians told me she was in critical condition, in a deep coma. Blood pressure could not be recorded for the past twenty-four hours. It appeared, they said, that she was waiting for me.

I went to her bed and leaned over her face. Immediately, her breathing became quicker. She opened her eyes, whispered my name, and lifting her paralyzed arm around my neck, pulled my face towards her and kissed me on the cheek. Then she fell back and stopped breathing.

The nurses, doctors, and all the onlookers couldn't believe their eyes. Neither could I. How could it have happened? Her will, so dynamic and strong, must have been operating from outside her individual consciousness, from what I could only think of as the cosmic level, directing the paralyzed limb of the pulseless body to lift and embrace me.

I kissed her face over and over again.

Ever since, she lives in the recesses of my heart. She has been and is directing me in my day-to-day life. If I have failed, as I surely have on a number of occasions, if the implementation was not always up to the mark, the right intentions and directions were always there.

And as I was fortunate to be given a direction in life by so pure a mother, so I have been equally blessed in marriage. In December 1995 Pushpa and I celebrated fifty years of marriage. She has stood firmly beside me in whatever little I have done in my life. She is deeply religious, and has a tremendous faith in God. Her definition of religion has meant no love for material wealth.

She has a warm heart. If a neighbor's daughter is leaving her parents after her wedding, Pushpa cries as much as the girl's mother. Though she is very sattvic, there have been times when rajas has dominated, making her abrupt in her speech or actions (see pages 82–6). But ninety-nine times out of one hundred it has turned out that she had a good reason.

She has always had intuitive insight into things. When the doorbell rings, she tells me who is at the door; when the telephone bell rings she tells me who is calling before I pick up the phone. She has almost always been right.

Whenever I have been at a crossroads in my life, standing still for a while, not knowing which road to take, I have always consulted Pushpa, taken her advice, let her make the decisions, and we have never regretted them. Her personality is reflected in Deepak and Sanjiv's life and way of living. The grandchildren are deeply in love with her. That is her Dharma.

4

Family and Children: Your Children Come Through You, Not from You

Your children come through you but not from you.
You may give them your love but not your thoughts.
You may strive to be like them, but seek not to make them like
* you.*
For life does not go backward nor tarries with yesterday.
You are the bows from which your children as arrows are sent
* forth.*

—KAHLIL GIBRAN

Late one afternoon, when our eldest son, Deepak, was just three years old, my wife Pushpa and I were walking with him towards the car parked outside the house. I had bought an Austin 8, a small car, and also had a government car for my use as a staff surgeon. Deepak said, "Daddy, which car are you taking? Sometimes you take the white car and other times the green car."

I said, "Deepak, these are both your cars. You select the one for us to use this evening."

Three-year-old Deepak stopped walking, looked straight into my eyes and said, "These are not my cars, they are yours,

Daddy. You drive the one you like. When I go to school, study, and then grow up and earn a lot of money, I will buy a big car. I will make you sit by my side and drive it and then I will call it my car."

Pushpa and I stood there for a long moment completely dazed before we climbed into the car, and once seated we did not talk for quite some time. We were struck by the clarity of Deepak's mind, and the future he could visualize at the age of three, even before we had mentioned the word "school" to him. The sense of dignity and the vision of the ultimate goal were already there. On some level of his being the future was planned; only the details had to be worked out.

When he was in high school, he was intent on becoming a writer. He was a voracious reader, devouring Shakespeare, Tagore, Kalidasa, Somerset Maugham, Thomas Hardy, Bernard Shaw, as well as Agatha Christie and one of his favorites, the humorist P.G. Wodehouse. He had a photographic memory and once, when asked to repeat a randomly chosen page from one of Wodehouse's books, he rattled off the contents verbatim, from the first word to the last.

Somehow or other I had a hidden desire that Deepak would become a doctor. I had come to love my profession over time, and like many if not most fathers, wanted my son to follow in my footsteps. But long ago I had decided it was best not to be an influencing factor in the children's decisions.

Parents through the ages have always had the notion that their children belong to them. The father tells his son, "When I was your age, I did such and such. I don't know what is the matter with you!" The result is that most children become imitators; they start behaving and even looking like their father or mother. As a parent, you tend to be happy and proud when your children resemble you, not realizing that you never gave them a chance to be free, to express their originality, to develop their own personalities and unfold and become better than you.

You cannot hasten the unfoldment and blossoming of a flower bud. If you try to force it, you will ruin the beauty and fragrance forever. The inner personality and potential of a child is a million times more delicate than an unopened flower. Therefore you should not try to enforce your opinions on children. You can guide them with tender love, and let them blossom into fine human beings on their own.

I know that my father, for instance, loved and cared for all his children, but he was a very disciplined and matter-of-fact man, strict in many ways. He insisted that everyone in the family eat, walk, talk, and even think as he did. That made me a rather timid and compromising individual as I grew up. My mother's unbounded love was my saving grace; it modified me and made my personality acceptable, but there was precious little original about me anyway. I had many inhibitions and had to gather courage to express myself and even to think as I truly wanted. I was okay as a doctor but was definitely not born to be a teacher or speaker, though I have learned.

Because of my background, Pushpa and I decided upon our course of action regarding our two children: we would not interfere with the growth of their minds and their potential. I never imposed myself upon them in any way. All we could give them was love. And in the course of time, both have reached the pinnacle of achievement in their chosen fields. But I am getting ahead of my story.

Deepak, Sanjiv (our second son), Pushpa, myself, and my mother were all fast friends. There were no secrets in the family; we shared everything, including our thoughts. So when the time came for Deepak to choose a course of study, we decided to have a dialogue.

Despite my own preference, Deepak insisted that he did not want to become a doctor. He wanted to see people happy and laughing, and not see misery and helplessness on the faces of patients, as his Daddy saw all the time. He wanted to take English literature as his major in the university, and be a journalist and writer, the author of successful books that would make people happy.

He was (and remains) a terrific storyteller, and had already started writing short stories. In light of his natural flare for literature and his own view of his future career, we all agreed not to discuss the subject further. But I wasn't quite ready to give up, and decided to involve the principal and the senior teachers at his school.

They told me that Deepak wrote for the school magazine, that his articles were widely appreciated, and that he was an eloquent speaker in school debates. He also acted in school plays and had recently given an excellent mime performance. His decision to make journalism and writing his career rather than science and medicine, they told me, would take him in the right direction. What could I do in the face of all this, but let go of my personal desire?

But then—soon after his graduation from high school—Deepak came to me and said that he wanted to become a doctor at all costs! He was so determined that there was no room for discussion.

He jumped into it with all his energy and intelligence, got first position in the pre-medical examination in the university, and gained admission to the All-India Institute of Medical Sciences through a national-level competitive exam.

While in medical school, he won numerous awards, including winning the All-India students' debating competition for four consecutive years. He also worked as a part-time news reader and commentator for All-India Radio. After graduating from medical school he went to the USA for his postgraduate studies, and began a successful career in traditional medicine. Within a few years he held a distinguished position.

But Deepak was a rebel. He saw the flaws in mainstream medicine, and refused to compromise. Instead, he chose the groundbreaking path of combining mind-body medicine, human potentiality, and spirituality. He refused to confine himself within the traditional mold of modern medicine, and dared to innovate.

Now he is a prolific writer, an eloquent, inspirational speaker, and the bestselling author of more than twelve books that deal with revolutionary ideas linking ancient wisdom with modern science. His lectures and seminars are as popular as his books and tapes, all around the world. His work combines a deep knowledge and understanding of medicine (modern and ayurvedic), Vedanta and the philosophy of the Vedas, and spirituality in its true sense. Along with his own original ideas, an appreciation of the works of ancient sages, contemporary scientists, and poets and writers of all ages and parts of the world are reflected in his works.

How much of all this did that three-year-old boy know when he looked me in the eyes and told me that some day, after he went to school and studied and made a lot of money, he would buy his own big car?

Children Have Their Own Destiny

According to the law of karma, a child is born to particular parents and a particular environment because his karma—the accumulated impressions of all his past actions and experiences —requires him to acquire certain physical and mental characteristics and have certain opportunities in this lifetime. He does not get a good or bad environment because of his parents, but because his own karma places him in a situation in which he can, if he so desires, utilize his accumulated knowledge and capabilities and add to them.

Some children are gifted, or are even born as geniuses. In such cases, an atmosphere of warmth and love in the family is certainly helpful. Research suggests that gifted children are usually brought up in a varied environment with plenty of opportunities. The value of a supportive family atmosphere cannot be denied, but there are innumerable families with such an atmosphere from which geniuses do not emerge, so this alone could not be responsible for the flowering of these great personalities. I am convinced they must have brought a lot from their previous lives.

In May 1995, seventeen-year-old Balamurli Ainhati graduated from the Mount Sinai School of Medicine of New York University and created a world record as the youngest person ever to become a doctor. The average age for medical school graduation in the USA is twenty-six or twenty-seven. The young doctor moved from India to the United States at age three, finished two elementary school grades each year, and graduated from high school at the age of eleven. He said that he knew by age four what his profession would be, and at age twelve declared that he wanted to break all records and be the youngest doctor ever. He was a gifted child who knew all through his childhood what his future plans were.

Perhaps the outstanding example of youthful genius in Indian history is Adi Shankaracharya. That great sage and revitalizer of Vedanta wrote his first book at seven, and composed dozens of commentaries on the most important scriptures by the age of sixteen. He then spent the remaining sixteen years of his life traveling throughout India on foot, spreading the message of Vedanta and establishing *maths* (centers of learning) in the four corners of India. He completed his life's work by the age of thirty-two. Shankara could not possibly have learned all that he knew in his short lifespan, and his genes do not explain it either; his parents and grandparents were ordinary folk.

Whether our children are geniuses or not, to us, the parents, they are wonderful, and we feel very proud to have them. To an extent, this joy and pride are probably all right, so long as we remember what the poet Kahlil Gibran said: Our children come through us and not from us. "You are only the bows from which your children, as arrows, are sent forth," said Gibran. We can give them our love, but we must not try to influence them, as we might hamper their growth. They have their own destiny to fulfill. As a matter of fact, I must say that I have been striving now for the last many years to be like our children, knowing fully well that it cannot be so.

Children Have Much to Teach Us

Sanjiv, our second son, had started sucking his thumb as an infant, and as he was growing up I would occasionally tell him it was not a good habit. We realized that it was our fault, as we had given him a pacifier to suck when he was an infant so he wouldn't disturb us, but he was now two years old and the time had come for him to stop.

One day I had Sanjiv with me in the car. I noticed that he had put his thumb in his mouth, and I pointed to a truck that had suddenly come to a halt at the side of the road as we passed it. I said, "That truck suddenly stopped and is blocking the traffic because a little boy is sucking his thumb." Sanjiv abruptly pulled his thumb out of his mouth.

After a while the habit got the better of him and he put his thumb back in his mouth. I saw another vehicle parked on the roadside and I repeated the trick; he again pulled out his thumb. After a while I forgot all about it, and Sanjiv was merrily sucking his thumb. But while driving back home, I lit a cigarette (I had started smoking shortly after Sanjiv was born). Sanjiv noticed a vehicle parked on the roadside and he said, "Daddy, look at that bus. It has suddenly stopped because somebody is smoking a cigarette." Embarrassed, I quickly put the cigarette out.

Thereafter, whenever I reminded him about stopping the thumb-sucking, he would tell me, "Daddy, you should stop smoking, it is not a good habit." This conversation between the two of us went on for quite some weeks till finally Sanjiv gave up sucking his thumb and I gave up smoking.

In his innocent way, my son did me an enormous service. Who knows if I would still be here today if I had not quit smoking.

I encountered a similar example of a young child's wisdom in my practice. Eight-year-old Dinesh was my patient for a congenital heart defect. I had him operated on for it, and told the parents that if the child had any infection or even a sore throat, he must see his family doctor, as the infection could get into his circulation and damage the heart.

A few days later the parents brought Dinesh to my office, as he had developed a cough and fever. Before I could examine him, Dinesh said, "I don't want to be seen. Doctor, please treat my father. He smokes a lot and drinks every evening. The smoke in the house caused my sore throat and cough. That apart, I am worried about my father. He is sick with alcoholism. If something happens to him, what will we do?"

The parents of Dinesh were stunned. They never expected their son to burst out with anything like that. But the father learned his lesson and changed his life from that very day.

When our granddaughter Priya graduated from her term of service with City Year (see Chapter 15), the chief speaker at the ceremony was Marian Wright Edelman, the American author, educator, and champion of children's welfare. "Parents," Mrs Edelman said, "should listen to their children instead of just talking. They should be patient instead of angry, should encourage and appreciate when their children do anything good, compliment instead of finding fault, point out their accomplishments rather than their weaknesses."

She reminded parents that "we demand and expect much from our children and try to mold them into our image, rather than discovering and nourishing them as they emerge and grow spontaneously into fine human beings. We forget that children have unpolluted brains and come out with wonderful ideas and constructive suggestions."

Children can teach us a tremendous amount. In their openness to life they show us the path we adults sometimes cannot see. I was happy during the times I spent with Deepak and Sanjiv when they were little boys. It was great fun going places with them, and I learned a lot from their experiences at school. We laughed a lot together, sometimes for no obvious reason. Being with them put me in touch with my childhood, which had been buried under the unwanted, unnecessary worries of adulthood.

When they were older, sometimes when I came home from work at the hospital and found them playing cricket in the open ground outside our house, I would join them. They knew more about it than I did and were better than I was, but so what? We enjoyed playing together and that was the important thing. I would make silly strokes and gave easy catches. It gave them occasion to laugh aloud and gave me the opportunity to free the child within.

Somehow or other, we get convinced as we are growing up that we must look serious and behave in such a manner that people will take us seriously as adults. We learn to control our laughter so well that we forget how to laugh, until we reach a stage when we feel that if someone sees us laughing for no reason, he may think there's something wrong with us. We make an effort, put on many masks, and then gradually we lose the capacity to be open and straightforward. As a result, we also start doubting other people's intentions and end up not trusting people any longer.

> *Except ye be converted and become as little children, ye shall not enter the Kingdom of Heaven.*
>
> —JESUS

Being with my boys was like a mirror in which I saw these things, and I saw how much I had to learn from them.

Look at a child lying in his crib, looking at the ceiling, laughing blissfully. That is your real nature. You have forgotten it over the years. But if we could have such a silent and pure mind when we grow up, and such joy in merely being, there would be no problems in this world.

The Right Environment

As parents, the most important thing we can do is to set good examples for our children. Instead, we tell them lies, and they learn to tell lies. We smoke, they learn to smoke. We indulge in alcohol abuse and tell them, "This is an adult drink, it's not for you," and of course they start drinking stealthily. We preach to our children not to watch movies with violence and sex, but we produce them. We adults are hypocrites, and the children become the same as they grow up. We must do our best to be what we want them to become.

When my boys were growing up, Pushpa would recite to

them from Ramayana. It was a ritual they observed almost every day. Once when I entered the room, she was reciting the chapter in which Rama, Lakshman, and Sita were leaving Ayodhya to go to the forest for their fourteen-year period of exile. Rama had given up the throne, and the people of Ayodhya were very sad to see their beloved Rama going away. Deepak, Sanjiv, and their mommy were all crying, with tears rolling down their cheeks. Watching the scene, my mind flashed back to the days when I was their age, and I saw my own mother sitting in the kitchen; she too used to tell us children these same stories.

Ramayana depicts Rama as an ideal son, a loving husband, and later a great and just ruler of his kingdom. A model of Dharma or righteous living, he demonstrated in his life the importance of truth and basic human values. Sita, his wife, has been adored as the model of Dharma for countless generations of Indian women. Ramayana, as well as other scriptures filled with ancient wisdom, were often related to our children by their mother, and have profoundly influenced their lives, as they have influenced countless others for hundreds, if not thousands of years.

"Let them learn first," said St. Paul, "to show piety at home." Religion, and the higher values of right living, should begin in the family. As someone said, "the holiest sanctuary is the home, and the family altar is more valuable than that of the temple. The education for eternity should begin and be carried on at the fireplace."

Parents must foster a warm and friendly relationship with their children, and encourage them to develop diverse interests. It is also very important to make them feel contented with what they have. Provide them with the basic needs, but giving children too many things creates the illusion that acquisition is a valid source of happiness. They must know that if their happiness depends on acquiring a particular thing, especially something they don't really need, then they are on shaky ground.

The environment and family atmosphere play a major role in a child's development and future achievements in life, but as we were saying, every child has inherent potentials that he brings with him. We only have to offer opportunities. However, if these opportunities are scanty, the child's development may well be retarded.

The educational innovator Maria Montessori pointed out that the laws of nature inherent in a child flow like streams. If there is a block the flow does not stop, but continues in another direction. There are "sensitive" or critical periods during which a child's energies are naturally absorbed by one or another life process or area of development. For instance, at around three years of age the sense of order is heightened and the child needs many opportunities to create order in his environment. If this is not provided, the child's energies will flow elsewhere, but something vital in his development will be missing.

In school, the children must learn to participate, and should have the opportunity to exercise choice. They should be constantly guided with love and affection by their teachers, as they are very impressionable and can be easily influenced. One wrong turn at an early stage can change the course of a child's whole life and lead to great unhappiness.

At home, children should not be excluded from any decisions. Parents are the ultimate decision makers, but they must find ways by which their children can participate. These decisions should include such questions as when their friends may come to the house for play or meals, and so on. Also any change of residence, or questions about education and career, should be discussed openly together. Unless the child is taken into confidence, he may start having a feeling of powerlessness, and this feeling can make both his childhood and his later life unhappy.

I have already mentioned how our family met together to discuss Deepak's future, when he was determined not to enter medicine. I tried to learn from this when a few years later it was time for Sanjiv to make similar decisions. He had distinguished himself in English literature in high school, and I suggested to him to take it seriously in college. But he was determined to be a doctor!

He gained admission to all the medical schools he applied to, including the one in Pune where I was teaching medicine at the time. But he preferred to be in the All-India Institute of Medical Sciences. At his final interview the president of the selection board asked him, "Why don't you go to the medical college where your father is teaching?"

Sanjiv has always been precise, to the point, and confident in his speech. He replied, "My father is in the service and was given this assignment. He did not have the choice of being a professor in this particular school. I have a choice, and I want to attend the All-India Institute of Medical Sciences." He always had his eye on the finest institutions, and was fond of quoting the author and poet Henry Thoreau: "You can build castles in the air, provided you know how to put pillars underneath them."

Sanjiv built the pillars quickly. Soon after reaching the USA he was on the Harvard faculty and ultimately became an Associate Professor of Medicine at Harvard University School of Medicine. He has written a number of books on modern medicine, and has won numerous awards. Unlike many prestigious faculty members who look upon their teaching as a chore, Sanjiv is an outstanding educator. He won the George W. Thorn Award for Outstanding Contributions to Clinical Medicine, and the Excellence in Teaching Award of Harvard Medical School, which read: "Outstanding clinician, devoted teacher and mentor. We thank you for your outstanding dedication to excellence in teaching."

Just recently, Sanjiv was honored with the most prestigious Harvard Medical School award, the S. Robert Stone Award for Excellence in Teaching, which praised his "uncanny way of distilling a great body of information into a well-organized, coherent exposition which brings to life his subject matter and leaves his listeners not only well informed but eagerly awaiting the next teaching encounter." Sanjiv's students regard him with great affection as well as respect. They say his knowledge is not confined to his own branch of medicine, but that he is "a walking encyclopedia" with a vast storehouse of knowledge about medical history and discoveries. He is loved by his students, colleagues, and patients alike. It is certainly a good thing he didn't follow my advice and pursue English literature!

Both Deepak and Sanjiv were gifted children. My learning from them began when they started walking and talking, and has been a continuous process. It has gone on unabated ever since they emigrated to the USA more than two decades ago, through their books, through my grandchildren, and also whenever we meet, which is quite often. They both have given me tremendous insight into my day-to-day life as well as the dignity of my profession as a physician.

Sanjiv, for instance, always had a "beyond the textbook" approach. He always insisted that learning and memorizing facts and figures was okay, but not the ultimate, and believes that time spent in sports and in reading literature other than medicine is essential for real knowledge. I have come to regard his insistence on balance as very important not just for being a better doctor, but for living a full life.

5

Everything That Happens to Me, I Asked for: Karma and the Art of Action

A human being fashions his consequences as surely as he fashions his goods or his dwelling. Nothing that he says, thinks, or does is without consequences.

—NORMAN COUSINS

Good and evil do not befall men without reason. Heaven sends them happiness or misery according to their conduct.

—CONFUCIUS

Our fate is matched by the total freedom we have to react to our fate. It is as if we were dealt a hand of cards. Once we have them, we are free to play them as we choose.

—THOMAS SOWELL

We live in a rather modest house in New Delhi, with my office on the ground floor, where two colleagues and I consult with patients in the evenings from 4:30 to 7:30. One day I finished the clinic rather late, about 8:30 p.m., and went upstairs, had a wash, and changed my clothes. At about 9:00 p.m., as Shanti, the cook, was laying food on the dining room table, the bell rang at the main door. Shanti ran down the stairs to see who was there.

Suddenly Pushpa and I heard some unusual sounds, some thuds and grunts, and wondered what was happening. Soon three young men entered the dining room. All were armed with daggers and one held a revolver in one hand and was dragging Shanti with the other. Shanti was bleeding from scalp injuries and appeared scared to death.

The young men began shouting some abuses, but before they could say very much Pushpa said, "I know what you want. You need money and jewelry. We will give you whatever we have in the house. Your need seems to be greater than ours. Here you are." With that, on the spot in the dining room, she took off whatever jewelry she was wearing round her neck, removed her bangles and earrings and the ring on her finger.

"This is not enough," said the one with the revolver, who seemed to be the leader of the young armed robbers. "Get into the bedroom and hand over the keys to the safe." They pushed us toward the bedroom. One of them yanked the wires out of the telephones, disconnecting them; he tied Shanti's hands with a rope and pushed him under the bed. The fellow with the revolver was still beating him on his bleeding head with the handle of the revolver.

Pushpa had handed over the keys to the safe to the other two fellows and was helping them find the valuables in the safe when she noticed Shanti being beaten. She shouted aloud to the fellow doing it: "Stop that! Don't harm him. He is very young and has two innocent little children. If you want to beat anyone or kill someone, we two are here. We don't mind being killed. We have had a good life, we have no responsibilities, our children are well settled. But don't you dare beat this young fellow. And in any case, what has he done? You are getting what you wanted."

He stopped beating Shanti. I was astonished at the brave stance of Pushpa. She was courage personified. For fifty years I had always thought of her as a timid person. She was absolutely clear in her mind that it would be madness arguing with them, as they were young, strong, and armed, yet here she was, defying these desperate young men.

Suddenly the leader of the gang threw one small pair of earrings on the bed, touched Pushpa's feet, and said, "You have been very kind. It does not seem right for us to take away everything. You should have at least this." And turning to the others he said, "I now recognize this man. He is the doctor who treated my father seven years ago. Let's go."

Without ransacking the house any further, they tied both of us with rope and pushed us into the bathroom, took the keys of our car, and ran downstairs. We heard the car start and knew that they had gone.

Pushpa untied the knots of my rope with her teeth, and then I untied her and Shanti. We went downstairs to the clinic. The phone there was working. We called my two colleagues and our relatives, Pratibha and Vijay. They all came immediately to the house. Shanti was taken to the hospital, where the necessary treatment was given.

The police were at their job straightaway, investigating and trying to solve the case. From our descriptions they easily identified one of the fellows, the leader, who had been in jail previously for robbery. With the help of fingerprints and other circumstantial evidence, they caught all three within the next few days.

When the three robbers were lodged in Tihar jail, the ACP (Assistant Commissioner of Police) of the area came to our house to inform us about his success in solving the case. Pushpa had in her mind the effects of karma and how it influences the life of human beings when she asked the ACP how the men were getting on in jail.

"They are obviously misguided people," she said, "and I hope they are being looked after properly." She further asked if she could be of any help, such as by sending them something they required. "Some effort to reform them, to show them the correct path, might change the course of their lives," she said.

The police officer wanted nothing to do with this compassionate viewpoint. "Madam, what are you talking about? Once a criminal, always a criminal. These men are a danger to society.

They have to be punished and dealt with sternly, in accordance with the laws of the land."

"Won't that attitude make them into hardened criminals?" Pushpa asked. "You see, these young men did not kill us. They could easily have done so, but the leader stopped them from harming us further because Doctor saheb—my husband—had helped his father seven years earlier. This shows the fellow has some underlying goodness. Why not tap it and help him reform himself to a decent human being?"

"Madam, I cannot agree with you," the ACP replied. According to him, the fellow had been to jail for similar crimes and he was beyond reform. "He didn't spare you because of his father; he would have killed you if you hadn't handed over your valuables to him, or if you had resisted or struggled with them in any manner."

The discussion went on for some time, without any agreement. Recently, however, programs of rehabilitation, including meditation, have been started for inmates of Tihar and other jails. We hope they may have some salutary effect on the lives and futures of the inmates.

The Natural Laws of Karma

The word karma means "action." Stated in its simplest terms, the philosophy of karma explains that every action has its consequences. One of the most fundamental laws of physics is "Every action has an equal and opposite reaction." In the Bible, Jesus tells his followers, "As you sow, so shall you reap." This is the law of karma. We are all subject to it, just as we are subject to gravity. The *Laws of Manu* explains karma this way:

> Action, which springs from the mind, from speech, and from the body, produces either good or evil results. By action are caused the conditions of men, the highest, the middling, and the lowest. A man obtains the result of a good or evil mental act in his mind, that of a verbal act in his speech, and that of a bodily act in his body.

All beings perform action. As Lord Krishna says in the Bhagavad Gita, "No one can exist even for an instant without performing action." Even He acts, though He doesn't have to: "In the three worlds there is no action which I need do, nor is there for Me anything worth attaining unattained; even so, I am engaged in action." Throughout the Gita He urges Arjuna toward action for the sake of Dharma and enlightenment.

Activity is seen everywhere, both in nature and in man, who is part of nature. There is activity in the movements of the stars and the planets, in plants and trees, in the animal kingdom. Even space itself is vibrating and pulsating with energy.

For the body to remain alive, one has to be active all the time. Our body is active when we are awake, our mind is active both in waking and dream state, and our heart, lungs, and intestines, our immune and endocrine systems, our metabolic processes are active in waking, dreaming, and deep sleep. We are active at work and in relaxation and recreation. Talking, listening, laughing, walking, working, thinking—any physical or mental act is karma. Even worship, prayer, and meditation are forms of action.

All created beings are interdependent and sustain one another by their actions. By means of actions we promote the harmonious relationship between man and all beings, and keep the wheels of karma in motion.

Every action has its inevitable effects. Indeed, every action we undertake has a wide range of consequences, both for ourselves and for the whole creation. According to Maharishi Mahesh Yogi:

> Through every thought, word, and action a man produces waves of influence in the surrounding atmosphere. The quality of the influence depends upon the quality of action performed; the degree of reaction spread through the surroundings depends upon the strength of the action performed. Thus we find that every moment in life produces some influence in the atmosphere, by the actions of breathing, thinking, speaking, and behaving.

Knowledge of the inescapable law of karma is very helpful. It helps us to accept what has come to us, because we know it is the result of our own previous actions. At the same time, it cautions us to be sure that our actions now, in the present moment, are creating the most positive influence possible for the future, for ourselves and for all others. "Even if I can't change the direction of the wind," someone said, "surely I can adjust my sails."

Karma and Rebirth

The ancient rishis taught that after death the soul assumes a new body, and that this birth is governed by the law of karma. So long as a soul is not liberated (merged into cosmic existence), it will maintain its individuality in one body or another, accumulating experiences, performing action, and creating future karma, moving forward or backward on the highway of evolution according to the nature of the actions performed.

Those who have led a wicked life are born as subhumans. A fellow who has been sucking the blood of the poor all his life may well be born as a mosquito; if he has been hiding and hoarding wealth and not sharing it with others, he may be born as a rat, said to be the greediest of animals.

If you smoke cigarettes and get cancer of the lung, you are to a great extent responsible for it. Your karma has given you its fruit in this very life. But what about the innocent ten-year-old child who has cancer? This can only be explained by his karma in previous lives—and the karma of his parents, for they also suffer greatly when the child has a disease like that.

Indeed, the doctrines of karma and rebirth provide the only reasonable explanations for many facts of life. How is it, for example, that some people show prodigious ability, such as in mathematics or music, at the age of three or four? Adi Shankara wrote commentaries on all the great ancient scriptures before he was sixteen years old. Where could such people possibly have gained the knowledge and experience to know what they knew, if not in some previous births?

Why do innocent, good people sometimes have to face tremendous difficulties and suffering, while others who are not so good may prosper? There is no plausible explanation, if one looks only to this one single life. As Swami Nikhilananda says, "What does he know of life who only one life knows?"

People who don't believe in the law of reincarnation and karma squander away their lives, impressing others, pretending to be what they are not. For every unpalatable happening in life they blame their parents or their "fate." They believe "the world hates a loser and admires a self-made man," no matter how many victims he may leave in his wake. Such a person, no matter what he might believe, is building up a mountain of karma that will return to him without fail.

The aggregate of a person's actions—good, bad, and indifferent—over many lifetimes, creates the body, the personality and character, as well as the tendencies and desires that drive us to particular actions today. These abilities and tendencies may be building up over the course of many, many lifetimes.

Take the case of a Buddha or a Jesus. As Swami Vivekananda said in his book *Karma Yoga*, how can you expect a petty king, such as Buddha's father, to produce a son whom half the world worships as God? Similarly, millions of carpenters like Jesus' father had lived earlier, and millions of children must have played in their courtyards with blocks of wood. The rising of a gigantic figure such as a Buddha or a Jesus cannot be explained either by genetics or environment, "nature" or "nurture." The tremendous spiritual power that manifested in these two great beings must have been accumulating through the ages, growing continually greater until it burst upon humanity.

No deed, small or great, good or evil, can be without effect. If a person is happy in this life, it is because he or she has produced a good, harmonious, positive influence in the environment by virtuous thoughts and deeds. When someone suffers in the present, it is the consequence of his having generated an influence of misery, ill health, and negativity in times past. This is the only logical explanation for the great disparities between man and man in this life, the tremendous differences in economic status, environmental conditions, family life, physical and mental endowments, as well as happiness and unhappiness, that are evident everywhere on the globe.

On the long path of evolution as it is understood in Indian philosophy, the individual's consciousness slowly unfolds. Consciousness (or Atman) is present in the stone no less than within the plants, the animals, or in man, but the stone can never know it so long as it remains a stone. It must evolve through higher forms until at last it reaches the level of humanity. Only in the human mind-body can the individual ego know its nature as consciousness.

Throughout the long journey toward total awakening to Reality, the individual is always subject to the law of karma. According to this law, his own desires and actions regulate the speed of his progress. By his own actions he builds or removes his own obstacles to ultimate enlightenment. His present state is conditioned by the karmas (actions) of his past, and at the same time he is continually determining his future by his present actions.

V. Dwarakanath Reddy explains in his book, *The Physics of Karma*, that karma, like gravity, is inexorable and knows no partiality. "Its lofty working," says Reddy, "determines every event and occurrence everywhere and at all times. Not a blade of grass moves and not a sparrow falls without obeying the impersonal and infinite dictates of the law of karma. The nexus between cause and effect is always one to one."

All our actions involve three different instruments: mind, speech, and the physical body. Positive thoughts such as of love, compassion, and charity are good mental actions. Speaking softly and not angrily, using appropriate words that do not hurt anyone, not being sarcastic, all create good karma. On the other hand, negative mental karma, or speaking harshly, will lead to negative effects in the future. The same is true of actions on the physical level. Helping, serving, healing are examples of good karma; harming, injuring, destroying are negative actions that will lead to negative results.

All our actions will eventually bear fruit, according to their nature. Bad karma retards our progress and pushes us down the line of devolution; good karma in thought, word, or deed pushes us forward and upward in our evolution.

Neither death nor birth interrupt this ever-unfolding process. The accumulation of karma carries on from birth to birth, life to life. The individual soul, sometimes called the *jiva* or *sukham sharira* (subtle body), goes from body to body, carrying its karma with it. As the Gita says:

> Certain indeed is death for the born and certain is birth for the dead; therefore over the inevitable you should not grieve.

> These bodies are known to have an end; the dweller in the body is eternal, imperishable, infinite.

> As the dweller in this body passes into childhood, youth and age, so also does he pass into another body.

> As a man casting off worn-out garments takes other new ones, so the dweller in the body, casting off worn-out bodies, takes others that are new.

The conditions of each individual's birth—his body and mind, the parents he comes through, the nature of his circumstances— is determined by the sum total of his karma. Each person is born with a blueprint of his or her life already prepared by actions in previous lives. Some physical traits and mental tendencies seem to be structured in the genes—but a person's genetic make-up matches his karma.

Karma and Heredity

How does this happen? How does a person's genetic inheritance fit in with the laws of karma? Don't we inherit genetic patterns and predispositions from our parents and ancestors? What does this have to do with the *samskaras* (karmic impressions) the soul brings with it?

A child is born with certain tendencies and characteristics.

Modern science says this is due to heredity, whereas ancient Indian scriptures explain that these tendencies were acquired in previous incarnations as a result of thoughts and actions long forgotten. Are the two theories compatible?

It all fits together neatly if we view heredity as occurring when the individual soul is driven, by its existing samskaras, to seek rebirth in a particular family, of parents whose qualities are like its own, so that it can "inherit" the tendencies it already possesses! The "cosmic computer" links up the soul with suitable parents, so that its karmic tendencies, its "merits" and "demerits," can find an appropriate environment for expression. This means, as tradition asserts, that you have really chosen your parents.

Tendencies for some diseases, such as cancer, are seen in certain families, and researchers consider the genetic factor important. Medical experts have been able to locate mutated genes that appear to greatly increase a person's risk of getting breast cancer, colon cancer, melanoma, thyroid cancer, and others, and tests are being developed to pinpoint the presence of these genes in a person's DNA. There is increasing talk of testing people on a wide scale and informing them, if they have the mutated gene, that they are likely to get cancer at a future date. Early detection, the theory goes, will help the person receive early treatment.

I find this idea alarming and I believe it will have detrimental effects. The candidates for cancer will get cancer earlier and with more certainty. Why do I say this? On the basis of experience.

I know of a number of completely asymptomatic persons who got a coronary angiography done because of some non-specific changes in their ECG. The angiogram typically showed a 40 to 50 percent stenosis or narrowing in one or two of the coronary arteries. This is not sufficient narrowing to cause either angina or heart attacks. However, these people began imagining what the "blockages" could do to them, and soon began having real angina: their arteries went into spasm due to their fear. One can well imagine what will happen when a person is told after his genetic tests that he is likely to have cancer after some years.

Instead, all those people who have a family history of heart attack or cancer should be told that it is not their parents' fault. Rather, it is *they* who chose to come into this world through those particular parents, because their karmic samskaras were similar. They have every chance now of modifying these samskaras by taking care to avoid all known risk factors, such as smoking, a high-fat diet, getting angry, etc. Modifying the effects of your past karma and healing disease is possible by resetting your mind. The person who thinks of himself as prone to sickness is more likely to get sick than a person with a healthy, optimistic attitude.

Karma and Free Will

Samskaras are built up by the continued action of thought waves, which in turn create new thought waves and lead to concrete actions and physical conditions. Swami Prabhavananda offers an analogy. On a lake, waves do not just disturb the surface of the water, they also, by their continued action, build up banks of sand and pebbles on the shore. These banks are more solid and permanent than the waves, yet they are not the same forever; they are constantly being modified according to the height, frequency, and strength of the waves.

If you expose your mind to constant thoughts of anger and resentment, you will find these anger waves building up in your life and resulting in concrete actions, even physical diseases. But just as a sandbank may shift if the current changes, the samskaras may be modified by the introduction and repetition of other kinds of thought waves in the mind.

Frequent repetition of positive thoughts and emotions, even something as simple as "Every day in every way I am becoming better," can be very effective. There is ample evidence now from the growing body of literature on mind-body medicine that a positive mental setting has been responsible for many remissions and healings of even serious diseases such as cancer. We can all shift the sandbanks of our samskaras by changing our thought waves.

I believe that by changing our habits and our thoughts, we can not only modify our own samskaras and our own destiny, but also those of our children and our children's children. Souls with a better "samskara track record" will be attracted to parents with suitable, matching samskaras.

All this suggests that while the law of karma is always in operation, the law of cause and effect as it applies to human life is not rigid and mechanical. The "judgment" of our actions is not absolute and irrevocable; the individual soul can always get its sentence reduced for good behavior. One lifetime of good works for the welfare of others may equalize several sterile or negative lives. Free will, in short, is always stronger than karmic destiny. No soul is ever so encumbered with old debts that it must drearily resign itself to pay and pay and pay.

You had free will, and you used it to choose or create where you are at this moment. You are not the victim of some vengeful god, sitting somewhere in heaven controlling your destiny with invisible strings. If you have made some mistakes with regard to the laws of nature and the rules of the game of life, that does not mean you must remain where you are. Through your will and efforts now, you can certainly modify your lot in this life and in the life hereafter.

Karma and Fate

Karma, then, is not "destiny" or "fate." Fate implies the helplessness of man to determine his own lot. Quite to the contrary, karma makes him the *creator* of his own destiny.

Our present dispositions are the result of our past karma, our past actions. But our *present* actions create our future. What is called fate or destiny is really the accumulation of tendencies produced by past actions and thoughts. This "fate" can be altered by new thoughts and actions. Thus each man is the architect of his own fate and the builder of his own destiny. Accepting with calmness and strength his present experience, he can shape a better future for himself.

Once we understand that our lives are the product of free will, the laws of karma, and reincarnation, our attitude toward life is bound to change. Without this knowledge, some of us tend to blame fate, our parents, our heredity, or even the government for our suffering or our present condition of life. Others say that everything is ordained by God. Those who have less than others, in terms of good health, material possessions, economic security, satisfaction in love and family, may disclaim

Understanding the Laws of Karma

"For everything detrimental that happens to him, man wants to blame God—or if not God, then someone else. This is psychological and spiritual immaturity. When you go to a good psychiatrist, he will encourage you to place the responsibility for overcoming your troubles on yourself, not others . . .

"Neither God nor anyone else has caused the difficulties we face in life; if you think so, you have not understood the great truth of the law of karma, cause and effect. You are the way you are because you have behaved in a certain way, and the way you behaved determines the kinds of fruits you are reaping in your present circumstance. A seed produces its own kind. An apple seed does not produce a carrot; it produces an apple. In the same way, wrong thoughts produce wrong actions; and wrong actions bring forth a wrong result. It cannot be otherwise. So you can forever continue to blame your problems on God, or your parents, or your environment, but that will not remove your troubles. It is like trying to remove darkness by beating at it with a stick. You may do that through all eternity, but it will never drive darkness away. The only way you can remove darkness is to bring in the light. If people only knew that this is what religion is truly about, there would be a spiritual renaissance in the world."

—*Sri Daya Mata, spiritual successor of Paramahansa Yogananda and president of the Self-Realization Fellowship* responsibility for their condition and spend their whole lives sulking and cursing their fate.

But knowledge of the law of karma and of reincarnation strengthens our faith in justice and order in the universe. We realize that it is we, and not God, our parents, the government, or any other force or power that is responsible for our present state of affairs. We are simply reaping the fruit of the seeds we have sown. And it is we who can change it or at least modify it to a very great extent by modifying our actions.

The ancient scriptures unequivocally state that our good and bad actions (karmas) in previous lives actively affect and determine our present life. Each individual soul is its own judge and passes sentence only on itself. But our *prarabdha* karma, the tendencies both positive and negative that determine our present life, can be modified and even overcome once we accept that our problems are of our own making and are therefore responsive to remaking. We only have to make sincere and persistent positive efforts.

We cannot just drift with the current; in order to counter the effects of the actions which have determined the present state of our lives, we have to swim upstream. We have to exercise what the *Yoga Vasistha* calls "self-effort."

The Importance of Self-Effort

"In this world," says the great rishi Vasistha to his pupil, the young Lord Rama, "whatever is gained is gained only by self-effort." The discourse that follows is perhaps the most powerful exhortation to disciplined, persevering self-effort that you will ever find. Vasistha clearly and strongly states that self-effort in the present is sufficient to counteract the karma of the past. "What is called fate," he says, "is fictitious and is not seen."

What is self-effort? The *Yoga Vasistha* (I will be quoting from Swami Venkatesananda's translation, published as *The Concise Yoga Vasistha*) defines it as "mental, verbal, and physical action" that "springs from right understanding that manifests in one's heart which has been exposed to the teachings of the scriptures and the conduct of holy ones." We might safely substitute the phrase, "behavior in accordance with the dictates of conscience," or "doing what we know to be good and right."

Vasistha tells Rama, "There is no power greater than right action in the present. Hence one should take recourse to self-effort, grinding one's teeth, and one should overcome evil by good, and fate by present effort."

The great enemy to evolution and progress is lack of effort, and Vasistha has no patience with such a person. "The lazy man is worse than a donkey," he says. "One should never yield to laziness." He calls laziness "a dreadful source of evil" and declares, "It is because laziness is found on earth that people live the life of animals, miserable and poverty-stricken."

> As is the effort, so is the fruit, O Rama. This is the meaning of self-effort . . . When afflicted by suffering, people cry, "Alas what tragedy" or "Alas, look at my fate," both of which mean the same thing. What is called fate or divine will is nothing more than the action of self-effort of the past.

But, he insists:

> The present is infinitely more potent than the past. They indeed are fools who are satisfied with the fruits of their past effort (which they regard as divine will) and do not engage themselves in self-effort now.

Again and again Rama is taught:

> You are not impelled to action by anything other than yourself. Hence you are free to strengthen the pure latent tendencies in preference to the impure ones [coming on from the past]. Persistently tread the path that leads to the eternal good.

The result of your endeavors, Vasistha says, "will be commensurate with the intensity of your self-effort, and neither fate nor a god can ordain it otherwise."

The idea of fate or "divine dispensation," says the sage, "is merely a convention that has come to be regarded as truth by being repeatedly declared to be true." But, in fact, "no one has ever realized the existence of fate or divine dispensation." Because of this, he tells Rama:

> One who says, "Fate is directing me to do this" is brainless, and the goddess of fortune abandons him.

The Universal Nature of Individual Action

As we have seen, activity is present everywhere, on all levels of nature. By action the wheel of creation moves on. As part of creation, you are connected with all other human beings, all the other creatures on earth, the hills, the forests, the moon, stars, sun, the galaxies. Because of this interconnectedness, your actions, according to ancient Indian scriptures, have a cosmic significance.

When you drop a pebble in a pond, ripples spread outward across the entire pond, until they reach the shore. Similarly, all our actions create an influence in our surroundings that ultimately affects the whole creation.

As one action has vast and varied consequences, so also a myriad influences converge on any single event. When a cloud appears in the sky, it doesn't just pop into existence in a moment. Many causes, beyond one's comprehension, come together for the production of this single effect, the appearance of a cloud in the sky and the fall of rain. Such is the case with anything that happens anywhere in the world, including birth or rebirth. For someone to be born in a particular place in a particular time, with these parents and this vast storehouse of capabilities to unfold and desires to fulfill—for this to happen, thousands or perhaps millions of causes must have joined together.

We may seem to have cut ourselves off from the universal Being. We imagine ourselves to be individuals bound by time and space, but the connection with all other beings, nature, and the Supreme Being can never be broken. We are just not ordinarily conscious of it.

There is no such thing as a local event in this world. Every event is a universal event. Our concepts of individuality and separateness are based on limited perception. As a matter of fact, we should not regard anything or anyone as a local individual or a local event, for everything is interconnected, universal.

Consequently, every action performed should not be for individual gain alone; it should be performed with the aim that it might benefit all beings. He who ignores the cosmic significance of action and works only for selfish purposes lives and works in vain; he who cooks for himself alone, the sages say, vitiates the whole universe.

The Farther Reaches of Karma

Haji Mohammed Rahim, an eighty-year-old God-fearing man, was transferred to our hospital from a nearby town some time ago for implantation of a permanent pacemaker. After his recent heart attack, he had three episodes of what is called Stokes Adam's Syndrome, when his heart rate dropped to about twenty-five beats per minute, not enough for adequate circulation and perfusion of the vital organs. The brain does not get enough oxygen, episodes of unconsciousness occur, and one of these attacks may also prove fatal.

In the absence of a properly operating natural pacemaker, an artificial, battery-operated pacemaker is inserted in the heart to keep it beating at the desired rate. But after we implanted a temporary pacemaker and gave him two days of treatments, his own natural pacemaking mechanism started working normally.

"Haji" designates a person who has been on a pilgrimage to Mecca. Haji Mohammed Rahim was a very pious man and God was kind to him.

I told him, "You are fine now. You have recovered from your heart attack. You don't need a permanent pacemaker and we are going to send you home."

"That is news to me," he replied. "I thought this heart attack was my end. I came to your hospital because my son insisted, otherwise I was all set to leave the world and go up there."

I said laughingly, "But Haji Sahib, God refused to take you because there was no vacancy there in that world, so He has ordained that you'd better continue staying here in ours."

"I'm surprised," he retorted, "that there's no vacancy. There seems to be some miscalculation. Every day we see that the population on our planet, and especially in our country India, is increasing by leaps and bounds. One fellow goes up there, and ten fellows are born here at that very moment. How can I believe there's no vacancy up there?"

For a while I didn't have an answer, then I suddenly remembered what the great Urdu poet Sir Mohammed Iqbal had written six decades ago in his poem, "Sitaron se aage jahan aur bhi hain," meaning that there are many planets and galaxies in this universe, and there are endless, innumerable universes one beyond another (see Appendix 2). I recited the poem to Haji Sahib, explaining that the traffic of individual souls is apparently not confined to one or two planets. There may well be many other planets where we go to or come from in our previous and subsequent lives. That gave us both something to think about.

Action and the Three Gunas

The sage Patanjali, author of *Yoga Sutras*, the basic textbook on yoga, says that the quality of your actions depends on the gunas predominant in you. The three gunas—sattva, rajas, and tamas—are said to be the fundamental qualities of nature, or *prakriti*. To grasp this fully, we have to look at the Indian understanding of the creation and dissolution of the universe.

It is said that from time to time the universe dissolves and then is re-created. When in its undifferentiated, unmanifest phase, it remains in a seed state for a certain period. During that time the gunas are in a state of absolute equilibrium, and prakriti, or material nature, does not arise. As long as the gunas remain in balance, prakriti remains undifferentiated and the universe exists only as a potential. All that exists is consciousness, unbounded, unmanifest pure Being, Brahman, the changeless Absolute, which has no beginning and no end.

As soon as the balance is disturbed, a re-creation of the universe begins. From the changeless consciousness, the continuously changing universe is created anew. The gunas enter into an enormous variety of combinations and permutations, with one or the other predominating over the rest. This gives rise to the endless variety of physical and mental phenomena that make up the world we experience.

The gunas are sometimes described as energies, sometimes as qualities or forces. They represent a triangle of forces, at the same time opposed and complementary, which govern the physical universe as well as our personalities and behavior patterns in day-to-day life, giving rise to our achievements or failures, happiness or sadness, health or disease.

As regards action, sattva is the creative force, the essence of form that has to be realized. Tamas is inertia, the obstacle to its realization. Rajas is the energy or power by which the obstacle is removed and the form is made manifest.

Let us follow the example offered by Swami Prabhavananda and Christopher Isherwood in *How to Know God* (Patanjali's *Yoga Sutras*). Suppose a sculptor wishes to create a statue of Lord Krishna out of stone. The idea of the statue, the form that the artist sees in his imagination, the creative impulse and image, is inspired by sattva. The marble represents tamas, formless solidity, the obstacle that has to be overcome.

Prabhavananda suggests that there may also be an element of tamas in the sculptor himself. He may think, "I'm tired; why should I work so hard? This is too hard. Maybe I'll do something easier." But here the force of rajas comes to his aid. Rajas is manifested in the sculptor's energy and will, by which he conquers the tamasic lethargy of his mind and the solid inertia of the stone. It also inspires the physical, muscular exertion that he puts into his work.

If, says Swami Prabhavananda, a sufficient amount of rajas is generated, the obstacle of tamas will be overcome and the ideal form conceived by sattva will be created out of the granite block. This example demonstrates that all three gunas are necessary for any creative action. "Sattva alone," he says, "would be just an unrealized idea, rajas without sattva would be mere undirected energy, rajas without tamas would be like a lever without a fulcrum." And tamas alone would be inertia.

Sattva is often said to represent purity and tranquility; rajas refers to action, motion, and violence; tamas is the principle of solidity, immobility, resistance, and inertia. All three gunas are present in everything but one always predominates. Sattva predominates in sunlight, rajas in an erupting volcano, and tamas in a block of stone.

In our own minds, the gunas are found in rapidly changing interrelationship. Thus we experience many shifting moods during the course of a day. If sattva predominates, we may experience moments of inspiration, disinterested affection, quiet joy, or meditative calm. Sattva represents purity, light, intelligence, knowledge, contentment, clarity of mind, kindness, compassion, cooperation. Quietude and peace prevail in a sattvic person or a sattvic mood. As intelligence and clarity, sattva gives a right sense of direction. Qualities of a person with predominant sattva include fearlessness, uprightness, purity, forgiveness, and absence of passion, anger, and jealousy. Such a person is peaceful and happy.

When sattva dominates, the mind becomes steady like the flame of a lamp in a windless place. A steady mind is helpful for both activity and meditation, and he who is predominantly sattvic can meditate effectively and is capable of real concentration.

A person with dominant rajas never finds peace. Rajas brings on outbursts of rage or provokes intense desire. It makes a person restless and discontented, and spurs continuous activity. A person with dominant rajo-guna cannot sit quiet; he must continually have something to do. Great passion is rajasic, as are aggressiveness, greed, and anger. At the same time, rajas in its more positive expression, especially when combined with sattva, is responsible for constructive, creative activity, as it brings energy, enthusiasm, and physical courage.

A rajasic person loves power and objects of the senses. Constantly engaged in activity, he will crave more and more power to lord it over people, and is very much attached to worldly things. The direct manifestation of dominant rajas is the insatiable fire of desire. Desires must be fulfilled or the person's life is miserable! The more he fulfills desires, the more he wants. He becomes a "morest"—a little more, a little more, a little more . . . He is acquiring wealth, power, name, and fame, but it is never enough.

When rajas is intense it envelops knowledge and is the foe of wisdom. Under the pressure of rajas, a man harbors greed, lust, and anger. Rajas attacks a person through the senses, the mind, and the understanding, deluding the embodied soul. For a useful life, and to have peace of mind, rajas has to be pacified and balanced with sattva.

Tamas, says Swami Prabhavananda, is "the mental bog into which we sink whenever sattva and rajas cease to prevail." When tamas prevails in our minds and moods, we exhibit some of our worst qualities: sloth, stupidity, obstinacy, and the depths of heavy despair. Tamas is often described as darkness and inertia. Helplessness, dullness, confusion, resistance, and ignorance also characterize tamas. When tamas dominates, the mind may become forgetful, sleepy, dull, and incapable of any worthwhile thoughts or actions.

A person under the grip of tamas may be more like an animal than a human; without the power of clear judgment, he may fail to distinguish between right and wrong. Like an animal, he will live for himself and may hurt others to fulfill his desires. In his ignorance and darkness, he may perform vicious actions.

Sattva attaches to happiness, rajas to action, while tamas, verily shrouding knowledge, attaches to heedlessness.

—BHAGAVAD GITA, 14:9

Balancing the Gunas Paves the Way to Healthy Living

Successful action depends on having the right balance of the three gunas. Pure sattva, as desirable as it may seem, cannot stand by itself. It is always mixed with rajas and tamas. It is sometimes said that the right balance for a human being is to be dominated by sattva, but to have sufficient rajas to make action dynamic. Sattva provides the right direction, rajas the energy or motive power. Only a little tamas is needed. When sattva is combined with rajas, the result is positive and creative and will move swiftly toward fruition; if tamas teams up with rajas, the results will tend to be less desirable.

By pacifying and checking rajas and tamas, you can increase sattva. Thinking about and trying to develop virtues, such as forgiveness, compassion, love, empathy, generosity, truthfulness, contentment, naturally increase sattva. If you can get rid of unnecessary rajasic and tamasic thoughts, you can win the internal warfare among the gunas that goes on in our minds like the war between the gods and demons. Watch your thoughts through careful introspection.

Interest in music and the fine arts help to increase sattva, and regular yoga asanas and meditation help a lot.

When sattva dominates in your mind, thoughts of inquiry into Truth will manifest. Restlessness simply goes away. The mind becomes one-pointed, and a meditative mood will dawn upon you without effort.

The impurities of mind caused by tamas may be removed by purifying the mind in the fire of vairagya, or dispassion. Vairagya does not, as some people think, mean giving up anything in the world. It means that you must realize that all the material things in your life, including your wealth, your near and dear ones, even your body, don't actually belong to you: they belong to the universe. Like a stage actor, you may use these things and interact with them on the stage of life, but use them while remaining unattached. Since nothing belongs to you, what is there for you to give up? If you have that attitude of dispassion, you can be at peace with yourself and with the world, and spontaneous right action, right karma, will follow.

The ultimate secret of successful action, as described by Lord Krishna to Arjuna in the Bhagavad Gita, is not to balance the three gunas, or merely to increase sattva, but to go *beyond* the three gunas. As Swami Prabhavananda says, "Several chapters of the Bhagavad Gita are devoted to the gunas and their manifestations. The spiritual aspirant is advised to transcend them."

Since Arjuna is a warrior about to go into battle, Lord Krishna wants to give him the highest teaching, to inspire action that will be both successful and evolutionary at the same time. What He tells him is to step entirely out of the field of the three gunas, to transcend duality and enter Unity or Oneness, the field of Yoga, Union, the realm of the Self.

> Be without the three gunas, O Arjuna, freed from duality, ever firm in purity, independent of possessions, possessed of the Self. *(2:45)*.

Then, He says, once established in this state, perform action.

> Established in Yoga, O winner of wealth, perform actions having abandoned attachment and having become balanced in success and failure, for balance of mind is called Yoga. *(2:48)*

That, says Krishna, is "skill in action." In that state of realization, you are a witness, uninvolved in action. Then only can you be completely and spontaneously balanced in loss or gain, success or failure, pleasure or pain, because you know something greater, the Self, the Eternal Reality. In Prabhavananda's words, "He is like one who sits unconcerned, and is not disturbed by the gunas . . . He rests in the inner calm of the Atman, regarding happiness and suffering as one." This is the fulfillment of karma yoga: performing action (karma) established in Union with the Divine (yoga).

On Karma

The law of cause and effect is inexorable and unrelenting. You reap a harvest of suffering, poverty, pain, and sorrow because you have sown the seed of evil in the past. You reap a harvest of plenty and bliss owing to your sowing of seeds of good.

—*Sivananda*

Not in the heavens above, nor in the farthest reaches of the sea, nor by transporting yourself to the remotest valleys of the mountains, will you be able to hide from the consequences of your own evil actions. Likewise, certain are the blessings growing out of your good actions.

—*Gautama Buddha*

If you help others, you will be helped, perhaps tomorrow, perhaps in one hundred years, but you will be helped. Nature must pay off the debt. It is a mathematical law, and all life is mathematics.

—*G. I. Gurdjieff*

It is foolish to be surprised when a fig tree produces figs.

—*Marcus Aurelius*

We are the makers of our own lives. There is no such thing as fate. Our lives are the result of our previous actions, our karma, and it naturally follows that, having been ourselves the makers of our karma, we must also be able to unmake it.

—*Vivekananda*

6

Non-Attachment:
The Performance of Action
without Pain

The bird of paradise alights upon the hand that does not grasp.

—JOHN BERRY

For my yoke is easy, and my burden is light.

—JESUS

Jagdish was a famous actor working for a well-known theatrical company. A top performer, he played his roles well, whether the part was that of a beggar or a business tycoon.

One evening Jagdish was playing the part of a king. It was a powerful drama and he was at his best. The hall was full, the audience clapped a number of times during the performance, and as the final scene came to a close the hundreds of people in the hall gave him a standing ovation.

After the curtain went down, Jagdish remained sitting on the throne with the crown on his head. The stagehands, the prompter, and the other players were surprised. They reminded him, "The show is over, why aren't you getting up?"

Jagdish showed his displeasure and said, "You know I am King Bingarajan. You fellows do not know how to address a king. I will send all of you to prison for your behavior."

The workers ultimately had to use force in order to dislodge him from the throne. He completely forgot who he was, Jagdish the actor playing a role, and instead became completely identified with the role he was playing.

We All Identify with Our Role

Exactly the same thing happens to all of us in real life, and is the cause of our unhappiness and misery. We forget who we are— the blissful, unbounded Self—and we identify completely with our "role" as an individual bound by time, space, and all the many aspects of our personalities and circumstances.

Shakespeare said, "All the world's a stage, and all the people in it merely players." We all play many roles, in this life and in the lives we have lived and shall live in the future. Therefore we should not get attached to the role we are playing now, but the fact is that most of us do.

The actor Dennis Weaver has pointed out that when you are acting in a movie or a play, you have everything necessary to play your part—dialogue, props, the right costume and makeup, a good relationship with the director—but as you are performing, you know that it is not real. You know that when the curtain goes down, you will have to give your props to the prop man, your costume to the wardrobe lady.

It is the same with our life in this world, says Weaver, though we usually forget. The things we are using—house, car, clothing—don't really belong to us, they belong to the universe. They have been given to us as a gift, in order to help us play our part well. We ought to remember that when the final curtain comes down, we will have to give all these props back to "The Great Prop Man in the Sky."

And just as in a stage play, if we want to play our part well in real life, we need a good relationship with the Director; we have to surrender our will, our ideas and demands to the Director so that the entire play, with its many characters and scenes, will be a success.

When a person gets unduly attached to worldly objects—the costume and props, the house, car, clothing, relationships—he desires to possess them and not to lose hold of them under any circumstances. His success and failure, loss and gain, pleasure and pain, his possessions and plans, all become extremely important.

The world of objects can smother a man who gives importance to them. It is that importance that gives power to these objects. If he feels someone is likely to take them away from him or is in the way of his possessing them, he becomes angry or afraid. The mental disturbances caused by his negative emotion cloud his intellect, and stress takes hold of him. Whether or not his fears have any basis in "external" reality— whether someone is actually playing the role of his adversary as he imagines—is irrelevant to the stressful reaction he has.

But as the Gita says, "A man of disciplined mind, who moves among the objects of sense, with the senses under control, free from attachment and aversion—he attains purity of spirit. And in that purity of spirit, there is produced for him an end of all sorrow" (2:64–65). One who has learned to live among sense-objects in a spirit of least attachment or aversion for them, attains tranquility and peace of mind.

A ship with sails up without anyone at the controls would be completely at the mercy of a storm, with its strong winds and waves, and will not reach its goal in the harbor. That is what happens to a man who has no self-control, whereas a man who is anchored and rooted in the Self is destined to live a peaceful and purposeful life with enduring success.

The sense of joy or elation is a wave, and that of pain or sorrow another wave. Both are agitations, disturbing the calm silence of the mind. A person established in the Self is not thrown about by such stormy waves. He is fully awake in the radiance of the transcendental Reality, infinite and eternal, calm and balanced in the midst of all.

The sensations of pleasure and pain, joy and sorrow, gain and loss are impermanent, transitory. That doesn't mean we should turn away from pleasure returning to us as a result of some of our actions, nor that we can somehow escape the pain we will feel as a result of other actions. What the wisdom of the Gita and other scriptures tell us is that we should not get struck in either pleasure or pain. Let the river of life flow.

The sensations of pleasure are welcome, but we should not get too attached to them: we are going to miss them and become miserable when they go away, as they certainly will. When pain comes, don't oppose it, it has to be accepted. There is no choice, it is the result of our actions in this life or lives lived earlier. This sorrow or pain, though unavoidable, is also not permanent. It will pass, and while it is there you may or may not suffer from it, depending on your attitude of mind. As someone said, "Pain is unavoidable, suffering is optional."

The goal, then, is to accept pleasure as it comes and not oppose pain when it comes; both will come and go. No more reaching out toward pleasure (*sukha*) begging it to linger, no longer resenting the pain (*dukha*). Remain unshaken, balanced, free.

It is not easy to achieve or maintain this attitude, but meditation and the direct experience of the Self, the witness, help a lot. The more you know the Self, the less power pleasure and pain have to disturb your equilibrium and play havoc with your peace of mind.

Non-Attachment and Karma Yoga

When work is done without desire for personal gain it becomes a cosmic, spiritual action. Such work is utterly different from the mechanical or instinctive action characteristic of the animal level of life, or the egocentric action of the average man and woman. With such egocentric action one may accumulate riches that buy many comforts, a big house, an air-conditioned car, a large bank account, but one feels hollow inside and is comfortably unhappy.

Ordinarily karma has a binding quality. It leaves behind subtle impressions, which at a future time, under favorable circumstances, become the cause of new actions. The new actions likewise cause another set of impressions, which in turn become the cause of yet other actions. So the wheel of karma turns, and man performs actions impelled by the past.

How to avoid this causal law and perform action as a free man? The solution lies in karma yoga.

In describing karma yoga, the Bhagavad Gita says, "You have the right to your actions alone, never to its fruits." That is, you have to perform action to the best of your ability, but you have to accept whatever comes. This is because we can exercise quite a bit of control and direction over action, but over the results of our action we have no control at all. We just don't know how it will turn out. No matter how well we have done our part, undoubtedly our past karma will be influencing the results.

That is why the Gita says that those who are attached to the outcome, who act with their eye always on the results, are "wretched." They will never have peace, nor will they be able to act effectively.

When performing action, you need unshakable concentration and full control of your mind. It is crucial to focus your attention completely on what you are doing, not to be thinking about the results. Do the work to the best of your ability, with devotion to the task. Be "process oriented," not "goal oriented." The cause of failure in life, in undertakings both large and small, is often in our carelessness over the process, the many details involved.

Every action, following the causal laws of nature, will inevitably produce its fruits. The result will be in accordance with the laws of karma. These laws are not made by you, and they don't go wrong. Every result is the right result. So why be concerned? You have done your best. Now relax, let it go, and leave the rest to nature.

What matters most is the spirit in which we do our work. What's important is how we shoot the arrow. It really does not matter whether we hit the target or not.

This doesn't mean you shouldn't expect results. Non-attachment doesn't mean trying to act without desiring a certain result. That wouldn't be realistic. In fact, it is good to have a clear mental picture of your ultimate goal, so you know exactly what you are striving for. Idealize the real and you will realize the ideal. But once you have a clear vision of your goal, drop it and get to work. If you drop the thoughts about the fruits of action from your mind, you will be able to pay better attention to the details of your action.

Once the action is performed, you will get what you deserve, not necessarily what you desire. The results will be based on *all* your past karma, not only on the present action. And where other people are involved, as they usually are, the results will also reflect their karma.

Thus, the results may not be in accordance with your expectations. In that case, you may become frustrated, disappointed, even angry. This stressful reaction will adversely affect your mind and your body. So, rather than feel angry and disappointed, why not think it over? There may be something you overlooked, something you could have done better. Maybe there is a lesson for next time. In any case, there is no need to get frustrated. Rather, accept the result as cheerfully as possible.

The more you appreciate the workings of karma, the more you realize that action never fails, it only produces results. A given expectation may be said to have "failed" to occur, but *I* have not failed, nor has the action failed, only the expectations have been wrong. This is because I did not know all the factors that were involved in shaping the result. And indeed we can never know them all. It is far too complex for our human mind to comprehend.

That is why the Bhagavad Gita tells us that we must work to the very best of our ability in all spheres of our lives, and then offer it to the Lord. (It is obvious that we cannot offer Him our second best.) Having done that, we must not despair if our work has disappointing results, or if it is criticized or altogether disregarded. On the other hand, we must not give way to pride and vanity if the results of our actions are very fruitful and win popular praise. Only *we* know if we have done our best, and that knowledge in itself is our reward. All men of genuine greatness and integrity do their duty in this spirit.

If you want your actions to bring you happiness no matter what the result is, you have to offer your work to the Lord. You have to invoke His grace. The attitude of offering your work to the Lord and accepting the result as a blessing from Him removes all our anxieties, problems, and conflicts and brings a sense of security and a feeling of well-being.

Whether or not you belong to a conventional religion or creed, or whether you believe in a personal God or not, you can practice karma yoga by engaging in unselfish, dedicated action. This way you will gradually attain peace and freedom, like the peace that a devotee gains through meditation.

By performing selfless right action, one's mind becomes purified and one spontaneously starts to live the nobler values of life. The texture of one's emotions and thoughts changes. If there seems not to be any immediate reward, remember that good deeds are like seeds that await favorable conditions for germination.

Performing our actions while remembering our connection with the Supreme Being and invoking God's grace makes every task easier. He is always with you in your unselfish endeavors. "The breeze of His grace is always blowing," said Sri Ramakrishna. "We only have to raise our sails to catch it."

"It is not possible to detach completely from egocentric desires," said Swami Vivekananda. "The only solution to becoming as unattached as possible is to attach yourself to the Lord, the Self. This way you will be more successful."

Paramahansa Ramakrishna taught that we should play our part in the drama of life to the best of our ability, but our mind should be on God all the time. We should be reveling in divine consciousness all the time, while we are engaged in the affairs of this phenomenal world. The part, played well, will be useful to all the others around us, and we will have peace of mind.

Krishna says in the Gita that those who perform action

without devotion to the Lord are wasting their time. When action is performed without desire for personal gain, it gives the performer of the action evenness of mind in all circumstances, favorable or unfavorable, in gain or loss, success or failure. Why? Because your ego is not involved in the result.

Detached Attachment Should Be Our Aim

Let us sum up our discussion by looking at what non-attachment both is and is not.

First of all, non-attachment is not indifference. It is not cold, deliberate shunning of everybody and everything. Vivekananda at one time wanted to spend most of his time in meditation, but his master Ramakrishna told him it was inhuman to neglect the world, with indifference to everything, for the sake of personal salvation.

Running from life and its duties, giving up one's possessions or ignoring one's relationships and responsibilities, is not renunciation or non-attachment. Nor is non-attachment a kind of fatalism. A fatalist believes that it really does not matter whether he works hard, tries hard, or not. "Whatever happens has to happen," he says.

Action has to be performed with full dedication and devotion, but without attachment to the fruits of action. The attitude of a fatalist toward the fruits of action is not non-attachment but indifference.

Non-attachment also does not mean abstention from action. The Gita warns about this, and says that he who restrains the organs of action but continues to dwell mentally on objects of the senses deludes himself and can be called a hypocrite. Except in the deep silence of meditation, it is not possible to refrain from action; as we saw in Chapter 5, action is going on all the time; awake or asleep, we are thinking, talking, dreaming, digesting, and so on.

Non-attachment comes by discrimination. For one who has realized the Self, attachment to actions and their results naturally fades away. Such a man moves freely, without longing, without the sense of "I" or "mine," doing his work with peace of mind.

Non-attachment may seem difficult to achieve, but it is not really so. In fact, when your mind abides in the Self, non-attachment is automatic. Right from the early stages of experiencing the Self in meditation, non-attachment begins to grow, even if it grows slowly. From the beginning, it gives you a new sense of freedom and peace. By virtue of your expanded consciousness, you increasingly identify with the Self rather than your limited personality.

This attachment to a higher reality helps you to renounce "I-ness," "mine-ness," and lingering selfish desires, and to have a state of mind free from all impure tendencies. Then you can be in the world among worldly things, working happily amid them. It is the quietude and serenity of your mind that makes you happy and free and in bliss.

The deepest, most innocent and complete experience of non-attachment occurs when a person becomes Self-realized. When one is established in the blissful, expanded, peaceful state of pure consciousness, the "pairs of opposites" such as pleasure and pain, success and failure, gain and loss, fail to shake the mind. They are like candles held up to the sun.

If you are the ocean, any number of waves can rise and fall on your surface; any number of rivers can run into you, and your status as an ocean, your fullness, will remain. As it is said in the Bhagavad Gita,

> Water flows continuously into the ocean
> But the ocean is never disturbed.
> Desire flows into the mind of the seer
> But he is never disturbed.
> The seer knows peace.
> He knows peace who has forgotten desire.
> He lives without craving
> Free from ego, free from pride.

We will talk about this more in the following chapter.

7

Self-Realization: Master Key to Health and Happiness

The measure of human life is man transcending himself. This is ultimate Dharma.

—CHATURVEDI BADRINATH

Vast, divine, beyond all imagination, shines the truth of the Self, the supreme Reality, as subtler than the subtlest, farther than the farthest. It is nearer than the nearest here, within the body. The sages realize it verily seated in the cave of your heart.

—MUNDAKOPANISHAD, 111, 1:7

The learned Ashtavakra was a sage by the time he was twelve years of age. He, along with his father Kabor, lived in the kingdom of the sage-king Janaka. As often happened in those days, Janaka organized a debate in his palace between two renowned experts in scriptures, Kabor and Sri Vandin. When news reached Ashtavakra that his father was not able to answer a question that King Janaka had posed, he gained admission to the court and soon stood before the king, who then asked him the troublesome question.

One day after lunch, the king said, he was taking a nap in his flower-strewn royal bed. His servants were fanning him. After a while he fell asleep, and dreamed that a neighboring king attacked his kingdom and defeated him. He had to run from the kingdom, and soon was on the verge of starvation. He came across a field of corn, picked two ears, and was going to eat them when the owner of the field suddenly appeared and starting beating him severely. Shrieking with pain, King Janaka woke up and found that he was in his own royal bed, with the servants still fanning him.

"My question," said the great king, "is this: which was real, the dream or what I found when I woke from the dream? None of the courtiers or the wise pandits have been able to satisfactorily answer this question for me."

Ashtavakra replied, "O king, neither the waking state nor the dream state is real. When you are awake, the dream state does not exist, and when you are dreaming, the waking world disappears, so obviously neither can be true. What is true and real does not vanish like that.

"In the waking state we are totally immersed in outer experience and activity and we think it is real. When we are dreaming, our understanding and our activities are completely different; so long as we continue to dream, we think that is the reality, even though we may experience a lifetime, from childhood through old age, and wake up to find that only a few minutes have gone by.

"The third state is sleep. This also is not real, for then, when we are neither awake nor dreaming, we are not aware of the world around us or of dreams within.

"We ordinarily live in these three states of consciousness, but none of them is real. When you are in meditation, you can transcend these three states. You are alert, but your mind gets infused with the Self, supreme consciousness, our base and the source of all there is in the universe. Once we understand that, and experience the Reality, we no longer identify ourselves with our physical body. The three ordinary states of consciousness come and go, but we are separate from them, fixed in the Self.

"Eventually, a feeling of universal brotherhood dawns upon us, as we realize that the same stream of life runs through everybody's veins; each being in this universe is a manifestation of the Self, Consciousness, God. It is *that* state of consciousness, O King, and not the waking, dreaming, or deep sleep state, that is real."

The Search for Happiness

The search for Truth, for knowledge of what is truly Real, is a purely human quest. Most people, content with making a living and raising a family, never even consider it. People like King Janaka, and those souls in every generation who are consciously seeking Truth, are rare. But it is they who unlock the higher powers of the human mind and spirit and inspire the rest of us.

In reality, however, these seekers are just doing what everyone else on earth is doing, in their own special way. They are seeking happiness. Whether we think of it in terms of greater success, more love, more money, higher position, better health, a more contented family life, more knowledge or understanding, it is ultimately happiness that we are all seeking. What turns a man or woman into a seeker is the realization, common to people in all ages, that happiness of a lasting nature cannot be gained through the ordinary experience of the material world.

Try as you might, you cannot think of any object in this world, any person, any situation, that can bring you permanent security or happiness. Particular people, particular achievements, may give you joy, satisfaction, pleasure, comfort—but not lasting happiness or bliss. The world is simply not capable of bringing you unshakable happiness.

Success and failure, pleasure and pain are relative, like hot and cold. They are some of the pairs of opposites that form our experience of the external world. The sweet does not come without the bitter, the pleasant without pain or loss, success without failure.

A mother giving birth to a child has pain but does not suffer; there is a pleasant feeling of joy in that pain. Your child is moving to another town. You feel pangs of separation, but you are satisfied and happy he or she is doing well and you are proud of it. Your daughter has just been married and she is going to move away to live with her husband close to her in-laws. You have never been away from her since she was born. You do not know how you can bear separation from her, and you are not sure the in-laws will give her the love she deserves, so you are crying; but at the same time you are happy inside that your daughter has got married. Your son has been offered a job in another country, and will relocate, probably for good. He is a bright fellow and he will do well there; you are happy. But you are sad, too: who is going to look after you when you are old, frail, and alone and you fall sick?

This is life as we know it, these bittersweet experiences. Even when there is an abundance of the positive, we know that the sweetness, pleasure, success, all these experiences that we consider positive or attractive, are transitory. They simply do not last. The wheel turns.

The only true and lasting happiness is union with the Self, the Atman. All other happiness is relative, temporary, and therefore, ultimately false. Genuine happiness can come only from within yourself.

What is the Self?

The Bhagavad Gita and other classic texts describe the various layers of subjective life, from gross to subtle. Our body is our outermost shell. With its sense instruments for hearing, seeing, and touching, the body is a useful tool, through which we can perform actions and fulfill our desires. But it is "our" tool—"my" body—not my deepest self. This body is ever-changing, constantly transforming itself from infancy to old age. If this is "myself," which version of the body is me? If I am my body, am I still myself if the body becomes sick, or crippled, or loses a limb? There must be something deeper.

Subtler than the body and senses is the mind. This swiftly changing pattern of thoughts, memories, desires, perceptions, feels more intimate than the body, but it too is unreliable. What I believed in yesterday I now see was a mistake. No matter what thoughts or feelings pass through my mind, "I" remain separate from them; I was there yesterday and I am still here today no matter what goes through my mind, so "I" must be something other than this busy mind.

At a very fine level of the mind is the intellect, which discriminates and decides. It gives a direction to our thinking and action.

And what is beyond even the intellect? The Self, the silent source of intelligence before a thought even flickers, the underlying Reality of our life. From both experience and scriptural authority, the Self can be described as eternal bliss consciousness, pure awareness, pure being. It is One wholeness, universal intelligence, the underlying truth of myself and of all other selves.

Experience of the Self is gained by meditating. By directing the mind inward, away from the variety of life toward the inner unity, by sitting quietly and letting the ceaseless activity of the mind settle down, one comes to know one's innermost nature, the Self. That field is the organizing intelligence responsible for the orderliness of the whole universe. With continued meditation, as a person's intellect gets infused with the glow of this infinite intelligence, life moves ever more powerfully in an evolutionary direction. The channels of love, compassion, happiness, health, and peace open up. Life becomes increasingly whole.

Thus the first principle for acquiring Self-knowledge is the discrimination between the real and the unreal, the passing and the permanent. You have to realize that the real you is timeless, beyond birth and death. The body will survive as long as it is needed. It is not important that it should live long, only that so long as it lives it should live in accordance with the laws of nature, growing and evolving to life's ultimate goal, Self-knowledge.

The life of man should be a journey from hatred to love, from bondage to freedom, from ignorance to wisdom, from darkness to light, from weakness to strength, from pain and suffering to bliss. The central teaching of the Bhagavad Gita, *Yoga Vasistha*, and other great scriptures is that one should enjoy this develop ment by realizing the Self while living in this world doing one's duty.

The Long Path of Evolution

Enlightenment, realization of the Self, is the final step in the long path of evolution. The Western (Darwinian) concept of evolution simply describes the different levels of evolution evident in nature: rocks, plants, animals, man, and others. The Indian understanding is that the individual soul passes through all these stages, eventually becoming liberated when it realizes its true essential nature as pure consciousness, the universal divine Being.

The state of evolution is dependent upon the degree of awareness or consciousness something or someone can manifest through its physical and mental faculties. Stones display no obvious consciousness; they are inert. Plants are quite a bit more conscious. If you put a plant in the shade, it will turn its branches toward the light. A sunflower follows the sun in the sky millions of miles away. Many experiments demonstrate that plants apparently respond to music, reacting differently to different qualities of sound. Animals, another step higher on the evolutionary scale, are obviously far more conscious; they can respond to language, show feelings, learn new behaviors.

But man is a giant step higher. Human beings do not live merely by instinct and impulse, like animals. We have the capacity and the need to have a wider view of actions and their consequences. We can regulate our emotions, desires, and habits, using the power of discrimination that has been bestowed on us. We can reason, decide, create, and even fly to the moon. Most of all, we can realize our true nature. We can stand apart and be a witness to our thoughts, standing in the silence of the Self.

From this perspective man is certainly at the top among all the forms of life we know on this planet. Yet if you look around, it is quite clear that not all men have evolved to the same extent.

People evidence great disparities in intelligence, love, morality, and other crucial aspects of life.

Some of us, for example, cannot analyze a situation dis-passionately, nor discriminate between right and wrong. Some, although in human form, seem not to have gone beyond an earlier stage of evolution. Some seem to have the inert tendency of rocks; others are vegetable-men with a cabbage head and pumpkin body; they respond here and there and like a plant may turn toward the sun, but they cannot think properly and are quite dominated by tamas.

Still others are animal-men, having varied temperaments but largely dominated by rajas and tamas. There are serpent-men, scorpion-men, and tiger-men, with behavior like these animals. They have not yet developed the faculty of discrimination or a love for their fellow beings.

Among those who have evolved into the man-man stage, there are two types of people, the hawks and the doves. The hawks strive for possessions, for pleasure and power. They believe it does not matter if others suffer from their pursuit and achievement of these aims. The doves, on the other hand, are real men; they believe in the principle "live and let live."

Finally there are men in whom divinity has become manifest. We can think of them as fully developed human beings, or God-men. They lighten the darkness of all who come across them and enlighten them with knowledge about life and living, says Swami Chinmayananda.

This is a state possible for all of us. By choosing to be healthy and pure (sattvic), by learning to meditate and practicing meditation regularly to unfold that inner glory, we can grow toward an enlightened state of being.

The hansa is a stately water bird found in the Himalayas. Belonging to the swan family, it is snow-white in color and has a long graceful neck. Hansas appear in pairs as lovebirds in many legends. Poets and scholars have written love stories and fairy tales about hansas in ancient Indian literature and scriptures.

According to various legends, hansas are also endowed with

a great sense of discrimination. It is said that a hansa can dip its beak into a mixture of milk and water and drink only the milk, leaving the water behind.

Most people can discriminate between various kinds of material objects, or between material gain and loss. Some can discriminate between moral values of right and wrong. But only a very few are able to achieve spiritual discrimination, by which they can know the real from the unreal, the eternal from the false, bliss from the transient pleasures of life. Such beings come upon God.

Param hansa or Paramahansa (supreme or super hansa) is the name given to a person who knows the true happiness or bliss of reveling in the Self. Such a person serves as a model and a guide, a teacher and inspiration for all of us.

Living the Unity of Life

The deeper you go in your meditation, the higher you rise. The closer you grow to the invisible source, the greater the healing power. Fixed in the silence of the Self, you maintain equilibrium of mind under all circumstances, favorable and unfavorable.

You realize that the same stream of life runs through everybody's veins, and that He alone dwells in the heart of all beings. The whole universe, stones, plants, animals, all are alive. The universe is one unbroken whole. All there is, is the One, the uni-verse, the One looking at itself, interacting with itself. You comprehend the ancient wisdom of the rishis, or sages, who say in the Vedic texts that there is nothing other than Brahman, the cosmic Self, that appears in many forms and variations.

> You are man, you are woman, you are youth and maiden too. You are an old man who totters on a stick. You are born with faces turned in all directions. You are the dark blue butterfly and the green parrot with red eyes. You are the thundercloud, the seasons, and the oceans. You are without beginning and beyond space and time. You are "He" from whom all worlds have originated.
>
> —SHVETASHVATARA UPANISHAD, 4:4

So long as the mind perceives only the variety, the field of differences, so long will there be conflict and disharmony arising from variations and disparities. Sorrow will continue to haunt us.

All differences and contradictions dissolve in the light of transcendental unity consciousness. The mind becomes cleansed of impurities and stress, ignorance gives way to awakening. The small self shines in the pristine purity of the true Self as a result of the knowledge that dawns upon you. Realization of unity consciousness is the aim of meditation. The result of unity consciousness is an overflow of love toward one and all.

Unity in diversity was one of the great themes of Vedic India. One of the important contributions of the Vedas to the world is the insistence on this factor, both in terms of spiritual attainment—All this (diversity) is One—and as a social ideal, expressed in the phrase, "The world is my family." The prayer in the Vedas continues to be "Let the people of the entire universe be happy and prosperous."

> He who has recognized
> All beings in himself
> And himself in all beings
> Is no longer vexed by anything
> Here where the knowing Self
> Becomes all living beings
> How could error be, how pain
> For him who thus beholds unity.
>
> —ISAVASY UPANISHAD, 6 AND 7

PART THREE

WAYS TO HEALTH

8

Self-Discipline: The Best Way to be an Achiever

He who is self-disciplined, of firm resolve with mind and intellect dedicated to the higher Self, by whom the world is not agitated and who does not agitate the world, who is free from joy, envy and anxiety, he is dear to Me.

—BHAGAVAD GITA, 12:14–15

For progress in any field, self-discipline is essential. Life cannot go on without discipline. To win a soccer match, you have to have a captain and have to play your game in accordance with his scheme. You have to play fullback or be the goalkeeper if that position is allotted to you. You can't be roaming about all over the playing field, or you are sure to lose the game.

If a young man subjects himself to drastic disciplinary measures, including regular hours of sleep, controlled diet, and strenuous exercise to train for winning a trophy in sports, everybody understands. Self-discipline is necessary for winning a race. But when somebody talks of discipline in day-to-day life, many people find it unnatural. They think that not having regular hours of sleep, exercise, and work, and eating what one likes whenever one likes, is more natural and certainly more fun.

But that sort of irregular, erratic style of life only weakens the body and invites disease.

Just observe nature. There is discipline in the orderliness found everywhere. The planets are disciplined, and maintain their proper order and relationship as they revolve at tremendous speeds. The seasons are disciplined, and come in time. Day and night maintain their own disciplined sequence. Likewise the growth of every living thing follows its own order.

Lord Krishna says in the Bhagavad Gita that moderation and discipline are essential in life for health, happiness, and success. What he says about yoga is true for all aspects of life: It is not for the man who overeats, or for he who fasts excessively. It is not for he who sleeps too much or for the one who keeps awake most of the night. Let a man be moderate in his eating habits, his recreation, his activity, and in sleep and wakefulness.

One should have disciplined reverence for the seers, teachers, and sages. A man needs straightforwardness, harmlessness, physical cleanliness, and sexual purity. Speech, too, must be disciplined. One should always say something that is kind and beneficial, never anything that causes pain. As the saying goes, "The tongue is not steel, but it cuts." These disciplines give a person strength, whether for yoga or for any line of action and achievement.

Most, if not all things worth achieving, require disciplined action over time. You cannot build anything worthwhile in a haphazard way. Everyone accepts that training for excellence in sports requires strict discipline. The same is true for excellence in any work or profession.

Discipline Harnesses Our Energies

There is a well-known image in Indian tradition that symbolizes discipline and the need for it: the image of the chariot, pulled by a team of horses and guided by the charioteer. The horses symbolize the senses. The roads they travel are the avenues of desire. The charioteer is the mind, the inner man.

When a man lacks discipline and discrimination and his mind is uncontrolled, the senses are unmanageable like the wild horses of a careless charioteer. But when he has self-discipline, his senses are like the well-controlled horses of a masterful charioteer. The man who has sound understanding and a controlled, disciplined mind is the one who reaches the end of the journey successfully.

The mind can also be compared with a mighty river. Unharnessed, it can be the source of floods and can create havoc and misery. Once under control it can generate electricity for millions and irrigate vast areas of land through a network of canals.

The Sanskrit word used for discipline by Patanjali in the *Yoga Sutras* is *tapas*, which in its primary sense means that which generates heat or energy. Tapas means the practice of self-discipline and control of our physical appetites and passions, by which we generate energy and direct it to the achievement of right goals, ultimately toward union with the Self or Atman.

Self-discipline is not something grim or horrifying, like lying on a bed of nails or other such austerities. All that is unnatural. The result of such austere practices is to weaken the body and sense organs.

What *is* discipline? It is:

— bringing order into your life
— overcoming laziness (tamas)
— not letting passions (rajas) rule your behavior
— exercising watchful, intelligent control over thoughts and actions
— persistence and perseverance
— regulating daily life (diet, exercise, rest) wisely for health and success.

Once the mind is disciplined and organized, once you have negative thoughts and emotions under control and your mind is dominated by positive thoughts, you can make use of the tremendous untapped potential that human beings naturally have. Then you can do anything that is useful for the community; nothing seems impossible any more.

Creating Time

The US President, Bill Clinton, remarked in one of his speeches that every successful journey is guided by fixed stars. Any plan of action in any field must be based on sound, fixed principles, which must include discipline, simplicity, and responsibility.

If you have the capacity to work and you work with discipline and devotion, you will find all the time you need. A lazy man has no time, but a busy man finds time for everything. When you are disciplined and devoted to your work, and not concerned about the fruits of your actions, you are contented, free, and happy.

When you sharpen a knife, you have to put it at a particular angle on the sharpening stone, otherwise your knife will be blunted instead of sharpened. If you play the sitar in the right way, plucking the strings with precision, soothing music flows. Performance of right action in any field requires discipline. You

Some Thoughts on Discipline

Running away from a situation is never going to help. A mind that has equanimity can face any situation and find a solution.

If you fall down, get up and brush the dust off your clothes and keep on. A temporary setback is not defeat.

"There is no question of failure either in the short run or in the long run. It is like traveling on a long, arduous road. Of all the innumerable steps there is only the last step which brings you to your destination, yet you will not consider all your previous steps as failures, including the steps you took when you had to turn back to bypass an obstacle. Each step brings you nearer your goal, but you have to be always on the move. Learning, discovering, unfolding is your eternal destiny."

—*Nisargadatta Maharaj*

have to train your wandering mind to become one-pointed. Then, with discipline and devotion, it is amazing how much you can achieve.

One of the great scriptures of the Indian tradition, the *Yoga Vasistha*, contains an eloquent and convincing argument by Rishi Vasistha on the value of self-discipline and self-effort for growth, success, and spiritual development. If you haven't already read it, I quote extensively from his teaching in Chapter 5.

9

The Right Diet: The More We Eat, the More Quickly We Leave This World

From food all beings are born, and having been born, they grow by food. Food is that which is eaten by all beings, and also that which in the end may eat them.

—TAITTIRIYA UPANISHAD

At a dinner party one should eat wisely and not too well, and talk well but not too wisely.

—SOMERSET MAUGHAM

Suresh is an old friend. We were together in school and in medical college. Then we joined the Army Medical Service together. For a number of years we were in Pune at the same time, and now we both live in Delhi. He and his wife Shakuntala also have two sons, born about the same time as our two sons, Deepak and Sanjiv. Both their boys are brilliant and are doing extremely well.

Despite the fact that our way of life has always been somewhat different, Suresh and I get on very well with each other. He has always been a happy-go-lucky man, full of life and laughter. He is very social, and likes evening parties. He loves good food, though he never overeats.

Suresh was a bit upset with me for some time because whenever he would ask us over for an evening party, I would make one excuse or another, as my wife Pushpa and I are not fond of late nights. Delhi social life is awful in this respect. If you invite a few friends for a get-together over dinner, they usually start arriving after 9 p.m. and keep on coming to the door even after 10. Cocktails and drinks go on till 11 or 11:30. It is quite late when food is finally laid on, and you cannot realistically hope to get back home till well past midnight. That lifestyle does not suit us.

Some time ago we finally accepted Suresh's invitation to his beautiful house in south Delhi. There were about twelve or thirteen couples, including some familiar faces. All seemed to be enjoying the evening, and Scotch whisky was flowing freely all around.

Abnash Chandra was sitting next to me. I had been seeing him as a patient for the past two years. Chandra is thirty-eight years old. He is obese, has a potbelly, and looks much older than his chronological age. He has been treated for high blood pressure and angina, and had undergone balloon angioplasty about two months prior to the dinner party.

The procedure was successful, and his angina had disappeared. Now free of pain, Abnash apparently thought he had a new heart and that he could once again abuse his body just as he liked. He forgot all about the guidelines he had agreed to follow regarding his diet and drinking. He was in a good mood, sipping his whisky and munching potato wafers, salted cashew nuts, and mutton kebabs—precisely the items I had told him not to indulge in because of his obesity, high cholesterol, high blood pressure, and angina.

Abnash Chandra's brother had been admitted to the hospital for a liver disease that was due to alcohol abuse. Abnash explained to me that he expected his brother to have a problem like that. "The problem with my brother," he said, "is not that he drinks too much but that he doesn't eat good food. I consume about the same amount of alcohol but I eat well, and before I go to an evening party I take a thin slice of bread with a thick layer of butter. Then I know the whisky won't go to my head. I can have my drinks as I like, and I know my liver will be fine."

Abnash did not have an apparent problem with his liver, yet. But the problems with his heart were very real. Nevertheless he was indulging in his idea of fun—eating and drinking—neither realizing nor caring, at that moment, that his behavior could hasten the formation of a clot in the narrow arteries of his heart and bring on a heart attack.

Less is More

Abnash's overindulgence is completely typical. All around the world, whether we eat at home or in a restaurant, people who can afford to do so consume enormous quantities of food. And yet many studies have been conducted, both on animals and humans, which conclude that individuals who consume fewer calories live longer than those whose caloric intake is high.

A normal mouse, for instance, lives for about thirty months before dying of old age. But according to Dr. Akhouri A. Sinha, Professor of Genetics and Cellular Biology at the University of Minnesota, if its caloric intake is increased significantly, its lifespan shrinks to twenty to twenty-four months and it is likely to experience a variety of diseases and other health problems. Conversely, mice whose caloric intake is reduced will live an average of thirty-six months, in generally good health.

Studies with human subjects support this research. For instance, men who weigh less than 65 kg (about 143 lbs, or 10 stone, 3 lbs) live longer than men who weigh over 95 kg (about 209 lbs, or 14 stone, 13 lbs). Overeating, it seems, saps a person's vitality, ruins his health, causes diseases, and in the end kills him.

Michio Kushi and Stephen Blaur in their book, *The Macrobiotic Way* (1985), quoted from *Sugar Blues*, by William Dufty (Warner Books, 1975) that "Sugar is poison, you should not let it enter your house let alone your body. It is more lethal than opium and more dangerous than atomic fallout." That may sound frightening, although everyone knows how much better and lighter one feels when one stops eating cakes, pastries, and sugary sweets and switches to a diet consisting mainly of whole grains, fruits and green vegetables. What has modern scientific research to say about it?

Researchers, as reported by *Time* magazine in an article "Can Science Slow the Aging Clock?" (January 20, 1997), say when sugars bond with proteins, they attract other proteins that form a sticky weblike substance that stiffens joints, blocks arteries, and clouds clear tissues like the lens of the eye leading to cataracts. The same reactions occur in diabetics but more rapidly. It is possible that as the cells of non-diabetics metabolize sugars, the same glycosylation process might take place. It is only much slower.

The glycosylation process is like the free radical process and, according to Dr. Robert Butler, Head of the Research Center of Mount Sinai Medical Center in New York, it is a natural process of metabolism of sugar that keeps us alive but also leads to aging and can cause disease.

Inside the mitochondria of cells during normal metabolism, oxygen is split into unstable oxygen singlets. These unstable oxygen molecules are known as free radicals. They help normal metabolism but in excess amounts they go on the rampage and injure and damage normal tissues and the inside lining of the blood vessels and DNA. In due course this can cause premature aging, coronary heart disease, cancer and other degenerative diseases like cataracts and arthritis. Oxygen is a life-giver but can also hasten aging, cause disease, and kill.

One way to reduce excess sugar metabolism is to take less sugar—maybe take unprocessed sugar in smaller amounts and not take refined white sugar at all, as by refining and bleaching all the protective enzymes, minerals, vitamins, and tracer elements are taken away—and give the body cells fewer nutrients to process and metabolize in the first place.

Studies have shown that rats whose caloric intake is 30

percent lower than that of a control group tend to live 30 percent to 40 percent longer. In humans that would translate to a spartan diet of just 1,400 calories a day in exchange for thirty extra years of life. The rat experiment can, probably, not translate into humans but George Roth, molecular physiologist with the National Institute on Aging in Bethesda, Maryland, suggests that individuals who consume fewer calories have better prospects of survival. Eating less processed food will also result in a slower metabolism, leading to improved rates of survival. In Japan, the number of persons aged 100 years or more these days is around 7,400 but you rarely see a fat centenarian.

The answer in the present state of our knowledge seems to be that for healthy and longer life one should eat less sugar, especially refined white sugar, avoid refined carbohydrates, have fewer total calories per day and have plenty of fresh fruits, green vegetables, and sprouts that are rich sources of antioxidants, capable of neutralizing an excess of harmful free radicals. This way you can add years to life and life to years.

As gerontologist Leonard Hayflick points out, we should be careful not to think of the overfed mice, who correspond to the way most people live and eat, as normal; the mice on the restricted diet, he says, "are merely being allowed to reach the limit of their lifespan. It's overfeeding that kills the control group."

The physical body of man is born from food consumed by his parents. It is maintained and nourished by food consumed by himself, and ultimately the physical body of everyone goes back to the earth to become food for others.

The vital force of life (prana) comes to our body through food as well as air. Prana expresses itself as vitality in the body.

In the right amount food is a blessing, but overconsumption is a cause of disease and death. The more we eat, the more quickly we disappear from this world. One who has self-control and eats as much as required, not as much as he wants, who regulates the expenditure of his energy and vitality and avoids undesirable dissipations, is the one who lives a healthy, happy life to the full extent of his lifespan.

Advantages of a Vegetarian Diet

The fifty trillion cells in the human body are ceaselessly decaying while new cells are growing in their place. To maintain that continuous "Brahma, Vishnu, Mahesh" process of creation, preservation, and dissolution in our body, the right nutrients are constantly required. These can best be obtained from a vegetarian diet of natural foods. It is now known that a vegetarian diet is protective against heart disease. Dr. Dean Ornish, the American physician who conducted landmark research on treating heart disease with diet, exercise, and meditation, says that "people who eat a low-fat, low-cholesterol vegetarian diet have low blood pressure, low blood cholesterol levels, and low rates of heart disease." Many anthropologists, Ornish points out, believe that our ancestors were primarily vegetarians, and that our teeth and intestinal tract were designed "for the slow digestion of high-fiber plant foods," rather than to digest meat.

Dr. T. Colin Campbell of Cornell University, who has long been studying diet in China, states that "we are basically a vegetarian species and should be eating a wide variety of plant foods and minimizing our intake of animal foods. The higher the intake of animal products, the higher the risk of cancer."

The American Dietetic Association has made the following strong statement about a vegetarian diet:

> A considerable body of scientific data suggests positive relationships between vegetarian lifestyles and risk reduction for several chronic degenerative diseases and conditions, such as obesity, coronary artery disease, hypertension, diabetes mellitus, colon cancer, and others ... Vegetarians also have lower rates of osteoporosis, lung cancer, breast cancer, kidney stones, gallstones, and diverticular disease.

Paradoxically, the incidence of heart attacks is rather high among vegetarians in India. The reason seems to be that Indian vegetarians eat a lot of deep-fried food, such as samosas and pakoras, which have a lot of hidden fat. Also, the oil used for cooking these foods is used many times and becomes oxidized. Oxidized oil is very harmful; it can aggravate atherosclerosis and has been associated with the formation of free radicals, which contribute to cancer, heart disease, and other serious health problems. By contrast, the vegetarian diet that is emerging in the West is less greasy. Western fast foods (hamburgers, fried potatoes, etc.) are in a way like the Indian vegetarian deep-fried junk food.

Whether in India or anywhere in the world, once people experience some degree of affluence, they tend to give up the traditional, simple, wholesome and sattvic diet of whole grains, beans, legumes, fresh fruits, and green vegetables and opt for a diet rich in meat, processed cheeses, oils, fats, and refined carbohydrates and sugars. Much of this nowadays is in the form of fast foods. Now that we know that eating the right vegetarian diet is a preventive measure against heart disease, it is tragic for us to go on permitting a steep rise in the incidence of heart attacks due to the food we eat.

In the Bible (Leviticus 7:23–25) God admonishes Moses: "You shall eat no manner of fat, of ox, or of sheep or of goat . . . for whosoever eateth the fat of the beast . . . shall be cut off from his people." This must have been good, practical advice, for "Moses was one hundred and twenty years old when he died and his eyes were not dim nor his natural force abated." (Deuteronomy 34:7)

Animals Have Feelings Too

Like humans, animals have feelings and emotions. When they are used for medical research, even in the best laboratory conditions, with controlled temperature and music piped into the rooms (and animals love music), invariably harmful biochemical changes are produced in their bodies. This happens even before the experiment, when the animals are being held in confinement.

When an animal is slaughtered for food the chemical reaction is far more intense. The pain and fear felt by the dying creature cause powerful biochemicals such as adrenaline and noradrenaline to be released into the bloodstream. These chemicals—which cause reactions in the animal, such as a rapid heart rate and muscles tensed in the face of danger—then become an integral part of the meat consumed by humans, and they affect our physiology. Over a period of time our pulse rate, blood pressure, and tranquility of mind may be adversely affected.

I believe our minds may become easily agitated if a non-vegetarian diet is consumed repeatedly. Eating meat may make us more irritable, ready to fight on the slightest pretext. And in course of time, the brain may be robbed of some of its inherent power of creative thinking.

Could this be why, in ancient India, the brahmins—the learned men, thinkers, teachers, writers, poets—were generally not meat eaters, but were prescribed a pure, sattvic vegetarian diet? Only the kshatriyas, the soldiers and fighters of battles, were allowed to eat non-vegetarian food.

Certain physical features can be observed in animals because of the eating habits of their species over millions of years. Look at the eyes of a tiger or even a cat, and see how ferocious a look it has. Now compare that with the eyes of a herbivorous animal such as a cow, a deer, or a horse. How calm and innocent it looks! Man's eyes are more like the cow's or the deer's. Beautiful, they reflect the tranquility of his mind and the love in his heart.

It is obvious from this comparison, from the shape and functional anatomy of our teeth, specifically the incisors and the grinders, and from the anatomy and physiology of our digestive system, enzymatic system, and intestines, that man is by nature designed to be a vegetarian. But if we adopt a non-vegetarian diet and continue to eat like carnivores, over time we are sure to develop the looks, teeth, and anatomy of these animals and become ferocious like them. Perhaps in another million years, we will return to the jungles.

The evolution of a species takes a long, long time. We are very highly evolved, but we are killing innocent fellow beings.

There seems to be little hope for man to survive for long in our present condition. The devolution, the biological and moral degeneration of our species, seems to have already begun due to many factors, including our eating habits.

Tips for Healthy Eating

The food we eat, the water we drink, the air we breathe are transformed into our bodies. Healthy food, eaten in appropriate ways in pleasant circumstances, creates good health for body and mind. Food that is unhealthy for us, eaten on the run in unsuitable surroundings, lays the ground for disease. If you follow these common-sense guidelines for eating, your meals can contribute to your health and well-being.

* The food you eat should not be tasteless and insipid. It should be tasty, attractive, and properly cooked. Use fresh food whenever possible, not packaged, stale, or leftover food.

* Eat whole grains. Glue is made by mixing water and white flour. If you eat food made of white flour in any form, it tends to get stuck in the walls of the large intestine and does not get entirely eliminated. This waste product is poisonous if it remains in the gut for any length of time, and is the cause of diseases including cancer of the colon. Eating whole grains, such as whole wheat, will not only help regulate your blood sugar and serum cholesterol, but will also result in complete evacuation of the bowels—no constipation—and in this way many diseases can be prevented.

* Don't eat when you are feeling emotionally upset. When you are depressed, anxious, or irritated, your digestion is less effective. Then what is eating you up becomes more important than what you eat.

* Pay attention when you eat. Every time we take food is a holy occasion. If you eat throughout the day, nibbling here and there, watching TV . . . then you are not paying attention to this very purposeful, solemn event.

* Be thankful. Say grace before you eat. Someone may say, "I

work hard all day earning my daily bread. If I don't do that, I won't get any food. So why should I give thanks?" It is true that you earn your bread by your work. But don't forget, our Lord makes the sun shine, the rivers flow, and the rains fall. Not even a blade of grass can grow without His grace. So to speak (or quietly think) a few words of gratitude is an expression of the art of gracious receiving. Asking for His blessings will help you eat with a quiet, peaceful mind.

* Fasting about once every week gives a rest to your digestive system and increases immunity. You may take some fresh fruit juice two or three times on your fast day.

* Remember, the food you eat is going to be you. So be sure to choose fresh, nourishing, sattvic food. Tamasic (dull) persons tend to eat food that is tamasic: badly cooked, stale, or leftover. Rajasic (passionate, highly active) people relish food that is rajasic: sour, salty, or spicy. Only sattvic (pure, good) persons have a natural affinity for food that is pure and fresh, and which increases vigor, vitality, and joy.

We can all consciously *choose* foods that will increase sattva in us. Traditionally, that means not just foods that are fresh and pure, but specifically milk, ghee, almonds, fresh fruit (particularly oranges), and rice. Dates, honey, mung beans, coconut, and wheat are also considered among the most sattvic foods.

* Have a broader perspective. The food on your plate is not merely some rice and vegetables, it is part of the great fabric of the universe. Food, the Upanishads say, is Brahman: "All beings here are born from food, when born they live on food, on deceasing they enter into food." Brahman, the supreme, is the changeless substratum upon which all changes take place. Food is ever changing. Food is you, me, and all living beings. That is why eating is a holy occasion.

* Don't stuff yourself. Never reach a stage in eating when you feel your stomach is completely full. You will feel happier and healthier if you stop eating before that.

In the olden days, when people had to work hard and be physically fit just in order to grow, gather, or capture their food, there was little malnutrition and probably little heart disease. In the modern age, there is a virtual epidemic of heart disease, and two very different types of malnutrition exist in the world.

Despite food now being very plentiful, many people still suffer from malnutrition because they do not get sufficient calories, protein, and vitamins. But there is another kind of malnutrition, particularly common among well-to-do people, and this is because of eating too much.

Nature did not design our bodies to consume the large quantities of fat, sugar, and refined carbohydrates characteristic of the modern diet. Man has been eating fruits, nuts, and roots for thousands of years; even farming is a recent development. If our metabolic capabilities are overloaded with cakes, pastries, samosas, jalebies, parathas, poories, we must expect to pay the price in the form of heart disease and other illnesses sooner or later.

The problem is that the affluent don't eat to appease their hunger. More often, they eat for pleasure, for emotional reasons, or to satisfy social obligations. This is not the way to eat.

Before going to a particular social event, decide in advance what, and how much, you are going to eat. If you can't resist the pressure of the host and end up eating more than you require or feel you should eat, you are punishing yourself. If this happens to you regularly, then you should cut off or minimize your social engagements. What good is the pleasure of social events if it leads to disease?

We can share meals with friends, and it is good to take pleasure in what we eat, but we should be careful to eat in a way that will build our health and sustain a long creative life.

The Ethics of Our Food Choices

If Americans were to reduce their meat consumption by only 10 percent it would free land and resources to grow over twelve million tons of grain annually for human consumption, instead of for animal feed. This would be more than enough to adequately feed every one of the sixty million human beings who starve to death or die of one of the hunger-related diseases *each year* on this planet.

Our hunger for wholeness

"If we are touched by images of men, women, and children that we have seen starving for food, it is because they are a reflection of our own need. They are a reminder not only of that part of us that is hungry, but also of that part of us that needs to give in order to be whole."

—JOHN ROBBINS, in *May All Be Fed*

This shocking statistic is an example of the impact our eating habits have on the life of our planet. But these habits are being actively promoted by powerful commercial forces, as the American writer John Robbins explains in his book, *May All Be Fed: Diet For A New World*. The huge and powerful meat-producing industry, allied with friendly political forces, vigorously promotes meat consumption. Thus these interests are largely responsible for causing the more affluent people to suffer from heart attacks, osteoporosis, and other diet-related diseases, while at the same time the world's poor are deprived of a basic human right—having ample, wholesome food.

Millions of acres of land are being used to produce grain for animal feed, rather than food for direct human consumption. It takes sixteen pounds of grain to produce a pound of meat and only one pound to produce a pound of bread.

In addition to the overwhelming evidence that a diet rich in red meat and other animal fats causes heart disease and several types of cancer, there is now also clear evidence linking a high-protein (largely meat) diet with osteoporosis or thinning of the bones, a condition that often leads to discomfort and broken bones among the elderly. Large amounts of meat in the diet cause you to lose calcium (hence bone mass) as well as other valuable minerals such as magnesium.

A vegetarian (or at least largely vegetarian) diet is thus not only extremely good for our own health and welfare. If more people adopted this as a routine way of life, more land would be freed to grow food for people rather than animals, and the devastating effects of hunger around the world could be greatly reduced.

Food and the Laws of Nature

I met Mr. Frank Bracho at a conference on ayurveda and alternative medicine several years ago. At the time, he was Venezuela's ambassador to India. He had authored a book entitled *Health, Environment, and Economics* and another on ancient monuments of India.

Mr. Bracho was deeply interested in ancient cultures, the achievements of past great civilizations, their monuments and arts. He was also drawn to understand the wise and respectful relationship with nature exhibited by some of these ancient cultures. It was because of that relationship with nature and Mother Earth that they could acquire the physical, mental, and spiritual strength, the knowledge and wisdom that nurtured these great civilizations.

While in India, this lover of nature had his residence in a farmhouse with a beautiful vegetable garden and fruit orchard. We had a meal with him one evening and enjoyed the farm-fresh fruit juices and delicious vegetable dishes. Mr. Bracho explained that according to Luis Espinoza, a shaman in the Inca tradition, "at the time of a meal a bridge of light is created between the eater and the plant world. Then, if the circumstances are right, the magic flows; the subtle arrives and we all nourish our bodies."

"It is important to prepare food with love," he continued, "to ingest it with thanks, to energize it before assimilating it. It is important to be aware and mindful of nourishment, as if you were talking with the spirit of each food stuff. They must also be cultivated with tenderness, and our relationship with the earth must be that of reciprocity and love. Plants can live without man and animals, but neither man nor animals can live without plants."

All the nourishment we need comes from plants, which yield us various kinds of food through their sap, roots, bark, seeds, flowers, leaves, and fruit. Animal protein is not only dispensable, but for reasons of health is actually undesirable. All the basic nutrients can be obtained from a combination of food from plants.

> *Eat right, think right, act right. Meditate on the Self and live your life in divine joy and bliss day and night.*
> —PARAMAHANSA YOGANANDA

The sowing of crops has always been looked upon with reverence, and from this reverence wisdom has emerged. In ancient times we knew how to live in equilibrium with nature. The ancient peoples believed that plants are living beings that listened and responded to the human voice.

Today there are still native farmers who allow no one who is angry or ill-tempered to go on their fields during planting. "You will ruin the earth," they say as they turn the unwelcome presence away. On the other hand, before sowing, it is often customary to take children to the fields to play, because innocence is powerful energy and purity a valuable fertilizer for the soil, plants, and human beings.

I told Mr. Frank Bracho that what held true for Pre-Columbian peoples in Latin America was the truth for all great ancient civilizations. If we could respect and maintain a harmonious relationship with the mountains, forests, trees, and rivers of Mother Earth and all her beings, as our ancestors did, and live in accordance with the laws of nature, this world would certainly be a much better place to live.

10

Get a Good Night's Sleep

Yoga is not for him who eats too much nor for him who eats too little. Nor is it for him who sleeps too much or keeps awake too much.

—BHAGAVAD GITA, 6:16

Gentle sleep is nature's soft nurse.

—SHAKESPEARE

This happened in Pune soon after the partition of India. I was a young doctor working in the army hospital. We were living in a large, spacious bungalow on Prince of Wales Drive that had recently been vacated by a senior British officer. The house had an artificial pond stocked with goldfish, and a beautiful garden with flowers now in full bloom.

One evening we were sitting on the veranda sipping tea when I saw Mr. Bhide single-handedly push his little red Morris car through the main gate. He had one hand on the steering wheel and the other on the front window and sweat was pouring from his face and staining his clothes as he pushed.

Bhide was an insurance agent with whom I had become friends after he made two unsuccessful attempts to sell me a policy I really didn't need. He was a simple fellow in his early thirties and I liked him a lot. He was not a tremendously successful agent, partly because he could never get himself to offer rebates or cuts to his clients, as other representatives did. It was against his principles. But he was happy and contented with his lot.

Bhide joined us for tea. As we were sitting together, a brand new, shiny, sky-blue Hillman car drove up to the bungalow, and a young man in a stylish three-piece blue suit walked up to us and asked for Colonel Nelson, the former occupant. "He left India two months ago," I told him. Bhide recognized the gentleman, whose name was Dhanukar, and chatted with him for a few minutes before he drove off.

The two men had been together in school, Bhide told me. Dhanukar had built a beautiful new house and now had purchased this car, which cost at least five times more than Bhide's rattling little Morris. "They say he makes a lot of money," Bhide said. He sat quietly for a moment after telling me this. But then, true to his nature, he smiled and said, "It really doesn't matter. I am very happy, and I sleep well."

In that moment, Bhide revealed the secret of sound, refreshing sleep.

Sleep ordinarily means a period of rest for both body and mind. It appears to be a creative process, during which the mind rests and prepares you for the day's work. The rest gained during sleep is considered essential for the body and the ever busy brain. When you awaken from a sound sleep, you feel fresh and ready to tackle the world with renewed vigor.

But the truth is, fatigue and insomnia are among the most prevalent disorders of our age. Tiredness and lack of adequate sleep are two of the most common complaints made by patients visiting a physician's office these days. And both are linked with stress.

Stress is both a cause and an effect of poor sleeping. Although sleeplessness can be caused by fever, physical pain, or foods containing a stimulant such as caffeine, stress is a much more common causal factor. When you are stressed and anxious, you are likely not to sleep well. You may have trouble getting to sleep, or you may fall asleep at 11 p.m. but wake up again at 2 a.m. unable to sleep again. When you sleep badly, instead of waking up fresh and clear, you get out of bed feeling stressed and anxious, afraid of not being able to function well. It is a vicious cycle.

But it is a cycle that can be broken, and usually without sleeping medications. In this chapter I will share with you a number of very practical suggestions to help you sleep peacefully and well.

The Stages of Sleep

Sleep has been the subject of extensive research over the past several decades. It is now known that the brain, like the body's organ system (cardiovascular system, digestive system, respiratory system, etc.), remains active during sleep although we are not conscious of it. The activity of the brain generates faint electrical waves that can be recorded by the EEG (electroencephalograph).

Although the sleep research is still in its childhood if not its infancy, we know that there are several stages of sleep including a stage of REM (rapid eye movement) sleep, and at least four stages of NREM (non-REM) sleep. During the night we pass through several cycles of both REM and NREM sleep.

It is during the REM stage that we experience dreams. Behind our closed eyelids the eyes dart about and the brain engages in rather busy, even turbulent activity. Breathing is uneven, blood pressure fluctuates, body movements increase, and blood flow to the brain can increase by up to 40 percent. Paradoxically, it is also during this REM phase that we experience the deepest level of slumber.

REM sleep appears to be the most important part of sleep. As long as you have your quota of REM sleep and dreaming, you will have enough rest and energy.

Exactly why REM sleep is so important is not yet clear. The Nobel laureate Sir Francis Crick speculates that it is during this phase that the brain sorts information gathered during the day and "downloads" it into the cerebral cortex for permanent storage. We do know that there is a connection between REM sleep and memory, and it is postulated that during this phase of sleep the brain is actively involved in building neural circuits in order to consolidate the knowledge we have acquired earlier and accord it a permanent lodging. From a "psychological" point of view, during dreams we express our hidden thoughts, feelings, and unfulfilled desires, a process that may be vital for our well-being.

Whatever the reason or reasons, it is surely important to get our nightly "quota" of both NREM and especially of REM sleep in order to maintain health and creative living. But how much sleep do we need? And what can we do to ensure we get our full measure?

Myths About Sleep

People have many misconceptions about these questions. Here are several of the most common:

— Everyone needs eight hours of sleep.
— If I have a sleepless night, I will not be able to function the next day.
— Only sleeping pills can help insomnia.
— If I don't treat my insomnia, it will lead to illness or a poor diet, containing too many sweets, fatty foods, and deep-fried foods that have a lot of hidden fat, and a nervous breakdown.
— Insomnia is inevitable in old age.
— A few alcoholic drinks in the evening will help me sleep.

Let's spend a few minutes dispelling these myths. I'm sure you will feel a lot better once you know they are not true!

People have differing needs for sleep: Some people truly do seem to need eight or more hours of sleep in order to maintain health and clarity. Babies, of course, can easily sleep 18 or 20 hours out of each 24. (Interestingly, sleep is important for the production of growth hormone. Because babies need this substance in abundance, they need vast amounts of sleep.) But there are many people who seem to do just fine on six hours or even four. Darwin, Napoleon, and Churchill all slept very little but slept well.

The inventor Thomas Edison typically slept only an hour or two, but took a number of brief "catnaps" during the day to refresh himself. Most of us can get away with less sleep if we follow Edison's example. Whatever amount of time you typically spend in bed, it can be safely reduced by up to two hours on the condition that the lost sleep is replaced by one or two short naps of a few minutes each during the day.

Sleeping too long can make your sleep more superficial. Gradually reducing the duration will automatically make it more profound.

In short, some people are able to sleep much less than others without any harmful effects.

* There is no evidence that a person becomes unable to function effectively after a sleepless night: In an experiment several years ago in a school in California, a student remained awake for eleven days and was able to function normally. All the same, perception of fatigue and impaired ability in performance becomes apparent in a majority of individuals after two or three days of continuous deprivation of sleep. Good, refreshing sleep allows the body to recover from fatigue, prepares the body for self-repair, and is essential for the healthy mind and body. Dreaming enhances this process.

* Natural means of healing insomnia are better than sleeping pills: Sleeping pills are not really the solution to the problem. Most of us do not understand the natural, simple laws of good sleep. Once we do, tranquilizers and sleeping tablets should be unnecessary in all but the most extreme cases.

We consume sleeping pills and tranquilizers by the ton, but they can be quite harmful. When you use these medications, you really have dullness or drowsiness rather than good sleep, and you wake up with a kind of hangover. After eight weeks on tranquilizers or sleeping pills, most people get less of the deeper stages of sleep. They may sleep longer, but the quality of rest is not good and becomes gradually worse with continued use of the pills. People start to have periods of sleeplessness, tossing and turning. So they take larger doses of the pills, and may become addicted to them.

Unfortunately, physicians are taught quite a bit about sleep inducers, and very little about natural sleep. It almost seems as if modern doctors, who find it convenient to prescribe these drugs rather than spend time talking to their patients and educating them about how to sleep naturally, are a kind of legalized "drug pusher."

Nature tells us when to go to sleep. Our brain sends messages saying, "It's time to sleep," but we do not acknowledge them. We yawn, our head becomes heavy, our eyelids weigh down, we lose concentration. The messages are clear, but we ignore them or fight not to comply with them.

The secret of good sleeping is to recognize these signals and the body's natural rhythms, and to respect the laws of nature behind them. Each individual has a preferential time to go to sleep. You can't sleep when your body's clock says "wake up." When you begin to feel sleepy, that is the best time to lie down and sleep. When you sleep in accordance with your biological rhythms and the laws of nature, the sleep is gentle and refreshing.

* *Serious health problems—mental or physical—are unlikely to arise because of insomnia:* Michael Stevenson, director of the North Valley Sleep Disorders Center in Mission Hills, California says that no human being ever died from insomnia. Further, there appears to be no long-term or permanent damage in persons who have insomnia. If you stay awake long enough, you will simply doze off. Before you fall asleep, you may have some difficulty maintaining any kind of cognitive relationship with the world, but after you sleep for a few hours you will return to normal.

It is important to take the fear of not sleeping and the potential, imagined effects of not sleeping out of your mind. The fear of having a nervous breakdown or getting some disease as a result of not sleeping is unfounded.

* In old age, it is likely that people actually need less sleep: In old age it is likely that people actually need less sleep—that probably is true because the body metabolism changes, but the elderly who take regular exercise and keep occupied sleep well. Some of the elderly complain of lack of sleep although they have adequate sleep. A survey by the National Institute of Health, however, did reveal that 17 percent of the population in the USA suffers from insomnia and the incidence is 25 percent among individuals over 60 years of age, leading to anxiety and subsequent problems.

Many people resort to sleeping pills as a long-term solution to insomnia. However sleeping pills not only lose their effectiveness after a few months but they may also disturb your sleeping pattern and may even contribute to your insomnia. Of course the most effective therapy is to identify the cause of insomnia—identify the problem and solve it.

Besides anxiety, stress, and worry, smoking, alcohol abuse, and excessive caffeine in coffee, tea, and colas can cause insomnia in prone individuals. Breathing disorders, noise, and other physical disorders can cause insomnia. Extremes of temperature or light can interfere with the sleep pattern.

* Alcohol interferes with normal sleep patterns: It is popularly believed that a few alcoholic drinks in the evening or before bedtime make you sleep well. This is not true.

Alcohol is a central nervous system depressant. It makes you initially drowsy, and may actually help you fall asleep, but it disrupts normal sleep patterns later in the night. You usually awaken once the effect of the alcohol has begun to wear off. Even if you do manage to remain asleep, the deepest and most refreshing levels of sleep may be reduced or disturbed. These negative effects are more likely to happen if you had the drinks within two hours of bedtime.

Secrets for Better Sleep

I recommend that you do not use medications to change unhealthy or unwanted patterns of sleep. If at all, the use of *mild* tranquilizers or sedatives should be restricted to acutely ill patients, on a short-term basis. Instead, use natural relaxation techniques and cut down on food, drinks, and lifestyle habits that counteract sleep.

Natural relaxation techniques such as deep breathing (pranayama) and meditation are very helpful in falling asleep. A few minutes of alternate nostril breathing is very relaxing and can help you settle into sleep. *Japa*, that is, repetition of a mantra or a name of God makes your mind quieter and helps you fall off to sleep (see Chapter 15). It is said that the poet Tennyson could not sleep one night. He started repeating his own name, "Tennyson . . . Tennyson . . . Tennyson . . ." and fell asleep.

Cutting down or eliminating caffeine, in colas, tea, and coffee, especially after midday, is very helpful. Caffeine is a stronger stimulant than many people realize, and its effects last many hours. This may be all you need to put an end to insomnia.

As mentioned above, alcohol is a major hindrance to sleep. Evening or nighttime drinks are likely to reduce the effectiveness of your sleep by waking you up after a few hours, and by causing disturbances in the all-important dreaming stage.

It's better not to have a TV in the bedroom. The fast-moving images on the screen can interfere with settling into restful sleep. I suggest not watching TV at all, especially action movies, shortly before going to bed. Rather, read a book or listen to some soothing music.

Once you're in bed, don't keep looking at the clock. Anxiety about falling asleep will not help you sleep!

Similarly, trying to sleep never works. It's like taking a train. If you miss the ten o'clock, it really doesn't matter. There will be another soon. Relax, and step into the next one when your body's clock next summons you.

Regular exercise is very helpful in promoting better sleep at night. You will find that half an hour's brisk walking or cycling (in the morning, if possible) will help you enjoy more restful sleep. For more about exercise, please see Chapter 11.

Insomnia may have its roots in lack of fulfillment. When you enjoy your work and feel that it is worthwhile, you have what is commonly called "job satisfaction," an important factor in being at peace with yourself. Tranquility of mind, as the story of Mr. Bhide at the beginning of the chapter demonstrates, is very important to help you avoid insomnia and sleep well.

On the other hand, if you accumulate wealth by means that are not right, not in accordance with Dharma or the dictates of your conscience, you can never sleep well.

Even if you are earning your income by honest means, an increase in income is often associated with a decrease in sleep time. People use up some of their potential sleep time either planning how to increase their assets or working overtime. If you push yourself too much, fatigue is inevitable. The pressure to stay awake at all costs eventually impairs not only your ability to remain effective, but also the ability to fall asleep when you want to; overwork and its associated stress in due course leads to insomnia. According to Michael Aldrich, director of the University of Michigan Sleep Disorders Center, insomnia is often an early sign that a high achiever is on the road to "burnout."

So take it a little easier. It's not worth destroying your health to accumulate wealth. How will you be able to enjoy it?

If stress and anxiety are keeping you awake, it is important to treat the cause, not just the symptom. Simply taking some sleeping medication to knock you out will not help in the long run if the situation that is the source of your anxiety remains the same.

In olden days, grandmother used to say, "Take a cup of warm milk before going to bed. You will sleep better." Her advice was excellent and is now scientifically proven. Milk neutralizes the excess acid in the stomach and improves the quality of sleep. It has a pharmaceutically based value, as it contains traces of the amino acid L-tryptophane, which has been shown to promote sleep. Some sleep clinics have been prescribing 1,500 to 2,000 mg of L-tryptophane to induce sleep. Sleep is likely to improve after a week or so.

Another medication that has been used recently with success is a synthesized form of the natural hormone melatonin, which is available in the US but not in the UK (at the time of writing). Neither of these medications appears to have the significant negative side effects of most tranquilizers and sleeping tablets. But I believe it is better to take some warm milk than medications.

Some Questions about Sleep

* How much sleep is too little? It is difficult to be precise. Research suggests that two or three hours of REM sleep and dreaming may be adequate.

  * What about people who go to bed very late? Isn't it unhealthy? It's true that the natural cycles of nature suggest that we go to bed early and wake up early with the fresh morning air, and for most people this seems the most healthy pattern. But I know some very efficient and hard-working people who go to bed very late and get up late as a routine.

They are very successful in life, and appear to be quite healthy. There is probably nothing wrong with this; their biological clocks just got set that way.

  * Doesn't the yoga tradition see sleep as a different sort of consciousness? How does that relate to the scientific research? From the time of the ancient Vedas, tradition has described several states or stages of consciousness. Ordinary life is said to consist of three: waking, dreaming, and deep sleep, and modern EEG research has clearly delineated these three.

The Yoga Sutras of Patanjali, the ancient textbook of yoga, says that "sleep is a wave of thought about nothingness" (I, 10). That is to say, deep, dreamless sleep is not an absence of thought waves in the mind, but a positive experience of nothingness. (Research indeed shows that the brain is active even in deep sleep.) Sleep cannot, therefore, be confused with a waveless state of the brain. If there were no thought waves, we should not wake up remembering that we knew nothing during sleep, yet are able to say that we slept well! Sleep is a state of consciousness.

When you are sleeping you are in bliss. You don't remember the past and you don't worry about the future.

Burning the midnight oil, or using stimulants to keep awake, interfere with natural refreshing sleep. Why interfere with the laws of nature? You have done your bit from dawn to dusk. Now call it a day and have sweet dreams. Sleep, Shelley said, is the time "when gleams of a remote world visit your soul."

Tips to help you sleep

- Read a good book instead of fretting before going to sleep.
- People who are excitable, whose moods change quickly, who are prone to anxiety, worry, restlessness because of their particular body constitution and subtle physiology may suffer from insomnia more often as they grow older. Regular exercise in the mornings help these people to sleep better at night; of course it helps everyone that way.
- No exercise should be undertaken too close to bedtime.
- Avoid alcohol two hours before bedtime. Excess alcohol may make you drowsy and sleepy. This sleep, however, is not refreshing.
- Established bedtime rituals like a warm bath, a cup of hot milk, a few minutes of reading are all helpful.
- It is better to wake up at the same time in the morning regardless of the time you went to sleep.
- Remember everybody's cycle of sleep is different—five hours' sleep may be more than enough for one person, while eight hours may not be sufficient for another person.
- Do not self-medicate with tranquilizers or sleeping pills.
- If you are a regular meditator you should have no problem with sleep.

11

Regular Exercise: An Important Key to Healthy Living

All parts of the body which have a function, if used in moderation and exercised in labour, become healthy and well developed and age more slowly. But if left unused and idle, they become liable to disease, defective in growth, and age quickly.

—HIPPOCRATES

By physical exercise one gets lightness, capacity to work, firmness, tolerance of difficulties, diminution of impurities, and stimulation of digestion and metabolism.

—CHARAKA SAMHITA, 5:32

People have always admired an athlete. In the Bhagavad Gita, Lord Krishna addresses Arjuna as "O Maha Baho," the one with mighty arms. The heroes of ancient Greek history were all examples of physical strength and valor. Since the early days of recorded history, sages have prized exercise as a virtue for its fruit of radiant health and longer life.

Throughout millions of years of evolution, our cardiovascular system and metabolism were used for vigorous physical activity. High levels of endurance were essential in hunting for food, and to run away from wild animals or human enemies. Until the nineteenth century, vigorous physical activity remained an integral part of everyday life, necessary for subsistence, travel, housework, and recreaction.

Then, the Industrial Revolution brought motorized transportation and labor-saving devices of every kind that have reduced physical activity to a minimum. Leisure time, which was once spent in games and sports, is now spent watching television; even the little exercise once required to get up and change the channel is no longer necessary, because of remote control devices. People are getting into the habit of using the elevator just to go up one or two floors, instead of climbing the stairs. And we want to park the car right in front of the store when we go shopping so we don't have to walk even a few yards.

In Delhi, where I live, only a very small fraction of people can be seen walking or jogging in the early hours of the morning in the parks. The rest are all lying in bed, perhaps watching the morning news.

Most people explain this away by saying they don't have time for exercise. Some say they don't have the energy. The truth is, we have become inactive and lazy. We are all spectators, preferring to watch a game of tennis on television rather than playing it. But perhaps the reason so many people lack both the will power and the interest in exercise is that they haven't grasped how important it is for health and long life.

Health Hazards of Not Exercising

As the saying goes, "Whatever you don't use, you lose." This holds true for our physical body as well as our mental capacities. Exercise has a direct impact on our health and well-being. For example, a study in London showed more heart attacks among bus drivers, who sit still at the wheel, than among bus conductors, who walk up and down collecting fares. Studies comparing mail clerks to mail delivery men, and railway clerks to laborers, both showed similar results.

Epidemiological studies indicate an inverse relationship

between physical activity and coronary artery disease. The incidence of heart attacks is half and mortality one third in active people as compared to those who are inactive (though in all fairness, the precise benefits of exercise are difficult to evaluate, as people who tend to exercise also tend to eat the right kind of food and usually don't smoke).

When healthy men were assigned to bed rest for a few weeks as an experiment, they suffered rapid deterioration of their cardiovascular and respiratory functions. Similar weakening of cardiorespiratory functions was noticed among astronauts until regular in-flight exercise programs were instituted.

A loss of minerals and proteins from the tissues and skeletal muscles leads gradually to a loss of muscle tone and strength and decreased ligament flexibility. Thinning of the bones (osteoporosis) and easy fracturing of the long bones can occur, especially among older people.

Lack of exercise wreaks havoc on the whole system. Loss of smooth muscle tone in the veins leads to varicose veins. There is increased risk of deep vein thrombosis (DVT), which can lead to pulmonary embolism, a potentially lethal disease.

Metabolism is also adversely affected. Abnormalities in carbohydrate, fat, and lipid metabolism can occur, leading to weight gain, a typical condition among sedentary people. Obesity is a well-known risk factor for coronary heart disease and atherosclerosis.

Until about two or three decades ago, people who suffered an acute heart attack were given strict bed rest for a minimum of six weeks. This inactivity turned out to be responsible for many complications, including DVT and pulmonary embolism. Prone, inactive people can also fall prey to insulin resistance, glucose intolerance, and diabetes mellitus. Some amount of exercise is so important that, these days, patients with uncomplicated heart attacks are asked to start walking a little on the third or fourth day, and are discharged from the hospital within a week to ten days.

The Benefits of Exercise

The health and endurance of our heart and lungs are built up by prolonged and repeated aerobic exercise of moderate intensity. This involves rhythmic contraction of large muscle groups, during which the circulatory and respiratory systems maintain blood and oxygen delivery to the exercising muscles, including the muscles of the heart. This most important aspect of a healthy body and a healthy heart is attained by exercises such as jogging, walking, swimming, and bicycling. Another excellent exercise is "wagging"—"wa" from walking and "gging" from jogging— meaning very brisk walking. Such aerobic exercises make the muscles and joints more flexible and the body more agile. Excess fat is shed.

These exercises don't build muscle mass. Rather, they increase the muscles' endurance and capacity to burn carbohydrates and fat. They benefit not only the musculoskeletal and cardio-respiratory systems, but the endocrine and immune systems as well. Oxygen delivery to the skeletal muscles and the body's cells and tissues is increased. Improved muscles tone helps in pumping blood back to the heart, thus benefiting circulation and cardiac endurance.

The heart, like all other muscles, can be trained with regular exercise. As it becomes stronger, it performs better and more reliably. Thus the chances of heart attack are less in people who are engaged in regular exercise. And even if an attack occurs due to another risk factor (such as smoking), the heart can be retrained with gradual exercise.

Regular exercise reduces your resting heart rate. Moderately high blood pressure gradually settles. The heart's work load and oxygen requirements are reduced, and its "stroke volume" and cardiac output (the amount of blood the heart pumps with each contraction) increase.

Another major advantage of regular exercise is that it reduces the blood's coagulability. This is valuable because it is a blood clot in one of the narrowed, atherosclerotic coronary arteries that is responsible for a heart attack.

The body's enlivened metabolic ability results in reduced fat stores. Triglycerides are reduced, and HDL cholesterol (the "good" kind) is increased. Both of these changes are protective against heart disease.

The feeling of well-being commonly experienced during and/or after exercise is due to the tranquilizing effect of endorphins secreted by the brain. The depression that often accompanies inactivity disappears, and self-confidence improves. People who exercise regularly feel better, sleep better, and think better. Sexual performance also improves, because of increased circulation in the pelvic region and increased feelings of vitality. Appetite also often increases—so be careful not to overeat!

These subjective benefits are usually reflected in improved relationships with family and friends. Aging is retarded, and older people who exercise regularly are more fit than their younger colleagues who don't. People who exercise can manage stress much better than those who don't. In short, exercise improves life and health in countless ways.

Determining Your Exercise Prescription

Here are some suggestions to help you determine what type of exercise to do and when to do it.

* As a general rule, regular continuous aerobic exercise for a minimum of 20 to 30 minutes, at least four or five days each week, is essential for heart care. The amount and intensity of exercise, however, needs to be regulated according to each individual. Factors such as age, current state of health, and past medical history must be given consideration.

* Such exercises as "wagging," walking, bicycling, or swimming are excellent for most people. More demanding sports such as jogging or tennis are fine for young people or older people in a high state of fitness.

However, jogging has no definite advantage over wagging, and it jars the knees and sometimes interferes with the menstrual cycles of young women, though the cause for this is not yet known. Rope skipping is a demanding aerobic exercise but has a jarring effect on the hips, knees, and feet.

* Swimming is an excellent form of exercise for cardio-respiratory fitness. The benefits of 100 yards of swimming are equal to about 400 yards of jogging. The musculoskeletal system benefits, and the buoyancy of the water stimulates deeper breathing, which helps increase vital capacity.

* Aerobic dancing was popularized by Jane Fonda, and her video tapes (as well as many others) have sequences of aerobic dance and exercises along with music. The music helps regulate your exercise in time with its rhythm. A vigorous aerobic dance workout for 20 minutes burns calories and improves circulation. The heart and various organs become stronger. It makes you feel good!

* Yoga asanas are an excellent form of stretching exercise that tones up the muscles. The bending and stretching provide a kind of internal massage that improves the functioning of the vital organs. They also produce a feeling of tranquility of mind. I will discuss their benefits later in the book.

* Leisure activities, such as gardening and hiking, walking at work, and going up and down the stairs during coffee breaks and lunch breaks are helpful supplementary exercises but in no way replace regular continuous exercise.

* If you haven't been exercising regularly, ask your physician's advice before setting up an exercise routine. Even after a heart attack a certain amount of exercise is helpful and important, but it must be in accordance with the instructions of your doctor. Remember, you have to handle life carefully.

The Times in London reported that a man in his seventies, an avid tennis player, was urged by his doctor not to engage in such a vigorous sport. "Take some milder form of exercise, such as walking," the physician advised.

The man replied, "Doctor, nothing will make me happier than to hit a winning smash and collapse on the court." And so it came to be—almost. The man collapsed and died on the tennis court, not after hitting a winning smash but after serving a double fault.

* Be consistent. Most people who begin an exercise regimen, including heart patients, find some excuse to drop it after a few weeks. Following through with your exercise program is very important. The right kind of exercise in the right amount is the first essential for a healthy life.

* Avoid unaccustomed exertion. If you are not regularly exercising, sudden strenuous exertion can be disastrous. Your body is simply not ready for it.

Vikram, a fine man and a very successful, affluent young businessman, came in for a general checkup. He was overweight, but had no evidence of any disease and was not a smoker. His treadmill stress test was negative.

Vikram had done no exercise at all since his school days. He was advised to begin with very mild exercise and work up to more in a graduated manner. He went to a health club and over-enthusiastically involved himself in a strenuous crash exercise program. He died suddenly while running on the treadmill.

* Exercise during very hot weather should be avoided, though it can be undertaken in the early hours of the day before the heat builds up. Mr. S. N. Haldar, aged sixty-five, was driving back from Faridabad at noon on a very hot day in June some years ago when he got a flat tire. He hadn't changed a tire by himself in forty years but he assured himself that he could do it. However, the lug nuts were very tight. He pushed himself to do it in the smoldering heat but collapsed on the road and was taken to the hospital suffering from a heart attack. He could have taken a taxi back home and sent an auto mechanic to do the job.

* The duration of each exercise session is important. For a significant improvement in cardiorespiratory function and endurance, regular exercise of 20 to 30 minutes is required, at least four or five times a week but preferably every day. Glucose tolerance and lipid profile (cholesterol and triglyceride levels) improve with a minimum of 40 to 60 minutes of moderate exercise daily. Regular brisk walking for three miles each day

Beware of sudden exertion

One of the greatest dangers to health occurs when a person who has not been regularly exercising engages in a sudden exertion, such as racing through an airport to catch a flight or participating in a sport or other vigorous activity. Likewise, occasional indulgence in a strenuous game of squash or football by people who are otherwise sedentary is not desirable, especially in persons who are middle-aged or older. Unaccustomed strenuous exercise can be disastrous, particularly if it is done with a competitive spirit. Healthy limits are forgotten, and one is likely to ignore even the warning symptoms of an oncoming cardiac problem, such as discomfort in the chest.

Mr Agnihotri, fifty-eight, was the managing director of a large business concern. He had sedentary habits, and had not undertaken any regular exercise since leaving Doon School decades earlier. One weekend he traveled from Delhi to Dehra Dun for a school reunion consisting of special events such as sports, seminars, and evening parties. He was very happy to meet old friends from all over India there.

In the afternoon there was a cricket match between the students and alumni. In cricket matches, especially "friendly" matches, if a player has a minor injury or is unable to run for any other reason, a healthy young man can be the "runner" and run for him between wickets. Other older men of his age took runners for the match, but Agnihotri, who had been good at cricket in his younger days, refused one. He played hard and enjoyed himself, running up and down more than was really necessary. After the match, the "old boys" got together to tell stories of their achievements over a pint of beer. Suddenly Agnihotri had an onset of pain across his chest, with profuse sweating. He was rushed to the hospital, where he was diagnosed with a massive heart attack.

Agnihotri had no known risk factor for heart disease. It was only the afternoon's exertion that brought on the attack.

Intermittent participation in sports cannot replace regular exercise. A regular routine of moderate exercise is an important key to a healthy life.

can help you lose over 2lbs of excess weight every thirty-five to forty days.

At any age—childhood, adulthood, middle age, or ripe old age—appropriate exercise can help you to be healthier, happier, and more vibrant with life.

12

Alcohol and Tobacco: The Biggest Preventable Menaces to Our Health

The twentieth-century epidemic costs more than you think. Tobacco is an insidious danger. Smokers do not keel over after the first cigarette. The use of tobacco products causes a delayed reaction with approximately 20–30 years passing between smoking initiation and resulting deaths. Ultimately the end result is devastating.

At present, tobacco products kill about three million people a year. This decade about thirty million people will be killed by tobacco products; tantamount to wiping out several of the world's largest cities.

—DR J.R. MENCHAEA, WORLD HEALTH ORGANIZATION

S ome years after I took early retirement, my wife and I were attending a party at a beautiful home in south Delhi. The room was filled with successful, affluent business people, along with about half a dozen retired major-generals and lieutenant generals, real army types with stern faces and whiskers. The room was filled with cigarette smoke, and rare brands of whisky and champagne were flowing freely. Even the disciplined military men were gulping Scotch and smoking.

I wondered, "Is nobody telling these people how many people die every year—and every day—because of excessive smoking and hard drink?" The combination is particularly lethal. Even comparatively younger people, in the prime of their life, when they can be most useful to their families and society and have the potential to be really happy, may die rather suddenly from heart attacks because of these destructive habits.

Didn't they know what smoking and alcohol abuse can lead to? I was convinced that they could not, or they would not behave as they did.

Self-destructive habits such as smoking and alcohol abuse do result in premature death for many. For those who survive this onslaught on their mind and body when they are young, misery and disease degrade the later years of their lives. They may survive into old age, but they are likely to suffer from breathlessness, fatigue, and debility in their later years because of chronic lung disease and declining functioning of their vital organs. They may not realize until it is too late that it is all the result of the terrible violence they have committed against their bodies by these addictions, which are totally against the laws of nature.

The Dangers of Alcohol

Alcohol has been used for rituals and ceremonies since ancient times. The Bible tells of wine-making in Palestine, and ancient Indian texts talk of "Soma rasa" and the use of wine in medicine. But never has alcohol been abused the way it is today. Drinking may not be bad in small amounts. It may even have some positive value. But most people cannot keep within their limits, and then it becomes a complete villain. As a result, millions of people are marching toward misery, ill health, and premature death under its influence. Alcoholism is a serious disease.

So-called "social drinkers" don't tend to take the dangers of alcohol seriously. But millions of people have slowly drifted, usually without realizing it, from taking an occasional drink to alcoholism. Heavy drinkers have a much higher death rate than non-drinkers, and their deaths are not easy: suicide, automobile accidents, digestive system diseases, and severe malnutrition are among the likely causes. Other destructive effects of alcohol include the degeneration of heart muscle, brain tissue, liver, pancreas, and stomach.

Wine—and particularly red wine—has attracted a lot of attention as being beneficial and protective against heart attack and stroke. The protective factor is a compound called quercetin that occurs naturally in wine. Another substance in wine, reveratrol, apparently helps to control cholesterol and fat levels in the blood. Professor R. Curtis Ellison at the Boston University School of Medicine believes that the incidence of heart disease in France and some other European countries is less than half the rate of that in the United States because people in those countries drink much more wine than people in America, where the accent is more on hard liquor or beer.

However, if you want the protective effects of quercetin and reveratrol, you can get them from safer sources. Quercetin is found in fresh grapes, and is also available in asparagus, onions, apples, the rind of citrus fruits, and tea. Reveratrol is found in grape juice and in raisins, and is particularly abundant in purple grapes. Thus, whatever little benefit can be derived from a moderate drinking of wine can also be obtained from these foods without exposing oneself to the manifold risks of alcohol consumption.

In addition, studies have shown that when beer or wine—white or red—are taken in large amounts, the risk for cancer significantly increases. So one may be somewhat protected against heart attack through moderately heavy drinking, but the risk of dying of cancer (especially when combined with smoking) is increased.

It is very difficult to get over an addiction to alcohol. "Once an alcoholic, always an alcoholic," the saying goes. It is preferable by far not to risk alcohol abuse, which results in devastating changes in a person's economic, social, and psychological life.

As I mentioned, the correlation between alcohol abuse and cancer is high. Malnutrition is also common among heavy drinkers. Experts say that chronic alcohol abuse reduces life expectancy an average of fifteen years.

Quite often the life of an alcohol abuser is cut short abruptly by an accident. Vasu, a young businessman twenty-eight years of age, came to the outpatient department because he was having heart palpitations and nausea. He had a history of drinking a bottle of whisky a day, starting early in the morning. He told us with pride that he could drive a car better than a professional driver. That very evening he hit a lamppost and was brought in to the hospital in a coma with serious head injuries.

So very many serious road accidents are a result of drunk driving. Tragically, not only the drinker is injured or killed, but many completely innocent people. Errors of judgment, capable of affecting driving ability, do indeed occur even after two or three drinks, but most people won't admit to this fact. Only a few are conscious of it and allow themselves to be driven home after a party.

Some research suggests that addiction to alcohol has a genetic component. But often the main factor in alcoholism seems to be not so much the family genes, but the family eating and drinking habits and the social popularity that drinking has somehow acquired.

The only solution for this terrible problem is the inculcation of yoga and meditation at a young age, along with other components of a healthy lifestyle.

Smoking: A Most Hazardous Affliction

Mr. Mahajan, a young business executive thirty-two years of age, came to us for a routine physical checkup and cardiac evaluation. He had no diabetes and had normal blood pressure. All his tests, including a treadmill exercise stress test, were negative for coronary heart disease. We declared him fit.

He was, however, a heavy smoker and had been smoking for the previous fifteen years, since his school days. I gave him a long talk on the benefits of not smoking and the hazards of continuing. He promised to kick the habit.

Two months later Mr. Mahajan, a promising, upcoming young man, the pride of his family, recently married and the father of two young children, dropped dead after a game of squash. What could have happened?

When a person smokes, carbon monoxide from the cigarette smoke forms carboxyhemoglobin, which replaces part of the hemoglobin that carries oxygen to all the fifty trillion cells of the body, including the cells in the muscles of the heart. Carboxyhemoglobin is not capable of carrying oxygen. When the demand for oxygen increases, as is always the case during strenuous exercise, the oxygen supply may become insufficient.

I found out that Mr. Mahajan had not given up smoking. When his need for more oxygen was not met, his heart muscle apparently fibrillated, that is, for a while there were ineffective, irregular contractions, followed by cardiac arrest and death. This happened even though, only two months earlier, the coronary arteries and heart were found relatively healthy. His death was a self-inflicted tragedy brought on by smoking.

I wish I could say that this was an isolated and unusual case. But the fact is that every single minute, six people die in the world due to smoking. The Health Education Authority esti- mated 120,000 deaths attributable to smoking in the UK in 1995. And in the USA tobacco use kills more than 400,000 people each year. The number is proportionately larger in the "developing" countries like India. According to World Health Organization figures, one million and eighty thousand persons die every year in India as a result of smoking.

Mrs. Bhat, forty-five years old, was admitted to our hospital with lung cancer. She was a non-smoker, but both Mr. Bhat and their son, Mehar, twenty-six, were smokers. Mr. Bhat was a successful businessman, and Mrs. Bhat assisted him in the office. For the past three years Mehar had worked with them too.

By the time Mrs. Bhat came to the hospital, the lung cancer was in an advanced stage. Surgery was ruled out. Medical treatment was instituted, but she succumbed to the killer disease within a fortnight of her admission to the hospital.

It was obvious that Mrs. Bhat developed lung cancer due to passive smoking. She was exposed to a great deal of smoke both in the office and at home. Apparently Mr. Bhat had stronger immunity than she had. Research has shown that some people's bodies can produce more superoxide dismutase (SOD) than others. This enzyme is a natural protection against free radicals, which are released by tobacco and tobacco smoke. They can initiate and propagate both heart disease and cancer.

Research has also shown that passive smoking can be even worse than active smoking. The so-called "sidestream" smoke that is inhaled by passive smokers has finer particles, which passive smokers innocently inhale deeper down into their lungs. This smoke contains more than 4,000 carcinogens, including polycyclic aromatic hydrocarbons, nitrosamines, and many other harmful chemicals that induce cancer.

Mrs. Bhat was not a smoker. But as I mentioned in Chapter 1, more and more women are taking up the tobacco habit. Tobacco companies have spent millions on advertising to promote smoking as a sign of women's independence and equality, and they have succeeded. The tragedy is that smoking does not confer any benefits; rather, it will bring millions of women and their families increased suffering and death from lung cancer and heart disease.

In addition, many women who, like Mrs. Bhat, do not smoke themselves, nevertheless suffer and may even die because of passive smoking when their husbands smoke. Men need to be educated not to smoke for the protection of their wives and children, as well as to protect themselves from future heart attack or cancer.

Mr. Haria, fifty-six years old and a chronic smoker, was admitted to our hospital with cancer of the larynx. He was successfully operated on; that is, the cancer was removed and he seemed to recover, but without the larynx he was unable to speak. Haria was miserable about losing his voice. He learned to speak through his esophagus with the help of a battery-operated electronic gadget, but the artificial voice had no inflections or subtleties, and could be understood only with difficulty.

"What is the use?" he complained. "I cannot shout at anyone when I am upset, I cannot laugh, and I cannot cry." A year later he developed cancer of the colon and died.

It is rare for one person to have two different types of cancer, but this does occur in smokers who are also alcohol abusers. This combination is particularly lethal and can be a major factor in cancer in various organ systems in the body.

The Single-Most Important Preventable Cause of Death

Tobacco smoking is the most hazardous human affliction of all time. It has also been described as the greatest *preventable* menace to mankind, and the most preventable of all the risk factors for heart attack and cancer. The Surgeon General, the highest-ranked medical officer in the United States government, has said that "smoking is the single-most important preventable cause of death" in American society. It is the same in countries around the world. If you are a smoker, quitting is almost certainly the best thing you can do for your cardiovascular system and for your overall health.

Deaths around the world from smoking are fifty times more than accidents in this modern era. Out of 1,000 smokers, half will die of heart attacks and cancer before they reach middle age. Heart attacks are ten times more common among smokers of thirty to forty cigarettes a day, and twice as frequent among those who smoke only five to ten cigarettes daily. Smokers also have a lot more complications when they have a heart attack; sudden death is not uncommon.

Yet how many people realize the tremendous danger that cigarettes pose? Having a smoke seems relatively harmless. Professor Richard Peto, epidemiologist and statistician at Oxford University, says that the relationship between smoking and disease is largely misunderstood because there is a gap of many years between the start of the killer habit and the appearance of one of the terrible and lethal diseases that result from the habit. One may begin smoking as a teenager or in one's twenties, but heart disease, cancer, chronic bronchitis, gastric ulcers, emphysema, or some other disease may not strike for twenty, thirty, or more years.

We are sitting on a time bomb: The big increases in heart attack and cancer because of smoking are still to come.

How to Quit Smoking

To prevent further tragedy, the benefits of not smoking and the terrible dangers of smoking must be explained to children. Smoking, which is itself highly addictive, can be the gateway to other drugs, which can ruin the life and career of our children. Once a person is addicted to nicotine, it is not easy to give up the habit. Therefore it is of the utmost importance that we motivate and educate children in their teens, and even before, never to take up the habit.

For those who want to quit, a firm resolve is the most important step. Once you realize the health disasters that are waiting to happen to a smoker, you will be motivated to stop. It can be done. People quit every day. In the United States, it is estimated that over fifty million persons have quit smoking.

Here are some time-tested guidelines gathered from experts on smoking cessation to help you drop the habit:

* Don't underestimate the challenge. Quitting smoking isn't easy. Nicotine is a physically addicting drug, and a smoker's body craves regular doses. "Smoking cigarettes is as physiologically and psychologically addictive as smoking crack cocaine or injecting heroine," says Dean Ornish, author of *Dr. Dean Ornish's Program for Reversing Heart Disease*. Admitting that you're physically hooked will increase your determination to break free.

* Don't try to quit until you're really ready, but when you are, make a firm commitment and don't waver. Many experts

believe that the most important factor in quitting is your own personal decision and resolve.

* Make a plan. You wouldn't build an addition to your dwelling or sew new clothes without making a plan. If you are a smoker, quitting smoking is one of the most important things you will ever do, so don't just jump into it unprepared. Decide whether you will quit all at once—"cold turkey"—or whether you will gradually taper off. What day will you quit? How will you avoid starting up again? A well thought-out plan will greatly improve your chances for success.

* Pick a "Quit Day" and write it on your calendar. Make it soon, no more than two weeks away, before your good intentions wear off. Then stick to it. Suggestion: Quit on a weekend when you can have better control of your time, surroundings, and circumstances.

* Tell your family, friends, and co-workers you're going to stop smoking. This will elicit their support as well as their sympathy and understanding if you're irritable for a few days after you quit.

* Plan to quit "cold turkey." Research shows that most people who successfully kick the smoking habit quit this way. Tapering off rarely works. When your "Quit Day" comes, just quit!

Here are some more brief tips to help you stop:

* Get rid of any cigarettes you have in the house.

* On the day you quit, do something enjoyable to keep busy. Avoid social situations where there will be smokers. If possible, go some place where smoking isn't permitted. This will be a good strategy for several weeks after you initially quit.

* Have snacks on hand. Fruit is especially good.

* Consider using nicotine patches. These patches, which are placed on the skin, are effective for some adult smokers who have been motivated to quit. Further damage to the lungs, and risk of lung cancer are both reduced, but the ill effects of nicotine continue until the dosage is gradually reduced and the use of the patches has ceased.

* In my experience and the experience of other observers, what really works is a change of lifestyle. Regular participation in sports, yoga exercises, listening to good music, all are very helpful in quitting smoking. Meditation appears to be one of the most effective things you can do. Jack Forem, in his prestigious book, *Transcendental Meditation*, cites studies in which 48 percent of the persons smoked before learning transcendental meditation, 27 percent heavily. After twenty-one months, only 16 percent still smoked, 5.8 heavily.

"It's hard to quit smoking unless you have something else that can provide the benefits of nicotine," Dean Ornish comments. "If smoking helps you relax, for example, then you're likely to feel more stressed when you quit smoking unless you have other ways of managing stress that aren't centered around cigarettes." If you don't already know how to meditate, see page 162 for some suggestions.

If you can keep away from cigarettes, and restrict yourself to moderate alcohol consumption or none at all, you will be well on your way to a long and healthy life.

13

Meditation: Experience of the Inner World

Behold, the Kingdom of God is within you.
—JESUS

The path of meditation leads inwards.
In prayer you are talking to God;
In meditation, God is talking to you.
—DEEPAK CHOPRA in
Instructor's Manual on Meditation

Imagine a calm, peaceful lake on a full moon night. The image of the moon in the water is perfectly reflected, round, silver white, cool, soothing, and beautiful. The look of it enthralls your soul.

Now throw a stone into the lake. Or imagine a wind whipping up waves. The reflection of the moon is disturbed, broken up into a thousand pieces, each shattered bit agitated. Of course, deep down, the lake is absolutely quiet and still. Soon the waves subside and the reflection of the moon is back in its full glory and splendor.

The human mind is in its essence, deep down, like the calm, silent lake. But on the surface it is troubled by ceaseless agitation. Every day thoughts, memories, concerns, keep up an internal chatter. A few unkind words may produce a rush of negative thoughts and feelings, rough waves further spoiling the calm waters. These waves, whether of anger, jealousy, worry, play havoc with you. Negative molecules rush through your system. If this process is repeated many times it stresses your body, buckles your immunity, and ultimately leads to ill health, even serious disease.

How can we prevent these negative emotions, these mental agitations, and the storms of molecules and chemicals in our system that are the cause of misery and ill health?

We have already discussed a number of techniques, including music and the arts, sports and exercise, laughter, etc. These are all helpful. But most helpful of all is meditation, the journey inward. For as the mind learns to go inward we fathom the deeper, more silent realms of our own nature. The deepest level is the unbounded, blissful Self, a field of quietness, silence, peace.

For a person who practices meditation regularly, day by day more of that inner silence "sticks" to the awareness as we go about our activities. Stability in the face of adversity grows; negative thoughts and emotions gradually disappear and give place to spontaneous positive thinking. The mind expands, happiness increases. You manage stress more effectively. As the American psychologist, William James, wrote:

> The turbulent bellows of the fretful surface leave the deep parts of the ocean undisturbed, and to him who has a hold on vaster and more permanent realities, the hourly vicissitudes of his personal destiny seem relatively insignificant things. The really religious person is accordingly unshakable and calmly ready for any duty that the day may bring forth.

In the usual course of events, we know our environment and our outer self, our body. We also know something of our inner self, our mind and intellect. But we do not know our real, innermost Self. With meditation, we come into contact with this part of our being.

The experience of meditation teaches you how to relax, not how to become lethargic; how to enjoy living, and how not to be afraid of dying; how to manage stress, not how to avoid it; how to live more fully in the world, not how to withdraw from it.

It also teaches how to take care of yourself so that you can be of maximum use to yourself and to others. Meditation is not a selfish withdrawal from life. The benefits you receive from meditating are not confined to yourself. You pass them on spontaneously to influence the surroundings and then on to the whole universe for the benefit of all beings.

When we meditate regularly, day by day we perform our duties with our mind more infused with the peace and love of the Self, the supreme level of consciousness. As the Isavasy Upanishad says:

> Meditation and action—
> He who knows these two together
> Through action leaves death behind
> And through meditation gains immortality

Growth of consciousness, spiritual development, requires both meditation and action. Real fulfillment comes from living both sides of life—a full material existence enriched and ennobled by a full spiritual life.

What is Meditation?

To some people, "meditation" is synonymous with contemplation (thinking deeply about something) or even prayer. I would like to make a distinction between such practices and what is called in Sanskrit *dhyan*, the term for bringing the mind to quietness or rest. Some techniques call for concentration, but what I will be referring to is much easier and more natural. It is a spontaneous way of allowing the mind to transcend or go beyond its usual limits and attain *turiya* or the fourth state of consciousness.

Life is ordinarily composed of three states of consciousness, known as the waking state, dreaming, and deep sleep. Meditation is a means of allowing the waves of the mind to settle down to the silence of a fourth state, inner wakefulness without the constant activity of thoughts and feelings, pure inner calm. Someone said, "In prayer, you talk to God. In meditation, God is talking to you." And his language is silence.

> There is something behind the mind which abides in Silence within the mind. It is the supreme mystery, beyond thought. Let one's mind and one's subtle body rest upon that and that alone.
>
> —MAITREYA UPANISHAD, 6:19

Those who advocate concentration and discipline for reaching this inner silence say that the mind must be tamed, like a restless monkey or a wild elephant. The elephant must be tied to a stake and allowed to shriek and trample until it is totally exhausted, then the training can begin.

The truth is that the mind, which is endlessly seeking satisfaction, wants to find the fourth state, which is known as *sat-chit-ananda*, or bliss consciousness. If left to its natural tendencies, with a little guidance, the mind will indeed experience that bliss. Meditation is only a vehicle to point the mind in the right direction. It is a kind of letting-go, allowing yourself to be. Your attention learns to fly in the silent, peaceful, unchanging Self or consciousness that is the home base of the mind.

By turning to the Self, the mind becomes infused with the peace of the silent lake, free from ripples and waves. This silence is very refreshing to the mind. With continued regular meditation, the mind comes to abide in it; awareness gets rooted in the Self.

The Vedas say that thoughts are like ocean waves, rising and falling. Knowing only their own motion, they say, "I am a wave." But the greater truth, which they do not see, is "I am the ocean." There is no separation between the two, whatever the wave may suppose. When a wave settles back down, it instantly recognizes its source in the ocean, infinite, silent, and unchanging.

With regular meditation, you still the oscillations of the mind and learn that you are not the waves but the silent ocean.

> As a lamp in a windless place does not waver, so the yogi whose mind is controlled remains always steady in his meditation on the transcendent Self.
>
> —BHAGAVAD GITA, 6:19

How to Meditate

Now let us consider some of the "mechanics" of how you can actually meditate.

To begin with, you will sit down and close your eyes. (Closing the eyes helps to shut out many external distractions.) The place where you meditate should be quiet. Sit with your back straight on a seat above the ground. The spinal column should be erect, with head, neck, and chest in a straight line. If you can, sit in the lotus posture, the half-lotus, or the *sukham* pose (see Appendix 3). If you cannot do any of these, sit in a chair. Sitting in the same place every day is preferable, but you can meditate in any place when you are away from home.

The basic principle of meditation is to observe your thoughts as they emerge to the surface of your mind. Observe them one by one, as they arise, but do not judge any of them. Don't attach any feelings to them. And of course, don't act on any thought. Just sit quietly and watch them as a *sakshi* or witness. That means don't be a participant in any of the thoughts. Just observe. When you find yourself caught up in a flow of thoughts, simply return to your post as the witness.

At first, it may not be easy not to attach any feelings or judgments to your thoughts. You may find yourself feeling that some thoughts are good, others bad. But they come and go, take shape and float away. Just let them go.

In order to enter the fourth state of consciousness, turiya, you have to set aside your little time and space-bound self and allow the unbounded state to happen by itself. Of course you have to intend it to happen, but at the same time, not make an effort. Be willing for it to happen, and allow it to happen.

If you make an effort, it is not going to happen. Some time ago I heard a story that illustrates this. Once there was a centipede who used to dance extremely well with all her hundred legs. Different animals used to assemble and watch her dance with admiration, and all sang her praises except one tortoise who was jealous of the centipede, as he could not dance at all. One day he went and slyly told the centipede that he was a great admirer of hers, but he wanted to ask her one question. He had been watching her closely, he said, and he wanted to know, did she lift leg number 51 before lifting leg number 79? The centipede starting thinking about what she actually did when she danced. The result was that she never danced again.

Something similar can happen to us if we become too engaged in analyzing our meditation process. We just have to be effortlessly willing for it to happen and allow it to happen spontaneously. You have to get out of your own way.

Now let me be more specific about what to do. In the following practice, you will simply follow your breathing. For years your breathing has functioned without any assistance from you. Now you will be paying attention to it. That does not mean that you need to interfere with it. You will notice that as you pay attention to it, you will be, in effect, setting yourself aside so that you can watch without interfering.

It is natural for your mind to generate thoughts, even about your breathing as you observe it. That's all right. Your mind will naturally wander about, thinking about other things. After all, your breathing is not that interesting! Whenever you find yourself thinking, let the thoughts go and gently let your attention return to your breathing. Let your attention be on the comforting rhythms of the breath.

Never fight a thought. A group of people were told that during meditation they could think of anything they wanted, except one thing. They were not to think of a monkey. They could not get rid of the thought of the monkey despite pushing it away repeatedly. Your mind will wander into its own thoughts. Gently return your attention to rest on your breath. Simply practice the willingness to have your attention attuned peacefully to your breathing.

Instead of your breathing, your attention can be on the silent recitation of a mantra, or on the primordial sound, Aum. The practice will be the same.

Another form of meditation, which I will not discuss here, has been taught by great modern masters, including Sri Ramana Maharishi and Sri Nisargadatta Maharaj. This kind of meditation belongs more to gyana yoga, or the path of knowledge. It involves deep introspective thinking on such questions as, "Why am I here in this universe?", "Where have I come from?", "Where am I going?" Most particularly, it involves looking inward to answer the question "Who am I?" This method emphasizes the application of discriminatory intelligence to achieve liberation from imaginary bondage to the body and the world, rejecting all that is transitory. According to these two great modern saints, it was all they needed to attain liberation.

Ideally, meditation should be learned from a qualified teacher. Swami Prabhavananda, recounting the Indian practice whereby a disciple who comes to his teacher for initiation is given a mantra, says the mantra "is the essence, as it were, of the teacher's instructions to that particular disciple, and the seed within which spiritual wisdom is passed down." Mantra meditation is centering the consciousness within, through repetition of a certain root sound representing a particular aspect of the spirit. With practice, in due course of time, you lose the mantra, transcend, and have a glimpse of the Reality.

If you are meditating with Aum (or with a different sound or mantra), when other thoughts come up, bring your attention back to Aum. Let Aum echo in your mind. You may hear many repeating echoes. Listening to these echoes allows your mind to think the same thought over and over again. This is much easier than trying to focus your mind to concentrate on something. Make no effort to concentrate, only pay attention to the sound.

As you see, meditation is not emptying the mind. It is not making the mind go blank. The goal is to attune your mind to your chosen ideal. It may be the breath, but it may be the oneness of spirit, or love, or the sound Aum, or some other sound or image. It is not the discipline of making the mind blank, but the willingness to listen to the reverberations of your ideal and bring the mind back to it if it strays to other thoughts.

It may happen during meditation that your mind will be occupied with thoughts racing one after another, including some thoughts we would rather not think, perhaps "negative" or distressing, such as painful memories. This is not wrong or bad; it is a useful purification process.

When we recently renovated our house, we found a lot of things we had acquired years earlier. Perhaps we had used them once or twice and then we stored them away. Why did we hang on to those useless things? They were only making the house dirty, cluttering it up. We did not even remember that we had them. It wasn't until we started cleaning up that we got disturbed by the muck we had been accumulating.

Similarly the mind is a storehouse of memories, good, bad, and indifferent. When we go deeper in meditation, we find that some of the stored thoughts and memories may reappear, and some may not be pleasant. We have to throw them away and forget about them. Like vomiting when you have taken in some undesirable food, "throwing up" unpleasant thoughts and memories is a cleaning-up operation and purifies the mind.

Another thing that may happen is that you may fall asleep, because meditation is very comforting and relaxing. That too is all right. It will help relieve your stress, and unless you are living an unusually tiring lifestyle, it will not happen often.

Once you sit down, just do your practice. Don't worry about what is happening, or judge it. When your mind becomes quiet, meditation will happen by itself. No effort, no forcing. If you don't have a deep, peaceful experience on a particular day, don't worry. Don't be frustrated. Perhaps it will happen the next day, or the day after. Before you set out on the water, you have to make your ship seaworthy, your plane airworthy before taking off. You just have to close your eyes and make yourself meditation-worthy and it will work.

And don't lose heart and discontinue your practice. In Chapter 6 verses 33–39 of the Bhagavad Gita, a doubt is cast about the seeker's success in meditation. Though he possesses faith, if he is unable to control his wandering mind, may he not wander from the path of meditation and yoga practice? Perhaps he may lose hope of experiencing the infinite joy of Brahman or the Self, and perish like a wind-torn cloud, supportless and deluded.

Preparations for Meditation

Here are several things you can do to make your meditation period more rewarding.

- Gradually train the body to sit in a comfortable, erect posture for a substantial length of time.
- Perform yoga asanas before meditation. They tone up the whole physiology, including the nervous system, and help the mind to be more relaxed. Endorphins are secreted, and a feeling of well-being comes.
- Between yoga asanas and meditation, practice a few minutes of pranayama or breathing exercises. They make the body feel light and help the mind settle down. (See Chapter 14 for more about yoga postures and pranayama.)
- Eat sattvic food. Light, fresh, wholesome food is good for meditation. Heavy food dulls the mind.
- Don't eat too much (again, you will feel dull and heavy), but don't eat too little either.

Doing these things will help prepare you for meditation. It is helpful to create a conducive physical and psychological atmosphere for meditating, with no activity on the emotional level, your mind quiet, and your body relaxed. Before you sow seeds in your farmland, you construct a fence around the land, make sure about the water and sunlight in the area, then sow the seeds. Then you just leave them alone and pray; with God's grace they will sprout and blossom.

Lord Krishna quickly dispels this doubt. In verse 40 he says, that neither in this world nor the next is there any destruction for a true seeker of truth. None who strives to be good ever comes to grief, in this life or hereafter. No seeker is ever lost. Though you may slip today, the effort you have put in is never wasted. So continue on: you are bound to achieve the bliss of the Self sooner or later.

Benefits of Meditation

Although you do very little or nothing at all during meditation, a lot happens to you. As your mind becomes more quiet, your breathing becomes softer and more regular. Heart rate and blood pressure decrease, the breathing rate is reduced, and there is reduced blood lactate and oxygen consumption, all resulting from a reduced metabolic rate. The overall effect on your physiology is relaxing and restful.

The benefits of meditation help us to understand that mind and body are one whole, not different from one another. You perform a simple mental process, but your body is very much affected. The relaxation and healing rest you get during meditation helps to reduce stress and negative thoughts and feelings, such as fear, anger, guilt, and grief. These stress-generated emotions lead to low self-esteem and poor relationships with the people around you.

Once these unwanted feelings start to diminish, the innate love and bliss inside you surfaces. Basic human virtues, such as compassion, forgiveness, peacefulness, come intuitively to you because they are your nature. The peace and bliss you attain enhance your self-esteem and give you a sense of security. You find that you cannot be hostile to others; you are relaxed and without stress while you engage in your work throughout the day.

As I mentioned at the beginning of the book, you cannot— and you should not—avoid or run away from stress or stressful situations. As the novelist Joseph Conrad commented, "Facing it—always facing it—that is the way to get through it. Face it."

Stress is essential for progress in life. With the quietude of mind and the intuitive faculties you unfold with continued meditation, you can manage stress to your advantage and lead a creative, healthy life.

Meditation also allows you to observe the dynamic nature of your own thoughts, how they come and go. The insights you gain help you to improve your thought process.

Deeper than thought, however, is the Self. As we said earlier, during meditation your attention goes to the silent, peaceful, unchanging Self. The Self is the home base for the mind, and by returning to it you infuse your mind with peace and silence, and open your awareness to good, creative thoughts right from their source.

As you gradually get to know the Self, your real nature, you experience increasing bliss. Every cell and atom in the body begins to resonate with it during meditation. You enjoy increasing quietude of mind during meditation, and carry the meditative mood with you during the rest of the day.

Old thought patterns and self-destructive habits like smoking and alcohol abuse fall off. You are no longer like a little pond that swells when the rains come and shrinks when there is no rain. Now you are like an ocean. Whether it rains or not does not matter; the streams flow in from all sides and you are not affected. You are no longer like an autumn leaf at the mercy of the wind, being tossed all over. You have a stable place to stand, in the silence of the Self, and you have a sense of direction; you know where to go.

In due course one is pleasantly surprised that there are moments when the "right" thoughts seem to flow freely, and you find yourself saying wise things, things you did not realize that you knew but must have been lying dormant within you. These thoughts apparently flow from a deeper level. You are not consciously thinking them, although you recognize them and you realize they are right. Now they have come up to the surface of your mind, at the right time, because your mind is no longer turbulent.

As feelings of well-being replace your formerly agitated state, your immune system becomes stronger, and health improves in many ways. Even serious illnesses can be reversed. For example, revolutionary research by Dean Ornish, first published in the prestigious medical journal *The Lancet* in 1990 and now the subject of several books, has shown that with a low-fat vegetarian diet, yoga asanas, and meditation, you can prevent, retard, and even reverse heart disease.

Both during and as an aftereffect of meditation, the electroencephalogram (EEG) shows greater coherence between the left and right hemispheres of the brain. Roger Sperry was awarded the Nobel Prize for discovering that the two sides of the brain had different functions. The left side deals with language, numbers, analysis and logic, reading and writing, while the right brain deals with intuition, creativity, rhythm of music, spatial awareness, etc. The EEG studies showing a better coordination between the left and right hemispheres have been correlated with better emotional functioning and a greater expression of human potential.

Actions arising from a more coherent brain tend to be in the right direction. Just as the sunflower follows the sun in the sky millions of miles away, you go forward in life spontaneously in the right direction. Nobody pushes the Ganges from behind or pulls it from in front; it just flows toward the ocean, its destination. The river of your life flows in the same way toward life's goal.

The Goal of Meditation

The ultimate goal of meditation—the goal of life itself—is to become an enlightened being, in conscious union with the blissful Self. Meditation enables one to perceive, right from the beginning, glimpses of this ultimate goal.

All scriptures declare man to be not a corruptible body with a soul, but a soul with a body. Meditation leads you to make this discovery yourself. You find that you are divine consciousness itself.

Awareness of the Self (pure consciousness) during meditation is known as *samadhi*, which literally means "still mind." Enlightenment is the state in which samadhi, inner peace, is permanent, that is, maintained along with all activity. As we have discussed, samadhi comes not by forcibly restraining the mind, but by allowing your attention to spontaneously shift from the phenomenal outside world to the inner depths of the mind. After meditation, when you return to the activity of everyday life, your mind is infused with the peace, love, and expanded awareness of that inner Reality.

> *Man bears the whole universe within himself and comes closest to the mystery of the world by stepping inside himself.*
>
> —NOVALIS (1722–1801)

During meditation you gently withdraw the mind from the plural world outside, the world of diversity and change, and turn it inward, where there is unity, oneness, wholeness, the Self or Atman, the pure awareness which is your true nature. In due course the awareness grows of unity in diversity, as the value of the inner Self is lived in activity. This is Self-realization, liberation from all bondage, life in real happiness and bliss.

If we divert the mind, through meditation, toward the One who is the source of all diversity, and come to know with unfailing certainty that the entire world is God Himself, then we have attained the goal of meditation.

So take a little time off each day to withdraw from the world. Interiorize your mind, and divert your attention to the presence of the Self. Then the difficulties of the objective world—the world outside—will not stress you. You will have the inner strength to look at the problems facing you and say, "All right, it is okay. I will face this obstacle also and overcome it." You will gradually cultivate positive thinking, and even if you cannot overcome the whole problem at once, start with the first step and tell yourself, "If I do this, my situation will be better tomorrow."

You are walking to your home. It is nighttime, and you have to walk five miles to reach your house. You have a flashlight in your hand. You don't say, "I can see only a few yards of the road with this light, I cannot see the entire five miles; how will I ever reach home?" You know that you will see the next few yards, and after you have walked those, the next. If you keep on walking this way, you are certainly going to reach your home.

The enlightened sages of all times have left us a record. They saw firsthand the entire long journey of the soul to its eternal home. And they have left us a torch to light our way. With continued meditation, you will arrive at the direct, intuitive experience of Reality, your home base, and establish a unified life in harmony with all beings.

14

True Insight into Life Comes from Yoga

For those who have conquered the body through self-control, through the fire of yoga, there is no disease, nor old age, nor death.

—SHVETASHVATARA UPANISHAD

In the early 1960s, when Deepak Chopra was a first-year student at the All-India Medical Institute, one of his professors invited a yogi to participate in a scientific experiment. The man was a wandering ascetic, a sanyasi, dressed like thousands of others in India in faded saffron robes, with matted hair and untrimmed beard.

The professor asked the ascetic to step inside a wooden box just large enough to sit down in. He did, and seated himself in the yoga posture known as the "lotus pose," with legs crossed, feet resting on the opposite knee, and closed his eyes to meditate. When he was settled comfortably, the top of the box was nailed on and the box was lowered into a pit dug in the courtyard. Earth was thrown on top so that the box was completely buried, and the professor and members of the class went about their business.

Six days later the class reassembled in the courtyard, eager to see what had happened. They watched in anticipation as workmen took half an hour to unearth and then pry open the box. There was the yogi, sitting completely still! After a few minutes he stood up slowly and, with eyes half-closed, allowed himself to be led to the physiology lab.

First measurements failed to detect a heartbeat, but a closer observation showed that it was fluttering in very light, rapid throbs. Tests of his breathing showed a level of oxygen consumption so reduced "that no bodily mechanism we had studied could account for. The simple fact was that the saint had lived peacefully for six days under conditions that would have destroyed a normal mind and body in less than twelve hours."

For thousands of years, practitioners of yoga have learned to control body and breath, and some have been reputed to develop unusual powers. Like Deepak's physiology professor, many researchers during recent decades have studied practitioners of yoga and meditation in an effort to objectively determine the effects of their practices. As the results become known, more and more people are recognizing that this ancient tradition holds great benefits for health and the possibility of developing more of our full human capabilities.

What is Yoga?

In a world beset with stress, unrest, and conflicts, the ancient knowledge of yoga is more relevant today than ever before in human history, and many people around the world are realizing this. Not only is yoga becoming increasingly popular in India, the land of its origin, but according to a recent survey, at least six million Americans already practice yoga postures regularly, and more and more people are similarly turning to yoga in the UK.

But postures, or asanas, are only one of the limbs of yoga, which is far more than some physical postures and breathing exercises. It is a complete system for the development of consciousness to the highest level of enlightenment.

The word yoga comes from the root "yug," which means to join, yoke, or attach. Yoga thus means the union of the limited individual mind with the universal or divine mind, the joining of our individual will with the will of God, the union of the small self with the Supreme Self.

Yoga is one of the six systems of classical Indian philosophy. The basic work on yoga is the *Yoga Sutras* by Patanjali, consisting of 185 aphorisms which lay out the disciplines necessary to achieve union with the Divine. The path is described in terms of eight "limbs" as follows:

1. *Yama*: universal moral principles or disciplines, including *ahimsa* (non-violence, non-killing); *satya* (truthfulness); *asteya* (non-stealing); *brahmacharya* (continence, celibacy); *aparigraha* (non-covetousness, non-accumulation).
2. *Niyama*: self-purification. The five niyamas are *saucha* (purity of body and mind); *santosa* (contentment); *tapas* (austerity, intense self-discipline); *svadhyaya* (study of the Self); and *Isvara pranidhana* (devotion or dedication to the Lord).
3. *Asana*: posture. The traditional yoga postures promote good health and bring lightness to the body and steadiness to the mind. Perfection of the asanas makes one capable of remaining in a steady posture for a long time.
4. *Pranayama*: breathing exercises. Prana, as we shall see, means not only breath, but also vitality, energy, or spirit. It is the science of breath which allows the practitioner of yoga to purify the body and calm the mind.
5. *Pratyahara*: control of the senses; withdrawal of the senses from their objects; retirement from the field of the senses. This allows the mind to experience pure consciousness without the distractions of outer objects.
6. *Dharana*: concentration, one-pointedness, or steadiness of mind.
7. *Dhyana*: meditation, the flow of the mind from the turbulent surface to its own silent depths.
8. *Samadhi*: absorption in pure consciousness, transcendental consciousness, unboundedness, the mind and senses quiet and at peace.

This is a capsule of the great system of yoga and its lofty goal.

What people usually think of as yoga, and what we will talk about in this chapter—that is, the asanas or postures and the breathing exercises—are only two of the eight limbs.

Yoga Asanas

Yoga asanas affect every aspect of the human physiology. They help to regulate the body's metabolism, harmonize glandular secretions, and burn up extra fat. Performing the postures makes the joints more limber, improves circulation and digestion, increases coordination of different parts of the body, and energizes and enlivens the brain. The asanas balance enzymatic and hormonal secretions, relax and tone up the muscles, give the body's internal organs a massage, and benefit the nervous system.

During the practice of yoga asanas, energy is preserved rather than spent. The body becomes relaxed and the mind calm.

As the noted yoga teacher B. K. S. Iyengar has observed, one practical advantage of performing asanas is that "To perform them [all] one needs [is] a clean airy place, a blanket, and determination—while for other systems of physical training one needs large playing fields and costly equipment." Of course there are many other advantages. By the practice of yoga asanas alone one develops strength, agility, balance, and endurance, as well as greatly increased vitality, better health, and a feeling of well-being.

The asanas, says Iyengar, "exercise every muscle, nerve, and gland in the body. They secure a fine physique, which is strong and elastic without being muscle-bound, and they keep the body free from disease. They reduce fatigue and soothe the nerves."

It is very easy to find a good book or a competent teacher to help you learn yoga asanas. If you have never tried them, you might think they are difficult, but it is actually very easy to begin with simple postures and gain a tremendous benefit.

Pranayama—Breathing Exercises

Patanjali's *Yoga Sutras* says, "After being seated in a position that is firm but relaxed, one must practice pranayama (control of breath) by stopping the motions of inhalations and exhalations. The mind is calmed by expulsion and retention of breath."

In many of the world's cultures, breath has been associated with the force of life itself. The Greek word for breath is *pneuma*, which also means soul or spirit. In China this life energy is called *Chi*, in Japan *Ki*. Christians call it *the holy spirit*. In India for thousands of years it has been known as *prana*, and in yoga philosophy it is said that the knowledge and control of one's prana is the key to mental tranquility, physical endurance, and intellectual success.

Although the existence of this life force or prana has not yet been verified by scientific instruments—and its qualities may be too subtle ever to be measured by standard quantitative scientific means—nevertheless its existence and effects are well known.

Prana, the vital force of life, flows from the universal cosmic energy, the essence of all matter, to us, through our food, water, and air, and becomes our body's life force. Although it is carried into the system by oxygen, water, and food, in itself it is not any of these. Even so, liberal amounts of pure water and fresh, well-cooked food, as well as breathing exercises, are essential components in all the ancient health sciences.

As John Douillard explains in his book, *Body, Mind and Sport*, "While we breathe in through the nose, prana, which is carried by oxygen, enters the nasal cavity. The air while in the nose is prepared for exchange in the lungs, but the prana is said to travel into the brain along the olfactory nerve." The first step for the prana is the brain, which, when enlivened and energized by it, can co-ordinate with any or all parts of the body for its various functions.

When we breathe in through the nose, the air passes by small bones in the nose called turbinates, which swirl it into a refined stream most suitable for oxygen exchange. When we breathe through the mouth this does not happen. Instead, the prana, along with the unprepared air, moves directly into the lungs. It travels in and out of the body without going to the brain directly through the nasal passages. With proper nasal breathing, says Dr Douillard, "the role of prana is heightened as it is capable of nourishing the control centers of the brain as well as penetrating the deepest level of the lungs and bloodstream."

In situations of stress, rapid breathing through the mouth is triggered automatically. This may be a carryover from an infant's mouth breathing, a survival response to the threat of suffocation. This type of breathing is associated with fear and anxiety, and produces activation of the sympathetic nervous system with an associated rise in blood pressure and pulse rate. It has even been suggested that chronic mouth breathing represents a kind of sustained "fight or flight" response, in which the body is always in a state of readiness to respond to danger. This highly stressful state can be counteracted with the deep breathing described in the box below.

How to use deep breathing to calm yourself down

Deep, rhythmic nasal breathing produces a relaxed state of mind and body exactly the opposite of the anxious "fight or flight" response. When a person is overcome by stress, such as anxiety or fear, one of the body's protective mechanisms is faster breathing through the mouth. If we don't actually have to fight or to flee, the body may gulp so much oxygen that it cannot be exchanged for CO_2 fast enough. The resulting hyperoxygenation may cause dizziness or fainting, intensifying the panic reaction.

The way to pull out of this situation of panic is to hold the breath momentarily, and then take slow, deep breaths through the nose. This slow, deep nasal breathing will stop the panic reaction. It calms a person down and gives you back control over what felt like a completely out of control situation. The deep and slow breathing allows the life force or prana to have a direct calming effect on the emotions.

Your original emotional reaction to some situation caused a release of chemicals in your body, which in turn produced rapid mouth breathing. The fearful thoughts and responses you had affected the operation of the body. Conversely, you can maneuver the body's actions in such a manner—through this slow, deep nasal breathing—that they will have a positive effect on your emotions.

According to ancient scriptures, prana not only signifies human breath, but also the breath of the universe, the life force. It is the tendency of the unmanifest to vibrate and take form; it is the energy behind both mind and matter.

The creation of the universe, according to the Vedic rishis, begins with supreme, pure consciousness, a field of unified energy beyond space and time. It has no beginning or end, and is beyond attributes. It can be called awareness, creative intelligence, or God—the quantum source of all there is, was, and will be. It is also termed Brahman, which literally means "Bigger than the Big," or Purusha.

The divine will of this unbounded Purusha is known as *Prakriti*, which can be translated as awareness with a choice. The cosmic energy has awareness and a choice: it is the One who desires to become many. The universe is born out of the womb of Prakriti, the *Shakti* or Divine Mother.

The origin of all matter is thus at the level of consciousness, and is a vibration or wave pattern. When meditation is performed along with pranayama, with awareness directed to the breath, you may become aware of the vibrations of this cosmic wave pattern or soundless sound. These vibrations are one with the prana or life energy of the breath. Meditating in this way, your breathing will become quiet and your mind settled, and you will go beyond thought, beyond time and space, beyond cause and effect. All limitations vanish. You are no longer a limited person. Individual prana merges with universal, cosmic prana; individual consciousness merges with cosmic consciousness.

The Kaushitaka Upanishad speaks of prana as the life breath and the consciousness of all beings and explains that each sense (hearing, seeing, etc.) has its own prana, but that all stem from the one cosmic prana.

We don't see with the eyes, we see through the eyes. We don't hear with the ears, we hear through the ears. We speak through the voicebox, we think through the mind, but it is the prana seeing, hearing, speaking, and thinking. When the breath breathes, it is the prana breathing. And what is prana? Pure consciousness.

The Brihadaranyaka Upanishad also teaches that prana is the vital force of the universe, and that when it enters the human nervous system it energizes and enlivens the brain and manifests into several types of prana. These flow through the body's subtle channels (known as *nadis*) enlivening the subtle body (the *suksham sharira*) as well as the gross physical body. Prana makes the breath come in and go out, makes the heart beat, enlivens the senses, permeates our entire being, and enables us to function in the world. When the prana leaves the body permanently, all functions cease.

Prana and Kundalini

Coiled up at the base of the spine is a tremendous dormant storehouse of prana known as *kundalini* or shakti. This is the cosmic energy, the dynamic aspect of the formless, attributeless Absolute. It is God's creative power, which manifests the entire universe of forms. All forms of matter are simply the outer expressions of this energy.

The word kundalini means coiled up, and shakti means great power. This great divine energy dwells within every human being. The ancient rishis of India discovered that through yoga asanas, meditation, and pranayama you can awaken the stored energy of the kundalini. When kundalini rises from its dormant or latent state, where it is curled at the base of the spine, and rises to the top of the head, it brings creative power, health, and liberation.

The six *chakras* or spiritual centers along the spine are like way stations on the path of kundalini's journey to the crown of the head. When these centers are not yet enlivened, they act as blocks or obstacles. As these centers are purified and enlivened, the kundalini rises. As it rises, you see the world around you as more beautiful; you see the divinity in people, in nature, indeed in all things. Creativity increases, as well as inspiration and performance. Various subtle experiences and refined perceptions take place.

Dr Karan Singh, former Minister of Health and Ambassador of India to the United States, is a great scholar of Vedanta and Sanskrit. His knowledge of our ancient scriptures, including the Bhagavad Gita, Upanishads, and Vedas is superb. Dr Singh is deeply interested in the phenomenon of kundalini and is the chairman of the Kundalini Research Association International. The object of the research is to objectively validate the benefits of kundalini arousal and make the knowledge widely available, so people will realize that there is tremendous potential lying dormant in every person. This power, when used in the right way, can make this world a better place to live.

Siddhis or SuperNormal Powers

Book III of Patanjali's *Yoga Sutras* describes some of the subtle perceptions and powers that may occur as the kundalini rises and the chakras open, opening the door to higher states of awareness. These include clairvoyance (ability to have knowledge of things happening far away), knowledge of past and future, and knowledge of other people's thoughts. As the scientific study of the "paranormal" and ESP or "extrasensory perception" increases, evidence is mounting that people can actually gain these abilities, known in classical yoga as "siddhis" or supernormal powers.

There is now compelling evidence, for example, that two clairvoyants, Annie Besant and C. W. Leadbeater, using only their own mental or psychic powers, directly observed and documented in detail the nuclear structure of all the ninety-two naturally occurring elements down to the quark and subquark levels. Their work occurred at the turn of the century, near Madras. The atomic nucleus was not discovered by physicists until 1912 (by Rutherford), and quarks were not scientifically validated for three quarters of a century; Friedman and Taylor received the Nobel prize for this work in 1990. Leadbeater and Besant also observed the existence of isotopes of several elements, before the scientific discovery by Aston in 1912 using his newly invented mass spectrograph.

It was Annie Besant who "discovered" the renowned philosopher J. Krishnamurti when he was but twelve years old. She was impressed by the brilliant aura around Krishnamurti, which she saw by virtue of her refined perceptions. She stated that this boy would grow up to be a world teacher, and her prediction proved to be true.

Nicola Tesla in 1891 and S. V. Kirlian in the 1930s demonstrated scientifically the existence of an aura around a person. Recently, with the help of what has come to be known as Kirlian photography, Valerie Hunt at the University of California, Los Angeles has confirmed the existence of energy radiations that cannot usually be seen with the naked eye. Each of the energy chakras we talked about above apparently affects the physical and emotional aspects of the personality. Using special photographic techniques to capture the aura, much information is revealed about the personality and mood of the subject photographed, including whether the person is emotionally or physically tired or stressed.

How little we know what we are, and how less what we may be.
—LORD BYRON

Such discoveries, held up next to the enormous range of human capabilities described in the *Yoga Sutras*, Upanishads, and other ancient works, suggest how much the human being can develop. Abilities far beyond the usual can be unfolded, which will surely stretch our definition of what is "normal." What is now considered extraordinary and even impossible may well be viewed as part of normal human life as our full human capabilities unfold through the ancient knowledge of yoga.

If we practice meditation along with the other limbs of yoga, we will feel immersed in the infinite ocean of cosmic energy. By doing pranayama, we can eventually perceive prana in the air we breathe and feel its presence in the food we eat, in the fragrance of flowers, the sound of chirping birds, the murmuring of the rivers.

We realize that prana, the vital force of life, is the same in all living beings, and that our vital life cycle is part of the natural universal biological cycle. The same building blocks, oxygen, carbon, hydrogen, nitrogen, which make up our body are present in all beings, the planets, the sun, the stars, the hills, the forests, the rivers. With this realization we come to love all creation, and that is yoga—Union with the Creator, the eternally True, eternally Beautiful, and eternally blissful Reality.

15

Waking Up to Reality: The Power of Prayer

He who is in the sun and in the fire, and in the heart of man, is One. He who knows this, is one with the One.

—MAITREYA UPANISHAD

The one who prays and the one to whom prayers are addressed are one and the same.

—YOGA SWAMI

It was 10.30 at night when the phone rang. Joseph, a twenty-eight-year-old patient in the surgical ward under treatment for a leg fracture, had suddenly collapsed. I rushed to the hospital and found him unconscious, with cold extremities and sweating profusely. Neither pulse nor blood pressure could be detected.

The examination led to a diagnosis of acute pulmonary embolism. This is a very serious, catastrophic ailment, and especially at that time (the 1960s) bore an extremely high probability of death.

Pulmonary embolism occurs when a blood clot forms in one of the deep veins in the legs or thighs of a person who has been confined to bed, as Joseph had been because of his leg fracture. The clot gets dislodged, moves through the circulatory system, and gets stuck in one of the main arteries leading from the heart to the lungs. Blood flow to the lungs, back to the heart, and subsequently to the brain becomes severely curtailed, and the person collapses.

These days, clot-dissolving medicines are available and we can often save the patient with this form of treatment. At the time, the only treatment was surgical removal of the clot through open heart surgery, a major and very risky procedure. But it was the only option. I contacted the hospital's heart surgeon, who regretfully informed me that the necessary equipment—a heart-lung machine—was not in working order.

I started Joseph on oxygen, medications to raise his blood pressure, and heparin, which does not dissolve clots but can help forestall worsening of the existing clot. For two hours I sat by his side, but there was no improvement. He was pulseless and had fallen into a coma.

Joseph's wife, Mary, arrived at the hospital. When I explained to her what had happened as well as the possible outcome, she listened with a calm face, thanked me for whatever was being done, folded her hands, and started praying.

I spent the night sitting at Joseph's bedside. Whenever I stood up to stretch my legs I stopped at the door to look through the small window. Mary was walking up and down in the corridor. Once I went out to speak with her, but she was as calm as before, quietly repeating the name of Christ. When I returned to Joseph's bedside, without realizing it I found myself praying for him. There was nothing else I could do.

Joseph's pulse came back at 7 the next morning. It was feeble, and despite maximum doses of blood pressure-raising medicine being infused into his circulatory system, blood pressure could not be detected. I knew that even though there was now a feeble pulse, unless the big clot in the artery coming from the heart could be either dissolved or surgically removed, the outlook remained hopeless.

This troubled me greatly, especially because I had discovered something very special about Joseph. He was a very kind man, soft-spoken, compassionate, and always concerned for the welfare of the other workers in the factory where he worked. What made the situation even more tragic was that he had fractured his leg while saving a child from being run over by a speeding car.

Twenty-four more hours passed, with no improvement. Joseph remained unconscious. We could not go on infusing fluids into his veins because he had passed no urine for twenty-four hours. If his condition persisted, his kidneys, liver, heart, and eventually his brain would begin to fail, one by one. And there I would be, unable to do anything, watching him wither away in front of my eyes.

Mary asked me no questions, only continued to pray and pray all the time.

After about thirty-six hours, Joseph began blinking his eyes. His pulse was very fast and thready but was definitely stronger, and his blood pressure could be recorded at a very low 40 or 50 mmHg, systolic. There was a flicker of hope in my mind: was the clot being dissolved? In some rare cases, a process known medically as spontaneous lysis (dissolution) does occur. It could be happening now, and the heparin being constantly infused could be preventing cascading of the existing clot.

After seventy-two hours, Joseph's body was no longer cold and his blood pressure was at a reasonable level. He was murmuring, but was completely incoherent.

On the fourth day he continued to maintain his progress, although there was a renal shutdown (kidney failure). I could see a twinkle of a smile in Mary's eyes as she earnestly continued her prayers.

Joseph passed urine on the fifth day, and to my surprise his mental condition also started improving. Within a week he was mentally coherent, and before another week was done he had made a complete recovery, with all his vital organs functioning normally. How this had happened I could not understand. Why, for instance, had there been no permanent damage when there had been no pulse and no blood pressure for days together? I could only conclude that it had been the intense prayers Mary offered to the Lord.

Joseph went back to his job as an engineer a month later. Three months after that, Pushpa and I were leaving Pune, where we had lived happily for many years. As we were boarding the "Deccan Queen," I saw Joseph walking briskly along the railway platform with Mary and their two beautiful young boys. Mary had a gift for Pushpa.

"I have brought a silver candleholder for you, Mrs. Chopra, as a token of gratitude," she said. "I have a pair of these. I am keeping one, so that whenever I light a candle we'll remember that Dr. Chopra brought light into our lives." I knew it wasn't me. It was Mary, and Mary's prayers.

We still have the beautiful silver candleholder and we cherish it.

Ever since that time, I have been trying to understand the phenomenon of prayer. According to modern science, there is insufficient evidence that prayers can bring on a cure. And yet I knew, from that experience as well as many others, that prayer could have a definite healing effect. Being a man of science as well as man of faith, I wanted to understand why.

The religious man in me might say, "Prayer works because God is everywhere, and God is love—so if someone prays to God, He hears the prayer and responds." That answer satisfies the heart, but not the scientific mind.

A Scientific Approach to Understanding Prayer

Recent advances in science are opening up possible avenues of understanding. In several fields, from physics to ecology, scientists are suggesting that all things in the universe are interconnected. Like the ancient proverb, "If you cut a blade of grass, the whole universe shakes," leading-edge thinkers are saying that every part of this universe is connected with every other part.

The entire universe, some say, is a single quantum field, a "unified" field, in which events in one part influence all other parts. Bell's Theorem, one of the most interesting concepts in modern physics, states that once objects have been in contact, no matter how far apart they may be in the universe, a change in one causes an immediate change in the other. This fact may help us understand why, in the words of Larry Dossey, M.D. "those who practice healing with prayer claim uniformly that these effects do not diminish with distance; prayer is as effective from the other side of the world as it is from next door or at the bedside."

Mind-body medicine has certainly shown the inter-connectedness of two fields that until very recently have been considered separate by science. As we discussed in Chapter 2, it is now evident that the mind can and does influence the body all the time, and that our attitudes, beliefs, and states of mind have a profound effect upon our health. The science of psycho-neuroimmunology is based on the fact that positive thought and imagery, through the complex mechanisms of neuro-transmitters, can act as powerful therapeutic agents to strengthen the immune response and help to heal disease.

Research has found that solely with their thoughts, ordinary people can influence not only the organic, living matter of their bodies, but also "inert" matter. An experiment at Princeton University showed that volunteers could sit down in front of a machine and influence its output simply by the power of their attention. If people can affect a machine with their minds, why couldn't they influence other minds and bodies with their thoughts and prayers?

These scientific insights throw fresh light on ancient knowl-edge. For example, the legendary Persian physician Avicenna (A.D. 980–1037) wrote that "the imagination of a man can act not only on his own body, but even other, very distant bodies."

And the notion of a quantum or unified field is reminiscent of the Vedic teaching about the universal, cosmic mind. The underlying, primal reality of the universe, the rishis taught, is pure consciousness, universal mind. All minds are expressions of the one universal mind. When, within consciousness, various vibrations begin, these creative impulses give rise to individual thought and action as well as to the whole material creation.

Great physicists have come very close to expressing precisely this insight. According to Deepak Chopra, "Niels Bohr compared the wave aspect of matter to cosmic mind," and Erwin Schrödinger "ended his life believing that the universe itself was a living mind (echoing Isaac Newton, who maintained that gravity and all other forces were thoughts in the mind of God)."

Prayer "works," then, because it puts the human mind in tune with the cosmic mind, the mind of God. This is possible because the individual human mind is inseparably connected to the cosmic mind, the pure consciousness from which it arises. We just don't ordinarily recognize the connection. Our individual mind is like a mirror covered with dust, which prevents us from knowing our true Self, what we truly are—pure consciousness.

When the dust is no longer there and the individual mind is one with the cosmic mind, it is in direct touch with the Self, the creator, infinite intelligence, or God: the supreme intelligence, the source of all energies, the source of everything. Then the energy from the cosmic mind, which is common to all beings, flows to the minds and bodies of those we pray for.

Another way to say this is that the one who prays, the one who is prayed for, and the one to whom we pray, are all one and the same, whether we call it the Self, God, or the Universal mind. A sage from India remarked a long time ago:

> Our little minds are part of the omnipotent cosmic mind of God. Beneath the wave of our consciousness is the infinite ocean of cosmic consciousness. It is because the wave forgets it is part of the ocean that it becomes isolated from the oceanic power.

As a result, our minds have become weakened by material limitations and function only at a local level. When our consciousness opens to unboundedness, we realize that we are part of the great cosmic mind.

Giving a direction to this universal power unleashes

enormous energy. As Mahatma Gandhi said, "Prayer is not an old woman's idle amusement. Properly understood and applied, it is the most potent instrument of action."

Love and Devotion Are the Purest Form of Prayer

Here is a story that, at first, does not seem to have much to do with prayer. But read it, and then decide what you think.

I had just finished the evening rounds at the intensive coronary care unit when a new patient was rushed in. Mrs. Om Prakash, fifty-two, was in coma. Her relatives gave the history: she was a diabetic, had a fever of a week's duration, and had collapsed two hours earlier after complaining of severe chest pain. Her blood pressure was not recordable. We soon discovered that she had suffered an acute heart attack and was in cardiac shock; to complicate matters, she had pneumonia and septicemia.

The outlook for a patient with such a diagnosis was grave. After starting treatment and giving instructions to the resident staff, I went out to meet the patient's husband, Mr. Om Prakash. He was very perturbed. I told him that his wife, Kaushalya, was critically ill. She had more than one serious problem, and, I said, "the chances of recovery in this type of patient are usually bleak. But we will do our best. There is always hope."

"Doctor," Om Prakash replied, "I understand what you are telling me. But please, tell me if there is anything I can do. Anything at all."

"Pray to God," I said, "for her recovery. It helps."

The man stood still for a while and then retorted, "But I am a communist and an atheist. I don't believe in God."

For a while I kept quiet and then I asked, "Why don't you believe in God?"

"I believe in something I can see," he said. "And I don't see him."

I did not want to enter into an argument with him at this delicate moment, but I replied, "True, you don't see Him. But

you are *able* to see because of Him. You believe in the existence of the moon, the sun, the stars, the hills, the rivers, and the
forests, right?"

"Yes, because I can see all of them."

"Then pray to them; they are all His expressions."

Probably I should have left it there. But instead I continued,
"What makes you see and hear is God. What makes the grass
and trees grow is God. What makes the birds chirp is God. You
don't see the butter in milk, but if you churn the milk, you will
see it. Churn your mind and realize the presence of God.

"The Upanishads say, 'The rivers flow, the wind blows, the
sun shines; we see this, but we don't understand that it is all
because of the presence of the Lord whom we don't see.' And
Jesus says in the Gospel of Thomas, 'I am the light that shines
over everything. I am the All. From the All came forth all and to
the All has returned. Split a piece of wood and I am there. Pick
up a stone and you will find me there."

> The subtle, the imperishable
> The unchanging Lord
> Everywhere you will find Him
> In the tiniest particle of dust
> In the hard wood
> In the tender blade of grass
> He is everywhere
>
> —ALAMA PRABHU

"You don't have to look for divinity only in lofty temples or the
mighty Himalayas, or in miracles performed by a saint," I said to
Om Prakash. "You can see it in all beings, in all things at all
times, anywhere and everywhere. Look at that tree," I said,
pointing out the window. "You believe in its existence. This
tree, like all other trees, brings the sky and earth together. It
takes the energy from the sun and the minerals and water from
the earth, gives you oxygen to breathe, fruits to eat, and provides
you with shade when the sun is hot. It teaches us that the sun,

the stars, the moon, and mother earth are all interconnected. That is why people worship a tree. It is an expression of God, right before your eyes. Go and pray to the tree for the recovery of your wife!"

The man was taken aback, and did not reply. Probably he didn't have an answer. Or perhaps he was so worried about his wife's condition that he wasn't really listening to me.

Later on, talking together in my office, Om Prakash told me a little more of what he believed. He was a straightforward man, who tried to be kind to his fellow men. But he believed that prayer was no better than wishful thinking. Of course he was worried and wished with all his heart for his wife to get well soon. One could call this deep wish of his a prayer, but he did not see it that way.

At one point he stared into my eyes, perhaps searching for some hope. I put my hand on his shoulder and spoke a few more words.

"Can you hear the rustling of the wind through the leaves of that tree?" I asked him. "That sound is the Lord. You can hear him in an infant's cry, in the mooing of a cow or a lion's roar, in the neighing of a horse, the trumpeting of an elephant, the song of a nightingale, the humming of a bee, the chirping of birds, the croak of a frog, and the hiss of a snake, in the breaking and lashing of the sea waves against the rocks, in the thunder in the clouds, the waterfall, and the murmuring of a brook flowing down the hills. All sound is one great symphony reciting His name and singing His glory. This is what the Upanishads teach us.

"He can be seen in everything. He is oneness in the many, unity in diversity. So if you pray sincerely to this tree that you can see and believe in, you are praying to Him. If you deny the existence of God, it is God in you that enables you to do so because it is God that illumines all thoughts and perceptions.

"We cannot see the sun when a cloud is covering it. That doesn't mean the sun is not there. We have to realize that it is because of the sun that we are able to see the cloud that is hiding the sun from our sight."

> That which speech cannot express
> But that by which speech is expressed
> Is Brahman
> Know that alone
> That which cannot be felt by the mind
> But that which enables the mind to feel
> That is Brahman
>
> —KENOPANISHAD

I couldn't help thinking how ironic it was that the name his parents had given him literally means "Light of the Lord," though I did not mention this. I found myself praying, "Lord, let him see you in all your expressions, the galaxies, the moon, the stars, the rivers, the trees, and all beings. And give him the strength to face whatever is ordained."

The ancient rishis believed that prayer is the most powerful form of energy we can generate. It is the expression of love, arising from the level of pure consciousness, the Self. From love arise all the positive values of life.

Love is the purest form of prayer. Om Prakash loved his wife very much and wished, all the time, for her to recover. That love itself was his prayer. Whether he believed in God or not really did not matter. That love *was* God. As the physician Larry Dossey wrote in his landmark book, *Healing Words: The Power of Prayer and the Practice of Medicine*, "Praying individuals—or people involved in compassionate imagery or mental intent, whether or not it is called prayer—can purposefully affect the physiology of distant people."

Mrs. Om Prakash regained her health. She comes to our clinic regularly now, every three months or so. Her blood pressure and diabetes are controlled, and she has no angina. Of the full month she spent in the hospital, she remembers nothing at all. She goes for long walks every morning and prays regularly. I don't know whether her husband does or not.

Prayer and Grace

God's grace and love are always available to help us; it is up to us whether to open ourselves and accept the gift. Prayer is the process of opening our awareness to God's grace. As Sri Ramakrishna said:
"The breeze of His grace is always blowing;
You have only to raise your sails to catch it."

Lessons My Mother Taught Me About Prayer

My mother was very religious. She would often recite Jap Sahib and chapters from Guru Granth Sahib, or tell us stories from Bhagavatam and various other scriptures. I have a very clear memory of a day when she was in the kitchen cooking while my younger brother, Madan, and I, and Madan's friend, Ilyas, were eating. Out of the blue, a local pandit dropped in for a visit. He was a sort of priest who would visit families and tell us about various auspicious days, when we should offer special prayers.

By definition, a true pandit is a man of knowledge, who sees beauty in everything. From his heart he gives knowledge to everyone, as he lives in the light of the Self and sees God or Self in everyone. He has clarity of mind and a sense of discrimination by which he knows what is of lasting value and what is only of fleeting value. This pandit, I am sorry to say, was one in name only. He gathered information here and there, and indulged in gossip.

Addressing my mother, this pandit said, "You pretend to be very religious, yet you have a Muslim boy sitting in your kitchen. God will never forgive you."

Hearing this, my mother went wild. "How dare you talk to me like that? Ilyas is my son's friend, so he is my son. What is all this Hindu–Muslim business? My God does not know about this. You get out of my house right now and take your God with you. Never, ever, shall you enter this house again!"

I had not heard my soft-spoken mother raise her voice like

that ever before. The pandit walked off. Mother hugged and kissed Ilyas and starting putting morsels of food in his mouth.

When we were just finishing our dinner, Gabo Maa walked in. I got up and touched her feet. Gabo Maa was a respected, trained midwife who served our town. She had helped in the delivery of all my brothers and sisters at home. (In those days, home deliveries were the rule rather than the exception. Nobody went to the hospital for childbirth unless there were complications.)

This God-fearing lady regularly offered namaz to Allah five times every day. When she prayed she asked Allah to be merciful to one and all. Mother explained that Gabo Maa never prayed for herself, she prayed for the welfare of all her children, and there were hundreds of them in our town of Rawalpindi, children she had helped the women of the town deliver. She loved them all as if they were her own.

Prayer as a means to effect a private end, my mother told us, is meanness and theft. It implies dualism, not unity. When man is one with God, he does not beg for private results; rather, he sees prayer in all actions. The prayer of the farmer kneeling in his field to weed it, the prayer of the boatman kneeling with the stroke of his oar, are true prayers heard throughout nature.

The Healing Power of Prayer, Love, and Care

When Mother Teresa fell seriously ill while visiting the USA several years ago, people in Calcutta and indeed all over the world prayed for her early recovery. She was a pure, God-realized soul and those who were praying for her were convinced that she was an apostle of peace, love, and altruism and that her work to serve the poor and downtrodden was not yet finished. It is only rare people like her who see God in everything and in all beings, and remind us of this truth with their lives as well as their words.

Mother Teresa was fond of the saying "The family that prays together stays together." Prayer generates faith and with faith the stream of love will flow, which in turn gives rise to compassion.

Love and compassion heal. I would like to relate an event in my own family that demonstrates this.

When our granddaughter, Priya, graduated from Boston University, Pushpa and I were thrilled to attend the ceremony. Priya was eagerly looking forward to starting work with City Year in the fall, but until then she would spend the summer doing voluntary social work.

Three years earlier, during her summer vacation, Priya had volunteered at Amar Jyoti, a charitable school for indigent children in Delhi (see Chapter 16). She loved the work and had set her sights on doing more of the same.

City Year works much like the Peace Corps. For a one-year period the young volunteers work with the elderly and look after disabled children. They help battered women, care for AIDS patients, and serve in programs to help drug addicts become free of their habit. The program is so successful, both for the volunteers and the people they serve, that it has become a model for similar programs in European cities.

Three days before she was to begin with City Year, while crossing the road after work, Priya was struck by a speeding car. She was hit so hard she was seen flying through the air.

Rushed to the hospital, she was found to have multiple injuries, including a concussion, a fractured leg, and severe internal bleeding in the pelvic region. She also was suffering from amnesia.

The entire first night was spent in the operating room. Her parents, Sanjiv and Amita, were by her side the whole time, as were her uncle and aunt, Deepak and Rita. As soon as they could, her cousins, Mallika and Gautam, flew in from California and New York. Other relatives, friends, and family friends were notified, and all, including her grandparents in India, were praying for her recovery.

There were some very anxious days in the beginning, but within a few days the infusions and transfusions could be stopped, and she was able to begin eating. From there, her recovery was fast and complete.

In the book on prayer and healing that I mentioned above, Dr. Larry Dossey has described three stages in the development of medicine. Era I he terms mechanical or physical medicine. All forms of therapy in this medical model are guided by classical laws of matter and energy, and it is considered axiomatic that to be effective, therapeutic methods must be physical. These include drugs, surgery, herbs, and acupuncture. The tremendous achievements of Era I medicine are well known to everyone.

"Some years ago," writes Dossey, "another unique period in the history of healing began to take shape." This is Era II or mind-body medicine, which has demonstrated that perceptions, emotions, attitudes, beliefs, and thoughts affect our bodies profoundly. The major diseases of our time—hypertension, cancer, heart disease, and other degenerative ills—are to a greater or lesser extent influenced by the mind. To incorporate this new understanding, many doctors are now using techniques such as meditation, biofeedback, and guided imagery to facilitate healing.

Era III medicine, according to Dossey, revolves around what he calls a "non-local" approach to healing. This approach views the mind as unbounded, the "cosmic mind" we talked about earlier. The cosmic or universal mind is without boundaries, and has a unitary nature. As a result, healing events that involve the mind, such as prayer, may connect persons who are widely separated from each other and have no apparent contact. In his research, Dr. Dossey has reviewed hundreds of scientific papers that point to this conclusion.

All three of these levels or stages of healing were vital to Priya's recovery. She had the best of doctors, who employed the most advanced surgical and therapeutic techniques. Whatever she needed was available, from the ambulance that rushed her to the hospital, to the surgeons and assistants in the operating room, to transfusions, and even to simple but vital aids such as crutches and a wheelchair.

But Priya had much more on her side. She displayed tremendous will power, vigor, and determination to get well. Her optimism and certainty of recovery were a source of inspiration to her parents and everyone else concerned about her. In the early hours, when her parents were in agony, it was Priya who cheered them up and boosted their morale.

Within a short time she wrote to us, "Dear Maa, Daddy (that is how she addresses us, her grandparents), I can tell you I have been in good spirits since the accident. I have not cried once. I don't remember the accident. I just remember walking back from work and then waking up at the Beth Israel Hospital with stitches near my left eye, a rod in my left leg, staples on my knees, my hand in a cast, and my aching pelvis.

"It is amazing how the body heals. It is a miracle, really, what the body can do in such a short time with the help of dedicated doctors and specialists, love and care and prayers of parents, family, friends, and well-wishers."

This is Era III, the new—and most ancient—model of medicine in which love and prayer play a significant role. In addition to the finest medical care (Era I) and her own determined spirit (Era II), Priya also had the loving attention of family and friends far and near. As she put it in her letter, "My whole family and all the family friends were behind me with their concern, good wishes, prayers, and love . . . I really felt sheltered in everyone's love and care."

I have been a practitioner of Era I medicine for half a century, and I know from thousands of patients I have been privileged to treat that it is powerful and effective. I also have clearly seen the efficacy of a positive attitude, a patient's determination to get well and faith that he will, as for example in the case of Shyam Sunder that I recount in Chapter 24. But I also know, as I have been trying to show in this chapter, that there is a truly unlimited power in prayer that can really heal.

I saw in Priya's recovery how powerful a combination these three kinds of healing can be, what love and prayers can do and how much perseverance, determination, and fortitude in a young and loving heart can achieve in a short time. As Priya closed her letter to us, "Don't worry about me and tell everyone in Delhi how splendidly I am honestly doing. I can assure you, Maa,

Daddy, that very soon I am going to be as healthy as before the accident. I am making and will continue to make the most of this miracle called life.

Love Infinite,
Priya Chopra"

A Powerful Method of Prayer

One of the most powerful ways to pray, and a method used throughout the world, is the repetition of the name of God. The *Book of Proverbs* says, "The name of the Lord is a strong tower," and scriptures in many religions speak of "taking refuge in his name." Swami Prabhavananda, in his commentary on Patanjali's *Yoga Sutras*, says that people who have never tried the practice of repeating the name of God are apt to scoff at it, but that it is a highly effective way of prayer.

Most of the time our minds are filled with disconnected thoughts, sense impressions, memories, fears, excitements. Many of these involve a kind of repetition of a name, but one over which we have no control: the name of a coveted object, an anxiety, a loved one, an enemy. And each creates its own sort of "mental climate." If we introduce into this mental soup the repetition of the name of God, we can change that climate and thus gain more control over our life.

Repetition of the name of the Lord is known as *japa* in Indian tradition. Various mantras, representing a name of God, can be used, if possible given by a teacher to a disciple. This repetition can be vocal or silent; you can use a rosary to count repetitions, or not. Tradition teaches that the practice is more powerful when purely mental, but each person has to do what works.

In Christian tradition there is a parallel practice known as the Prayer of Jesus, made famous by a monk who wrote a book called *The Way of a Pilgrim*. This technique is described in the book as follows:

> The continuous interior Prayer of Jesus is a constant uninterrupted calling upon the divine Name of Jesus with the lips, in the spirit, in the heart; while forming a mental picture of his constant presence, and imploring his grace, during every

occupation, at all times, in all places . . . The appeal is couched in these terms, "Lord Jesus Christ, have mercy on me."

You can use this simple method of prayer (using whatever word or phrase you choose or have been taught by your teacher) when you are sitting quietly in a meditative manner, or even when your mind is so disturbed that you feel unable to settle down for rational thought or quiet meditation.

John Climacus, one of the saintly "Desert Fathers" of early Christianity, taught his pupils:

> When you pray, do not try to express yourself in fancy words, for often it is the simple, repetitious phrases of a little child that our Father in heaven finds most irresistible . . . Wordiness in prayer often subjects the mind to fantasy and dissipation; single words of their very nature tend to concentrate the mind.

The contemporary theologian Henri Nouwen suggests, "The quiet repetition of a single word can help us to descend with the mind into the heart." Thereby we empty out "our crowded interior life and create the quiet space where we can dwell with God."

16

The Joy of Service

*I am only one, but still I am one. I cannot do everything, but still
I can do something. I will not refuse to do the something I can do.*
—ATTRIBUTED TO HELEN KELLER AND TO EDWARD EVERETT HALE

God helps those who help others.

—SWAMI VIVEKANANDA

Our five grandchildren, Mallika and Gautam, Deepak's
daughter and son; and Priya, Kanika, and Bharat,
Sanjiv's two daughters and son, have all come to
Delhi, sometimes in twos, sometimes alone, to spend time with
us. They have come most often during the summer months,
when they have a long vacation, and although they are not used
to the heat of Delhi, they don't seem to mind it.

In the summer of 1989 Priya came alone, with two months
to spend before beginning college. On her second day she
wanted to know what our plans were for her. "How am I going to
spend my vacation? Everyone should work during summer
vacation," she asserted. "This is a time when you can do
something different from your daily school or work routine."

When we asked her what she would like to do, she replied
that she would like to work in a center for handicapped children.
Immediately the name "Amar Jyoti" flashed into my mind.

Several months earlier I had heard about this institution, and Pushpa and I went to see it.

Amar Jyoti (the name means eternal guiding light) is a charitable trust, a voluntary organization engaged in the education and rehabilitation of orthopedically handicapped children, most of whom come from the less privileged sectors of society. Mrs. Uma Tuli started Amar Jyoti single-handedly under a tree, and through her dedication and her love for children, it is now a great, sprawling center for teaching, research, and rehabilitation.

When Pushpa and I visited, we walked around and observed the multifaceted activities of the center, including education, medical care, vocational training courses, and the manufacture of artificial limbs. The day we went happened to be the school's annual day, and the boys and girls staged a play in addition to a session of songs and music. It was an exceptional experience.

Priya started going to the center. She volunteered to teach English to Class I and Class II children, and in return received an unexpected bonus: the children helped her learn Hindi. Each day Pushpa gave her some snacks to eat during the morning break, but we noticed that she invariably brought them back when she returned home in the afternoon. When asked, she replied that she would eat them only if she took enough snacks to share with the children of her class. Her attitude endeared her to students and staff alike. She enjoyed her summer's work so much that it led her, after graduating from college, to spend an entire year in another volunteer position, this time with City Year.

Shortly after Priya's terrible accident (see Chapter 15), she was able to begin her year of service with the City Year program in Boston. Along with 350 other young men and women (seventeen to twenty-three years old) she worked in the schools, shelters, and urban parks to help improve life in the city of Boston. They tutored 11,355 children, and completed literally hundreds of service projects, such as renovating or helping to construct affordable housing for poorer families. They cleaned up and beautified more than fifty parks, built an outdoor amphitheater, worked with the city hospitals' child immunization project, served hot meals to people who were sick at home with AIDS, and built a new community center.

The commitment these young people made to helping others was summarized in the City Year "pledge," a few lines of which follow:

> That each of us can make a difference and everyone must try, and that there is nothing more powerful than people united for change;
>
> I will continue to strive to be quick to help and slow to judge;
>
> To serve my family, my friends, my community, and my nation;
>
> To stand up against oppression of any kind;
>
> And to be a caring force for hope and justice and positive change.

When Pushpa and I attended the graduation ceremony for Priya and the others who had worked with her, we felt that they would surely carry this ideal of love, compassion, and service before self throughout their entire lifetimes.

A New Perspective

In the summer of 1988, Mallika, Deepak's daughter, while still in high school, spent her vacation in a village outside Santo Domingo in the Dominican Republic as a volunteer health worker for an organization called "Amigos de las Americas." As she told us later, she set out on her trip to offer help to the people of the village, but she ended up receiving far more than she gave. This is the great blessing of performing service for others.

"We lived with families in the village," she told us, "and worked together with the people. The house I lived in was actually just a shack, made of wood painted with gaudy colors, red, turquoise, blue, and dark green splashed carelessly on the walls. Dust particles danced in the beams of sunlight that filtered through cracks and holes in the walls and the tin roof. Nine people, along with an assortment of goats, dogs, and chickens, lived happily in that little shack. The entire space was smaller than our living room back home in Massachusetts. There was no electricity or running water, and the only way to reach the village was by crossing the river and then walking or riding a horse along slippery paths.

"We talked to the people about the principles of hygiene and health. We discussed community sanitation and helped them make latrines, to prevent the spread of sickness. But what I learned in exchange was really worth much more. Not only did I meet new people and learn about a new culture, but I also gained a new perspective about life and human relationships.

"I arrived at the village self-assured, confident, maybe a little arrogant about my background, my education at Concord Academy, my knowledge about nutrition and hygiene, my 'sophistication,' my opinions of how things should be. I went with the idea that I would teach these people things they did not know, that I would show them the right things to do. But I was in for a surprise.

"My ideas about intelligence were shattered by a group of people who had never learned to read or write, yet there was a simplicity, and an innocence and sensitivity among them that immediately disarmed me. I realized that the easy spontaneity of these people, their careless laughter and their light-hearted joyfulness were attributes no amount of education or material affluence could buy.

"I was touched by their warmth, their openness, their acceptance of everything, and their intense feeling. These people were themselves. They did not put on a new mask for every situation, a new mannerism for every encounter. Suddenly I was totally at ease, totally at home, and I realized that true intelligence is the elegance of simplicity.

"At the end of my stay, when I was about to leave Los Guantes, Don Julio, the village elder, was the first to say goodbye. 'Mucha falta, mi hija,' he said. ('We will miss you a lot, my

daughter.') Then everybody gathered to sing a song of celebration and parting. The little baby girls pranced and danced in
joyful glee, the dogs yelped, and even Ninning, the retarded
boy, held out his hand and smiled with recognition. I asked Don
Julio if I could write to him, and what address I should mail
the letter to. 'A la casa cerca del rio' ('to the house by the river'),
he said.

"Two hours later I was on board a jet bound for Miami. A
very proper and polite stewardess was asking me if I would prefer
my Diet Coke without ice, an irate businessman was complaining about his cold coffee, and another couldn't wait for the
'No Smoking' sign to go off so he could light up the cigarette he
held in his hand. Slowly Los Guantes slipped into the back-
waters of memory as the jet surged forward into my hysterical,
uptight, but all-too-familiar reality."

Mallika's description of her visit to Santo Domingo reminded me that "culture," which usually means excellence in
arts and literature, can never replace the ancient wisdom of
simplicity, openness, love, compassion, and the pursuit of the
path of righteousness, the path of Dharma. I was happy that she
seemed to learn that lesson too.

Another Meeting Point between Science and Ancient Wisdom

Service to others, *seva*, has always been an important part of the
Indian tradition. Throughout the ages, our teachers have
recommended it for spiritual development, for becoming a better
person. And now science is finding that indeed, when we do
something good for others, not only do we feel good inside, but
those positive feelings of love and compassion also produce
biochemical changes that strengthen our immunity and improve
our health.

What this means is that the ancient principle of karma—"as
you sow, so shall you reap"—applies not only in the long run,
over many lifetimes, but *immediately*: if we sow good deeds,

performing service for others, we immediately enjoy the benefits in our own improved health and increased happiness.

For example, in a recent study it was discovered that the incidence of heart attacks was much less among a group of people who worked for eighteen hours a day performing community social service, as compared with a group of people who worked an average of six hours a day, but whose work was for personal gain. This confirms that work done without any desire for personal gain has an immediate benefit for the doer.

In past times, people understood that the way for society to function to everyone's advantage was for everyone to be guided by this principle of giving and serving. When people use every social interaction to give whatever they can to each other, everyone benefits. When everyone gives, then everyone automatically receives; moreover the giver receives in the very act of giving! Many people today seem more concerned with "getting" than giving. That is another reason I am so proud of my children and grandchildren for the lessons they have learned about service.

It is fine for young students to go hiking, or to travel and see new places during their vacations. It broadens their outlook on life. But spending a vacation as Mallika and Priya have done teaches all of us something vital about the secrets of life and living. Their experiences gave them a lot of satisfaction, and showed them the truth of our ancient wisdom and how it can influence our present lives. I was reminded by them that if you can do something for someone, even if you must suffer discomfort and inconvenience in the bargain, it is an expression of love and a real joy for the soul.

The Privilege of Service

When it comes to serving others, being a physician is filled with golden opportunities every day. But this profession also carries with it a kind of danger, if the sense of being "the doer" is not tempered. For many years I have been trying to tell my doctor colleagues that whether in our private offices, or working in large, premier institutions, we should not have the notion, just because we provide vital service and even save lives, that we should be treated as some kind of demigods. This haughty behavior—which unfortunately is not uncommon—indicates a deplorable state of affairs and should be condemned by all concerned. Patients and doctors are equal partners. They should share all information and enlighten each other.

Medical people, like other professionals, should not only accept their particular professional responsibility, but also tremendous additional responsibilities as members of the community and the larger society, as citizens of their country, and above all as members of the human race.

A doctor should never behave in a way that magnifies his egoistic self. Praising himself, wasting time in criticizing other members of his team, blaming someone else when things go wrong—such behavior is not becoming of a doctor, either as a professional, as a human being, or as a member of society.

In my practice of medicine I have had some very difficult and trying times. I've been through many a long night looking after or resuscitating a critically ill patient. I've had to face worried and anxious relatives, who were sometimes very harsh in their remarks, when my whole heart and soul were engaged in saving the patient. At such moments, which I know all doctors have to face, we should keep our cool and neither argue nor resent remarks made in moments of distress.

I have always looked at the anxious moments spent working to save a critically ill patient as a privilege. As a result of these ordeals I often developed a truly selfless, affectionate relationship with both the patients and their relations, which I felt professionals in other fields have no opportunity to enjoy. The "job satisfaction" has been tremendous.

As mentioned briefly above, a relationship based on feelings of love and compassion helps the helper as well as the helped. When a doctor cares for the sick with all his heart, he has a feeling of well-being due to the release of natural opioids—endorphins—which help to increase his immunity. This has been shown to be scientifically true, and works through a chain reaction of neuropeptides, neurotransmitters, various other chemicals and the immune cells.

Doctors, in other words, heal themselves in the process of healing others. This great principle applies to all members of society who help each other. I'll repeat here one of my favorite expressions, something that Swami Vivekananda said one hundred years ago: "God helps those who help others." This is a greater truth than the usual expression, "God helps those who help themselves."

When it comes to service vs. self-centeredness, it seems that there are three categories of people. The first sacrifice their own interests to the needy and to the good of others. Such people are rare. Like the Mother Teresas of this world, they are very dear to God, and have eternal peace and bliss.

The second lot consists of those persons who live happily, enjoying the fruits of their actions. They have material abundance but also help others. They are a good lot, and enjoy much inner satisfaction. As discussed, various studies show that the incidence of heart attacks and other diseases is much less in them compared to people of the third category.

People in the third group are essentially selfish and live for themselves, often at the expense of others. They frequently harm others by indulging in activities destructive of their interests.

As the great Buddhist teacher Shantideva said in *A Guide to the Bodhisattva's Way of Life*:

> The childish work for their own benefit.
> The Buddhas work for the benefit of others.
> Just look at the difference between them!

We should at least live up to the ideals of the second category. The right path for most of us is to live and enjoy the little pleasures of life but without getting too attached to them, to help others and live in harmony with them.

Adi Shankara insisted that right action and devotion to work are absolutely essential in the pursuit of Vedanta, the philosophy of right and joyful living and realization of Truth. We are all capable of doing something constructive, and we should do it.

17

Negative Emotions: A Slow Poison

To be free from thoughts that distract from Yoga, thoughts of an opposite kind must be cultivated.

—PATANJALI, YOGA SUTRAS, 2:35

If you aspire for peace and happiness my child, reject the objects of senses and negative thoughts as poison and seek forgiveness, straightforwardness, kindness, cheerfulness and truth, as these positive thoughts are the nectar of life.

—ASHTAVAKRA GITA

"Mrs. Raghuvir is on the line," the nurse told me as I was just finishing my round of the intensive coronary care unit. "She says Mr. Raghuvir has suddenly collapsed and she wants you to go to her place immediately." I picked up the phone, but it got disconnected.

I had known Raghuvir for many years. He was a successful businessman, a garment exporter, very social and popular among his friends. A few months earlier he had come in for a routine checkup, and all the tests were normal. He was in his late fifties, not a smoker, had no diabetes, and his blood pressure was normal. What could have happened to him now?

I was not happy about the way Mrs. Raghuvir had spoken to

the nurse on the telephone, and I rushed to Raghuvir's house after instructing the intensive care ambulance to follow me. When I reached the house I found Mrs. Raghuvir sitting on the floor crying. A few persons from the house next door were sitting in the room. Unfortunately, it was my job to confirm that Raghuvir was dead.

After a short while I got to know the story. At 8 that morning, Raghuvir, who had been a keen golfer, returned home after a game of golf. He was sipping some tea when an urchin threw some pebbles against the glass panes of his living room window. Annoyed, he opened the window and shouted at the boy, who appeared to be about twelve years old. The mischievous fellow ran away and Raghuvir returned to his easy chair.

A few minutes later the boy was back, again throwing little bits of stone at the window panes. Raghuvir got up, rushed out of the house, and shouted at him. He ran after the boy and could not catch him, but soon after he reached his chair, the urchin was back on his job, this time throwing bits and pieces of garbage at the window with a big grin on his face. Apparently the urchin realized that Raghuvir was getting irritated, and he seemed to enjoy it.

Raghuvir rushed out of the house in a rage. He ran after the boy, chasing him six or seven hundred yards up the road, and ultimately caught hold of him. He was very angry and abusive, shouting at the boy and beating him hard. People collected around him and wanted to know what had happened. They thought the urchin must be a thief. Some of the crowd pleaded with Raghuvir not to take the law in his hands and urged him to call the police.

While these arguments were going on, the urchin managed to escape the scene. Raghuvir, along with two or three neighbors, returned to the house. He was still enraged and could not forgive the fellow. As he finished relating the whole story once again to his neighbors, still shouting at the top of his voice and sweating profusely, he leaned back in his chair and died.

> *I have no time to quarrel, no time for regrets, and no man can force me to stoop low enough to hate him.*
>
> —LAWRENCE JAMES

The whole episode was rather surprising to me. Raghuvir always appeared to be as cool as a cucumber to his friends, at the office, or at social gatherings. Later, I learned that he had strong pent-up emotions; he was wearing a mask most of the time and looked calm, but on occasion he exploded and ventilated his anger. When he did that, he became so upset that he did not know what he was doing. He was very annoyed with his only son, who was in business with him, because he had married a girl he did not approve of. He never talked to her, with the result that the son and daughter-in-law were living separately.

Raghuvir had been declared fit only a few months earlier, after standard medical tests, including a stress test. Yet he had died of a sudden heart attack and cardiac arrest. How could this happen to an apparently healthy man?

It can and it does. Raghuvir was under great stress, although he never showed it. He also never shared his feelings, even with his wife.

"My Life is at the Mercy of Any Rogue Who Annoys Me"

The hassles of life, and negative emotions that arise in response to them, have a cumulative effect on our whole system. They create a certain amount of narrowing of the coronary arteries, though not enough to prevent adequate blood and oxygen from passing through and supplying the heart muscles, even during the increased exertion required by the stress test.

But if you undergo an unaccustomed level of exertion, such as running at a high speed after a young boy, and at the same time you are in a rage, the whole nervous system becomes alarmed. Chemicals, such as adrenaline, are released in large amounts in the body. Your pulse rate goes up and blood pressure rises. This can cause asynchronous, ineffective contractions of the heart muscles (a condition known as ventricular fibrillation), which in turn can lead to cardiac arrest and sudden death.

What then caused Raghuvir's death? Was it the urchin, the little bits of sand and paper on the window panes, the mischievous smile on the urchin's face? No, it was *choosing the wrong reaction*. If Raghuvir had ignored him the first time, the boy probably would not have returned. Or he could have spoken to the boy without flying into a rage.

You should never *react* to a stressful situation, you should only *respond*. Reactions tend to be what you regret later on. Never shout or answer in a hurry when you are having an argument in a stressful situation. Look before you leap. You are the slave of spoken words, the master of words still unspoken.

An immediate, overpowering negative reaction, an expression of rajas, was responsible for the violent behavior that cost Raghuvir his life. More sattva would have balanced his personality; tranquility of mind would have come to his rescue. Meditation is a highly sattvic activity; it can tilt the balance in favor of sattva, which pacifies rajas.

Suppose you pass a drunk and he showers you with abuse. If you can pass smilingly by, or ignore him, you'll have no physical or mental consequences. If you choose to fight back, verbally or otherwise, the sequence of events might be the same as in the case of Raghuvir. We get any number of heart attack patients who are rushed to the hospital from a company office or a factory following a fit of anger.

Just the other day, late in the evening, Ram Lal, fifty-four, was brought to the hospital with broken teeth, a bleeding nose, and a broken right forearm. X-rays of the nose and arm showed fractures. Ram Lal was known to have high blood pressure, and at this moment it was very high and the ECG showed a mild heart attack. His distressed wife was crying aloud. We had to report the matter to the police, as the injuries were a result of a fight Ram Lal had with Mr. Rajesh, his immediate neighbor.

It seems that an argument between Rajesh and Ram Lal began when Rajesh parked his car next to Ram Lal's house instead of next to his own. The argument was followed by shouting and verbal abuse, and then a fight ensued.

Ram Lal lost his temper, sustained injuries, had a mild heart attack, and could have had a fatal brain hemorrhage due to his dangerously elevated blood pressure, all because of a silly thing like somebody parking a car next to his house!

If you ask someone to remain continuously angry for a whole day without a break, it would be impossible for him to do so. But if you ask someone to remain quiet and peaceful for a full day, most people will be able to do it, because it is our true human nature.

Angry thoughts and emotions can play havoc in the human brain and throughout the body. Anger is thwarted desire, an impurity of the mind that serves no purpose and leads to the flooding of "jittery" molecules into the body of an angry man. These circulate and react with every cell, instructing the body to constrict the arteries, increase the pulse rate, raise blood pressure. The heart misses beats, and fatty plaque builds up in the arteries of the heart and brain.

Repeated episodes of anger have a cumulative effect and ultimately, unless you get control of this unnatural behavior, the resulting undesirable chemical secretions accumulate and wear down your immunity and your organs. It can lead to severe problems, such as heart attacks and paralysis.

The ancient sages have classified the negative emotion of anger (along with jealousy and guilt) as a slow poison that eats the individual over a period of time. Finally a fit of anger can be the straw that breaks the camel's back, leading to a heart catastrophe.

The renowned eighteenth-century Scottish physician, John Hunter, had a very bad temper. He knew the ill effects of anger and was heard to say one day, "My life is at the mercy of any rogue who chooses to annoy me." A few days later, during a stormy hospital board meeting, Hunter suddenly suffered a massive heart attack and died. The coronary arteries of his heart, investigated during an autopsy, were described as considerably narrowed, hardened, and ossified in places, the cumulative effect of previous fits of anger.

Research conducted by Dr. Gail Ironson at Stanford University School of Medicine and published in the *American Journal of Cardiology* revealed that when people with heart disease merely *remember* an incident that made them angry, the ejection fraction (pumping efficiency) of their heart was reduced by 5 to 7 percent of their already reduced capacity. This significantly lowered the blood supply to their heart and arteries. The patients tested said that they were only half as mad while recalling the episode as they were when it actually happened, suggesting that the pumping efficiency would be even more greatly reduced during an actual angry encounter.

The angry situations these patients were recalling were usually unresolved grievances, or injustices they felt had been done to them. One was still angry over an incident that happened years ago, when someone backed into his car, leading to a frustrating odyssey through insurance company red tape and various auto body shops, ending up with a high cost to repair his car. Afterward he got so upset every time he drove his car that he sold it!

These very patients whose cardiac efficiency dropped while even recalling anger showed practically no decrease in their heart's pumping ability during other psychological stressors, such as doing difficult arithmetic problems, giving a speech, or defending themselves against a charge of shoplifting. When they rode a stationary bicycle, their pumping efficiency actually increased by 2 percent. The study has shown that negative emotions such as anger are unequivocally bad for heart patients. Actual episodes of anger would be worse, in initiating and exacerbating coronary heart disease and precipitating heart attacks.

It is no use fuming or becoming furious. Don't lose your temper all the time. Preserve it, and then if once in a while, on a rare occasion, you do become angry, people will value it. Of course, *not* to get angry, not to react, requires more inner strength and balance. If you are quiet, your silence will unnerve the person who is annoying you. You react with anger if somebody criticizes you, but when somebody praises you, you never say, "What right do you have to praise me?" Why should you retort if someone criticizes you?

According to the ancient wisdom in the Bhagavad Gita, one who does not get agitated by the world when conditions are "good" or "bad" can manage all situations of stress and remain happy under all circumstances. This balanced, imperturbable state is worth striving for.

Rid Yourself of All Negative Thoughts and Emotions

Anger is bad for us, but so are many other negative thoughts and feelings. The Gita calls anger, greed, and lust the "triple gates of hell." Jealousy, hatred, fear, selfishness, self-condemnation, guilt, possessiveness, depression, anxiety, all are negative emotions which cloud our minds and hearts and lead to illness. These negative agitations of mind disturb our sense of discrimination, and they block our energy, our zest for knowledge, our happiness, love, health, and well-being.

A clean body, clean clothes, and a clean dwelling place make life more pleasant, Swami Dayananda points out. Inner purity, to which less attention is paid, means cleanliness of the mind. The smudges of envy and jealousy, spots of anger, streaks of ego and dust of guilt all spread around inside the mind and make it unclean.

If you want to get rid of negative thoughts and emotional reactions, patience, perseverance, and constant effort are required. The key to success is to notice any negative thought that arises in your mind and substitute it straightaway with a positive thought. This is like removing a small pebble from under your foot as soon as it irritates you. You don't wait for many pebbles to collect before you clear the irritating pebble away. So also you should not wait until your mind is full of negative thoughts and agitations that torment you. As soon as you notice some negativity rising, catch it before it develops into something bigger.

A whirlpool of thoughts roils the lake of the mind, constantly taking new forms. Most of the time, we have no control over what thoughts fill our awareness; the waves just keep rolling in. If you happen to think of an apple, the image of an apple will form in the mind stuff. Then if you think of grapes, the image of the apple will subside and grapes will appear. In this way, countless thoughts are arising and subsiding in the mind every day. But since it is our own mind, we can decide what we want to think; the thought waves can be *consciously* transformed and modified.

Take hold of your mind and become your own master! Any disturbing thought or agitation must be thrown away before it develops and leads you to an action you might regret later on. When you find yourself dwelling on something negative, simply substitute a positive thought or image for the negative thought.

> *A man is happy so long as he chooses to be happy, and nothing can stop him.*
>
> —ALEXANDER SOLZBHENITSYN

The best way is to start a parallel line of positive thoughts. If you try just to push negative thoughts away, you will rarely succeed. They will come back over and over again like monkeys. Any attempt to rigidly control negative thought waves, without raising positive waves such as love and compassion to oppose them, will not work. Any cold, stern effort to be "good" and not have negative thoughts is not practical. You just have to stand apart and watch your thoughts come and go, and raise positive thoughts of love, compassion, and detachment. This line of action was recommended long ago by Patanjali in the *Yoga Sutras*: "To be free from thoughts that distract from yoga, thoughts of an opposite kind must be cultivated."

For example, if you feel someone has wronged you and you

feel angry about it, rather than plotting revenge and tearing yourself up the way poor Raghuvir did, if you replace or substitute anger with forgiveness, peace will prevail in the mind. Each cell in the body will participate in that peace.

I met Mr. Harnam Das the other day. He is a retired senior civil servant, a very disiplined individual. He seemed very upset and started telling me about his nephew, Chandra, who was very close to him. Chandra had left his car behind when he went to the USA for a year, and Harnam Das had kindly looked after it.

"I got the car serviced regularly," he said, "and now he tells me that there is noise at the rear and the wiper isn't working. I gave him the address of the repair shop and the papers for the work done, but he's somehow blaming me. He's called me three times and disturbed me about it. He has no manners. I'm not going to forgive him when he comes to apologize."

Harnam Das is adamant about it. He is not going to forgive his nephew; instead, he will continue to harbor malice and burn inside. But what is the use of that?

In our day-to-day life, when someone does something wrong to us or hurts our feelings by saying something nasty, usually an angry and unforgiving attitude fills our heart. Even when we don't want to cry "Blood for blood!" or do something to get even, we are often unable to forgive and forget. Frequently it is someone who is or has been close to us, and, like Harnam Das, we make up our mind in advance that we are not going to forgive even if he or she comes to us to apologize. But this attitude starts eating our insides and all the joy of life starts vanishing, replaced by a crushing heaviness in our heart born out of bitterness for the person who hurt us.

In such instances, it is important to remember that everything that happens to us, we created. It is our karma, the fruit of our past actions, returning to us. If someone happens to be the one who delivers the karma to us, that is not his or her fault. We can judge the person's action any way we want—rude, unmannerly, even mean or cruel—but in fact they are not like that with everyone, or even with us all the time. We are just receiving,

right now, something we have earned; better to accept it
gracefully and forgive the messenger.

Once you do finally forgive, a burden is lifted, feelings of
light-heartedness dawn, and life has meaning once again. Forgiveness releases the grip of fear and anger and we start afresh in
life. Forgiveness should be without reserve; forget all your
previous resentment.

Look at jasmine flowers; you trample over them and crush
them, and they forgive you with fragrance. One should do the

The Jealous and the Greedy Neighbors

There once were two neighbors, a greedy man and a jealous
man. As the greedy man acquired more and more riches, the
jealous man became increasingly jealous. One day he noticed
that he had not seen his neighbor, the greedy man, for several
days; the man seemed to have disappeared. On investigation
he found that the greedy man was meditating in the Shiva
temple. The jealous man also went there and started
meditating on Lord Shiva.

Both went into samadhi. As their intense meditation continued day after day, Lord Shiva became very impressed by
their devotion to him. He appeared in person and addressing
the jealous man he said, "I will grant any boon to you that you
may desire to have. It can be any treasure, even a kingdom.
Whatever you want will be yours."

The jealous man was thrilled and was thinking about what
to ask for when Lord Shiva added, "There is only one condition. Whatever you ask for I will give you, but I will grant
twice that to your neighbor."

The jealous man's spirits fell to the ground. How could he
tolerate that his greedy neighbor should receive double the
wealth or blessings? He thought hard for a solution.

Lord Shiva was growing impatient, and when he threatened
to leave without granting any boon at all, the jealous man
suddenly said, "O Lord, you are very generous and kind. All I
want and wish is that I should become blind in one eye. Kindly
sire, grant me my promised wish."

same and forgive with love in your heart and blessings for the person you are forgiving.

Jealousy is another undesirable mental state that is all too common. It may start with feeling that, either literally or figuratively, the grass on your neighbor's lawn is greener than the grass on your lawn. Then you may start comparing yourself with your neighbor, forgetting that each individual is unique.

The pain, sadness, or longing that comes from comparing yourself with someone you see as superior or in a superior position, jealousy is a reaction to a lack you feel exists in you in comparison with the other person. It is usually some aspect of his skill, status, or possessions which makes you jealous, but the real source of the jealousy is a deep dissatisfaction with yourself, a sense of inferiority.

To overcome jealousy, as with all negative emotions, it is necessary to agree first that it *is* indeed negative: something that you don't want, that is not only eating you up emotionally, but is also creating unhealthy molecules in your body and lowering your immunity against disease.

Specifically, jealousy can be overcome in three ways:

* First, when jealous thoughts and feelings start to come up inside, substitute positive thoughts of appreciation for the other fellow, repeatedly and patiently replacing your obsessive jealous thoughts with appreciative, admiring thoughts about the other person and his accomplishments.

* Secondly, bolster your own self-esteem. Research suggests that this is an excellent method to save yourself from jealousy and envy. Turn your thoughts to your own good qualities and achievements, sources of pride and satisfaction.

* Finally, put your shoulder to the wheel and work harder at improving the quality of your life and work. The ancient scriptures tell us to rejoice in the other fellow's success, but that doesn't prevent us from improving our own quality of life.

Ultimately, the solution to negative thoughts is gained through discovering our real Self in meditation. Most people identify themselves with the body/mind and its agitations. The real you is behind the mind. If you identify with the mind and body, with all the emotions and agitations in the mind and the pains and shortcomings of the body, you will experience numerous kinds of miseries and suffering. Only when the mind's agitations subside can you attain real peace and happiness. Just as you can see the bottom of a lake clearly only when the ripples and the waves subside, so also you can attain peace and equilibrium of mind only when mental agitations settle down and your awareness opens to the Self, the inner divine Reality.

If someone has restless, scattered, passionate thoughts, his mind is never able to really concentrate or really become peaceful and contented. One who has pure thoughts, whose mind is still and contented, speaks powerfully and produces deep impressions in the minds of listeners. He influences multitudes through his pure thoughts.

We will talk about this repeatedly throughout the book, as it is a true master key to health, longevity, and happiness.

Cultivate your mental garden

A man's mind may be likened to a garden, which may be intelligently cultivated or allowed to run wild; but whether cultivated or neglected, it must, and will, bring forth. If no useful seeds are put into it, then an abundance of weed seeds will fall into it and will continue to produce their kind . . . Every thought seed sown or allowed to fall into the mind and take root there produces its own, blossoming sooner or later into act, and bearing its own fruitage. Good thoughts bear good fruit, bad thoughts bad fruit.

—JAMES ALLEN, in *As A Man Thinketh*

You Can Affect Your Mind and Mood Through Action

One effective way to prevent negative thoughts and feelings from taking over your mind and body is to raise a line of positive thoughts to replace them. The following is another practical strategy.

Mind, body, and spirit operate as a unit. Your body is the result and the end product, the physical expression of your ideas and attitudes in life. This inner, more subtle realm is more powerful (as the subtle atomic level is more powerful than the more manifest, solid material level), so it tends to determine the functioning of your body and the balance of health and disease in your life. If you are happy, the flow of happy and positive neuropeptides increases your immunity and feelings of well-being.

But this works in reverse as well. By taking control of our physical functioning, we can very well affect our feelings and thoughts. For example, you may have noticed that a person who slouches often has low self-esteem or feels depressed. If you find yourself slouching or slumping, notice how much better you immediately feel simply by sitting or standing straight up!

This is knowledge that we can use in daily life. By conscious intention, we can perform physical actions that correspond to certain attitudes, such as sitting up straight to produce more energy and alertness. In this way we can build or create a desired attitude or mood through bodily actions.

By acting bravely in a difficult situation we can actually begin to feel more courageous.

By smiling even when we feel downhearted, by laughing artificially when we feel anxious or worried, we activate centers in our brain which produce happy feelings. This strategy can help us to overcome depression and anxiety. Laughing can also give us more energy. It can change the chemistry of our body and help create happiness and health.

Every day I wash my body, put on clean clothes, dust my writing table. So long as my body lives, I do all that. So should my mind be cleansed of all negativity. There is no greater wealth than to possess a mind free from anger, fear, jealously, greed, and other negative thoughts and feelings.

18

Love and Compassion are the Nectar of Life

Heaven arms with compassion those whom it would not see destroyed.

—TAOIST SCRIPTURES

Born at the banquet of the gods, Love has of necessity been eternally in existence, for it springs from the intention of the soul towards its best, towards the Good. As long as the soul has been, Love has been.

—PLOTINUS

Mother Teresa was a legend in her own time. The frail-looking Mother was a living symbol, an embodiment of love and compassion, whose love overflowed to all who were in most need of tender care and affection. The fundamental objective of her work and her mission in life was to make men and women, and especially children, who were poor, destitute, and unwanted, the homeless, the sick, and the starving feel the dignity of being loved.

The Mother firmly believed that "faith in action is love, and love in action is charity." By charity she did not mean any form of pity for the downtrodden; it is not even sympathy. Rather, it is empathy, which means identification with or the vicarious experiencing of the feelings, thoughts, or condition of another person. She actually felt what the neglected, the destitute, and the sick felt; from that, her love flowed to them, and the action and service to them followed. That is what made her a living saint. Who else has looked after starving children by the roadside and the dying in the gutter? Her all-pervasive compassion went beyond our ordinary understanding.

Mother Teresa's Motto

The inscription on Mother Teresa's visiting card summed up her philosophy:

> The fruit of silence is prayer
> The fruit of prayer is faith
> The fruit of faith is love
> The fruit of love is service
> The fruit of service is peace

Out of the deep silence of meditation or prayer are born faith, love, and compassionate action, which give you peace. Peace and happiness are the aim of life on this earth.

Mother Teresa's simplicity, sincerity, and saintliness were overwhelming. Her life was a personal response to the verses in the Bible in which Christ tells his disciples to take care of the poor and disadvantaged: "I was hungry and you fed me. I was naked and you clothed me. I was lonely and you comforted me. For whatsoever you do to the poorest among people, you do it unto me." She served not only the hungry, naked, and lonely: even the dying were brought to her various homes. They were washed, their sores were dressed, and they were clothed. "Even if we cannot save them at this terminal stage," said Mother, "we can certainly help them die with dignity."

Over 50,000 dying poor of different religious backgrounds have breathed their last in peace in the ashrams run by her Missionaries of Charity. Mother recalled being especially touched by the words of a dying beggar: "I have lived like an animal, but I will die like an angel." Sister Marina of Asha Daan Ashram in Bombay said, "For Mother, the person in front of her is the most important. It may be the prime minister, or a beggar. She sees God in that person and for that moment he becomes very special." Another nun at the same ashram said, "Mother gives, gives, and gives love to all. And she gives me the inspiration to serve."

There was even a sort of joke about her, which went something like this:

Question: "Why did Saint Peter not allow Mother Teresa into heaven?"

Answer: "Because there are no slums there."

What would this beautiful soul have done without working for the poor in the slums?

Mother Teresa passed away on September 5, 1997. While the state funeral was being held at St. Thomas' Church in Calcutta, with dignitaries and celebrities from all over the world in attendance, the streets of Calcutta and many other cities were thronged by millions with flowers in their hands, tears in their eyes, and love in their hearts, mourning the death of an apostle of love, compassion, and peace.

People gathered in thousands in churches, temples, and mosques all over India, and prayed to God for the ability to contribute to Mother Teresa's missionary work and keep her legacy alive. Mother Teresa was a missionary not so much of charity as of love. Challenged by the love of Christ, she translated this love into a reality. Her love for God was always in action in the form of service to the needy. Our beloved Mother believed the rich and the poor all belong to God. They deserve equally to be loved and cared for. Mother Teresa was one of the most remarkable personalities of this century, and in death as in life she shows the path of love, sacrifice, and peace that is open to all of us. She lives on and will continue to inspire us to do our bit to bring joy to the lives of those less privileged, the downtrodden and the poor.

Compassion in the World's Religions

Mother Teresa's inspiration was completely from within the Christian tradition. When someone asked her what books had influenced her thinking, she replied, "The only book I read is the Bible." When asked, "Are there any people, such as Gandhi, Nehru, or anyone else, who have inspired you?" her answer was, "Only Jesus Christ." Her work, her homes for the sick and dying and the lepers around the world, is based on reciting the name of Jesus Christ and praying to Him all the time. Yet her mission of mercy never differentiated between creeds. Hindus and Muslims outnumber Christians in her various institutions.

Love and compassion, and the exhortation to care for the poor and hungry, are common to all the world's great religions. The teachings of Jesus, who was a Jew, embody the spiritual instructions of the great Jewish masters throughout history. From one of these, Rabbi Hillel, came the famous words summarizing religion: "Love the Lord thy God with all thy heart, and all thy soul, and all thy might: and thy neighbor as thyself." The Jewish people are known throughout the world for their charitable giving to the many hospitals and educational institutions they have built and continue to support.

Compassion is so central to Buddhism that the very founder of that religion, Sakyamuni Buddha, is universally recognized as "The Compassionate Buddha." At the core of Buddhist teachings is the effort to transform oneself into a person who is kind, loving, and compassionate to "all sentient beings," great and small.

Swami Vivekananda expressed the compassion in the Hindu tradition when he told his followers to "go onward forever with compassion for the poor and the needy and the downtrodden, even unto death . . . Have faith in the Lord. Feel for the miserable and look up for help; it shall come. I bequeath to you, young men, this compassion, this struggle for the poor, the ignorant, the oppressed." And he added, "When you pray for the welfare of others, God's grace and power will be operating through you."

The Bhagavat Purana expounds the path of doing service to

the needy, who are the visible forms of God, as a sure and easy means of experiencing God. The real devotee recognizes God in many manifestations, large and small, sentient and insentient, ugly and beautiful. The devotee washes the feet of the Lord by washing the feet of the weary traveler, feeds the Lord when he feeds the hungry, houses the Lord when he gives shelter to the unsheltered.

Similarly, the Koran shows great concern for the welfare of the weaker, less fortunate members of society. It refers to them as *maskin* (the poor, the needy, and orphans) and urges all human beings to have compassion for them. The Prophet strongly emphasized the utility of prayer, but insisted that those who pray only to be seen and praised, but who do not have compassion for the poor, are wasting their time.

Islam also rejects charity by those who exploit others. Prophet Mohammed preached that the conscience of man should not rest if he were to eat, drink, or be merry while his relatives and neighbors were unable to earn a living. He urges men to be satisfied with less, to curb their desires and help the needy and the suffering. He even decreed that the master should feed and

The Love of a Spiritual Master

Great spiritual teachers express their love by helping others to grow in consciousness, inspiring them to rise to the full value of human life and live in the light of the Divine. Swami Vivekananda exemplified this in the famous address he delivered to the World Parliament of Religions on September 11, 1893 in Chicago. He told his listeners, "God's compassion is unbounded. You are the children of God, holy and perfect beings, the sharers of immortal bliss. You must never say you are weak. Stand up, be bold and strong. Take the whole responsibility on your shoulders and know that you are the creator of your own destiny. All the strength and succor you want is within yourselves.

"Arise, awake, wake yourselves and awaken others. Achieve the consummation of human life before you pass off. Arise, awake, and stop not until the goal is reached."

clothe the servant as he would care for himself. His message clearly says that man should turn his back on pride and not exalt himself over his fellow human beings.

> Charity does not mean giving away old things you don't require. You will not attain piety until you spend and give of that which you love. And whatever you spend Allah is aware thereof.
>
> —KORAN, 3:92

The Biochemistry of Compassion

An important theme of this book is that our inner world of thoughts, beliefs, and feelings generates a flood of biochemicals which strongly influence our health. Negative emotions, and dwelling on dark thoughts, translate into suppressed immunity and may eventually lead to illness. Positive, happy, loving thoughts and feelings have a salutary effect on us.

So it may not strike you as totally amazing to find that even *thinking about* Mother Teresa can change your body's biochemistry and increase your antibodies against disease. Salivary IgA is an antibody that protects against upper respiratory infections. David McClelland of Harvard University showed a film about Mother Teresa to students and measured the amount of IgA in their saliva before and after they viewed the film.

Some students said they liked the film very much, and in them IgA levels increased. Others didn't like it, some even professing "intense dislike" for Mother Teresa, suggesting that she was a fake and that her work was not good. According to the research, even those students showed immune function improvement. McClelland believes this study shows how unconscious beliefs may affect bodily reactions more than our ordinary "surface" awareness. Perhaps the influence of someone like Mother Teresa reaches a part of the brain of the "disapproving" viewers, and the brain responds to the strength of her tender, loving care.

It is revealing to note that when McClelland tested the study's validity by having the students watch quite a different type of movie, *Attila the Hun*, a film with a violent message, salivary IgA levels fell.

Dr. Larry Dossey, commenting on this study in his book *Meaning and Medicine*, suggests that altruism affects us like a miracle drug that has beneficial effects not only for the person toward whom help is being directed, but for the person doing the helping as well. It can even stimulate healthy responses at a distance, as McClelland's study indicated.

Compassion and Healing

Any doctor knows from experience the tremendous benefit compassion has for his patients. A kind look, a sympathetic glance, or a bit of a smile cheers a sick patient with a withered heart, and goes a long way toward speeding his recovery and healing. If a busy doctor takes the time and care to stand near a very sick patient, hold his hand a moment, or sit on the patient's bed and ask about the welfare of his family, it alters the meaning of the experience of illness for the patient in a positive way.

No patient should ever feel that the doctor is in too much of a hurry to talk to him; he should always feel he is being lovingly cared for. This gives him hope and faith, and fosters assurance in the healing force, both his own built-in healing mechanism and energy, as well as the unseen superpower—you may like to call it God.

In his first book, *Creating Health*, Deepak Chopra wrote extensively about the meaning and value of compassion. Kindness and compassion, he says, are not accidents of human feelings. "They have grown out of universal tendencies in nature ... All living organisms display behavior patterns that favor the whole over the interests of the individual part." No healing, says Deepak, can occur without compassion.

Norman Cousins wrote of patients and their vast collection of emotional needs: "They want reassurance, they want to be listened to, they want to feel that it makes a difference to the physician whether they live or die. They want to feel they are in the physician's thoughts." These needs, Deepak notes, "ask for a flow of feeling from the subtlest level," for "compassion at the source of life," which brings comfort and healing.

Love, Human and Divine

Human love is the highest and finest emotion we can know. It frees us to a great extent from our egotism, in relation to one or more individuals. But human love as most of us know it is at least partly possessive and exclusive, whereas love for the Self or for God is neither possessive nor exclusive. As Elizabeth Barrett Browning urged (see below), we should love one another not for beauty, strength, intelligence, sense of humor, or any other quality, but simply for what a person *is*. And what people "really are" is the Self, the spirit, the one Reality.

To love the Self, the divine in ourselves, helps us to love It everywhere. Such love goes beyond any manifestation of nature to the Reality within nature. It is too vast to be fully understood or appreciated by ordinary agitated minds, yet most people do have a peep into that vaster reality, for to love someone, even in the usual manner, is to catch a glimpse of something within that person which is tremendous, inspiring, and eternal.

We think, says Swami Prabhavananda, that this "something" is unique. He or she, we feel, is like nobody else. This is because our perception of the Reality is clouded by the external manifestations, the individual qualities of the person we love.

If Thou Must Love Me

If thou must love me, let it be for nought
Except for love's sake only. Do not say
"I love her for her smile—her look—her way
Of speaking gently—for a trick of thought
That falls in well with mine . . ."
For these things in themselves, Beloved, may
Be changed, or change for thee,—and love, so wrought,
May be unwrought so . . .

But love me for love's sake, that evermore
Thou mayst love on, through love's eternity.

—ELIZABETH BARRETT BROWNING

Nevertheless, that flash of perception is a valid spiritual experience, and it should encourage us to purify our mind and make it fit for the infinitely greater kind of love which awaits us. This higher, divine love is not relative or transient. It is absolutely free from desire, because lover and Beloved have become one. Such a love is an eternal joy for the soul.

Persons who experience this level of love have no place in their hearts for petty jealousies or desires. They share their possessions, both material and spiritual, with others, and they have *seva bhava, sakha bhava*, and *prem bhava*, the attitudes of service, friendliness, and love toward their family, society, and all fellow beings.

In such a state, when the mind is infused with love, "happy" molecules flow throughout your brain and body, letting each of your trillions of cells know of your happiness. It has been shown scientifically that in such people immunomodulators increase, raising their immunity against disease. They are joyful, healthy, and more creative in life. And as a Jewish sage once said, "Charity lengthens one's days and years."

Opposite of Love is Not Hate

Love is the opposite of fear. These are the two basic human emotions from which all the other human emotions arise. Fear is created by the illusion of separateness, failure to understand that all of *this* (phenomenal world) is nothing but *That* (absolute, divine Reality, the Self). When we identify with the body, rather than with the Self, we see other bodies as separate from ourselves. This separateness makes us fearful; others can hurt us, take what is ours, deprive us of what we want.

From fear arises insecurity, which is the basis of other negative traits, such as greed, hatred, jealousy, anger, lack of contentment. These are all slow poison, the harbingers of disease and misery. Studies have shown that the incidences of angina, heart attacks, and even sudden death are more common among people who are repeatedly or habitually irritated, hostile, or angry. It is no use going to the temples and offering prayers if you cannot be kind to people or forgive them.

As fear is created through our identification with the body, with the surface expressions of life, love arises from the deepest level of the Self—Consciousness, the Truth, Reality, the Creator Himself. You go beyond the body level and your mind abides in the Self. Love, with all its fragrance, radiates and flows into your being. You then see the truth of what you are: you are not separate from existence, from Being. You are overflowing joy itself, a joy that has nothing to do with external material things. You are in love, which means, you are in bliss; you are bliss itself.

In love one grows and expands; in fear, one shrinks. In love you are open; in fear, you close your doors. Love is trust; fear is doubt. In love you are never lonely, for you are the universe. You can then love all human beings, the trees, the rivers, the forests, the birds and animals, the mountains, the stars, the galaxies, because all of these are the expressions of the same Self, the Self that you are. All are interconnected, not separate from each other or you. Endowed with true Self-knowledge, one sees all things in the Self, which is infinite. As the Isavasy Upanishad proclaims:

> The wise man who realizes all beings are not separate
> from his own self and his own self in all beings, does
> not, by virtue of that perception, hate anyone.

The man who knows he is in all beings and all beings are in him, by virtue of this is able to feel the hurt of others as his own. Deepak Chopra says that born out of love are charity, compassion, devotion, discipline, the ability to forgive and forget, and gratitude. You are generous and fulfilled, and you rejoice in the success of others. As the young sage Ashtavakra told Raj Rishi King Janaka, "If you drink this nectar of life that is love, you will obtain bliss, you will be in peace, and you will be free from all bondage."

19

Live in the Present

Forget the past.
The past of all men is dark with many shames.
Everything in the future will improve if you are making a
    spiritual effort now.

—SRI YUKTESWAR

The bridges you cross before you come to them are over rivers
    that aren't there

—GENE BROWN in *Danbury*

Happiness lies in good health and a bad memory.

—INGRID BERGMAN

It was the summer of 1944, during the Second World War. The Japanese were sweeping across India. Burma on the other side of Manipur had already been captured and occupied, and now the Japanese had captured Kohima, near Imphal, capital of Manipur state; the British and Indian troops were on the run in the valley beyond Kohima. Imphal came under siege, and all lines of communication between Imphal and the rest of India were cut off.

We got an urgent message that a fierce battle was raging in the foothills of the valley. The casualties were expected to be very high, and additional medical personnel would be required.

We were ordered to move to the front line and set up our field hospital.

The Japanese were fanatics as fighters. If a column of Japanese soldiers encountered barbed wire rolls blocking their way and their advance in that sector was deemed vital, the first dozen or so soldiers would simply lie down on the barbed wire and allow the rest of the column of soldiers to march over their bodies across the barbed wire barriers toward the enemy, without losing vital time. That was their training. Sacrificing their lives for the Emperor and the country was considered a matter of great privilege.

The *Prince of Wales* was the mightiest British warship the Allies ever had. It had tremendous firepower, and was considered invincible: no torpedo or missile would ever be able to pierce its armor. Then one fine morning it was blown to bits and scattered over the ocean waves along with the bodies of hundreds of British soldiers and sailors. How could it happen?

A small Japanese fighter plane belonging to their suicide squad, loaded with explosives, dived into the wide smokestack of the mighty warship. We heard later that more than a dozen volunteers among the daredevil pilots had vied for this mission; lots had to be drawn to determine which man would be lucky enough to help his country win the war and gain a place in heaven by blowing himself up along with the *Prince of Wales.*

That was the enemy we were fighting in the valley of Manipur after Kohima fell. It was the same battle, whether it was fought on the high seas, in the skies, or in the hills of Nagaland and the valley of Manipur. We had to face the same formidable enemy on every front.

I and another general duty doctor, Dr. Chattopadhyay, went right into the battle line. It was a foggy, hazy early morning, before dawn. The forest was thick. Our men were trained in digging and camouflaging the advanced dressing station (ADS) so that we could be close to the fighting men, but this time we had no time to dig, as we had to get to work soon after we reached our destination. We were attending to the wounded soldiers right out in the open.

When a wounded man staggered over or was carried to us, we would quickly dress the wounds, apply stitches, inject morphine to relieve the pain, put on a Thomas's splint or a bandage, offer a cup of tea, say a few comforting words to the wounded soldier, load him in an ambulance and send him back to the headquarters of our mobile hospital, where a surgical team would take care of him.

As day dawned, we could see some hand-to-hand fighting and shooting right nearby. Through the fog and drizzle, I saw some Japanese soldiers darting through our dressing station. I suddenly noticed that Captain Chattopadhyay was missing and the nursing attendants (male nurses) were doing all the work. I was told that he was feeling very unwell and a little while ago had gone back to Imphal in an ambulance along with the wounded. We were now running short of ambulance vans and were packing the patients off in whatever vehicle we could get hold of.

Around 11 a.m. the noise of the gunfire suddenly became less. It was still very hazy, but I could just make out a column of vehicles moving slowly on the road toward Imphal. A senior British officer from our brigade headquarters walked up to me and told me that I should pack as many wounded soldiers as possible into whatever vehicles I could lay my hands on and start moving toward Imphal. We were retreating.

As the officer was walking back toward his jeep, he was hit by a bullet. We crawled to him and dragged him inside our dressing station. The bullet had gone through his chest. We dressed his wound and put him in a three-ton vehicle along with other wounded Indian and British soldiers and joined the moving column. There was a shower of bullets among us as we started moving a little faster. The enemy must have known by then that we were on the run. After a while all became very quiet and still; probably we were getting out of their range of fire.

The pulse of the British officer was getting very feeble. I thought he, and some other seriously wounded patients, would be able to receive emergency surgical treatment when we reached our main dressing station. Ten doctors were there, including a surgeon. But when we arrived, we found the equipment and implements strewn all over; the officers, doctors, and men were gone.

We set out for the headquarters in Imphal, thinking they must have gone back there, but by the time we got to the base hospital, the officer was dead and everybody got busy with the treatment of those among the wounded who were still alive.

None of the missing people came back. Investigations by the brigade headquarters started. It was feared that all might have been taken as prisoners of war. Then in the afternoon, five British soldiers arrived, along with Captain Basu, one of our doctors. Basu was in a state of shock, and it was only the next morning that he was able to tell us the tragic story, which he had to repeat time and again, both at the brigade headquarters and at the corps headquarters, as the story sounded unbelievable to many people.

Basu's Story

"The Japanese soldiers ran through our field hospital and took all the officers and men as prisoners. They marched the men, with their hands tied behind their backs, to their own lines at the rear of the fighting front, then lined up all ten officers—two administrative officers and eight doctors, including myself. Our hands were tied, and it appeared they were planning to march us somewhere. Then they hurriedly conferred among themselves, and one of them, apparently the one who was in charge of the platoon, gave some orders in Japanese which none of us understood.

"Two Japanese soldiers took out their revolvers. They lined us up in a straight line. Each officer started at one end of the line, put his revolver to the temple of one of the officers, and shot him dead. Then he moved to the next in line.

"I was in the center. My turn, along with another colleague, came last. We were shot in the head almost simultaneously. The last thing I remember was the barrel of the revolver at the side of my head, a little in front of the upper part of my right ear. There was the loud sound of a gunshot, and I fell to the ground.

"It was evening; the sun had just set, and it was becoming dark. After a few minutes I opened my eyes and saw, in the semi-darkness, a Japanese soldier approaching where our dead bodies were lying. I realized that somehow or other I was not dead, and instinctively I managed to crawl halfway under my colleague's dead body, my chest and the upper part of my body mostly beneath his back.

"When the soldier reached the site of the massacre, he began stabbing each body in the chest, to make sure each man was dead. I somehow managed to escape this action, as my chest was under my colleague's dead body. I spent the night in the same posture, terrified to move a finger lest the Japanese were still around. It was painful to lie on my back for hours without moving, although I did eventually take the risk of slowly sliding out from underneath the dead body of my friend and colleague.

"I fell asleep. At dawn I awoke, to find myself lying on my belly with my head down, my face sideways. I was completely worn out, mortally afraid to lift my head from the ground.

"A little later, when the sunlight began filtering through the thick leaves, I instinctively lifted my head. Immediately my eyes met four eyes about thirty to forty yards away. I couldn't see their faces, as they had camouflaged themselves. I instantly lost consciousness, and came around only after I reached Imphal."

We later learned that the four eyes Basu's eyes had met belonged to two British soldiers who were hiding in a trench with bushes and leafy branches on top of them. They had been left behind when the British and Indian troops retreated, and they had witnessed the massacre from a distance. These soldiers, along with the stuporous Dr. Basu, somehow or other reached Imphal by that evening.

The British brigade commander, Brigadier Wilson, did not believe Basu's story at all, although his senior officer suggested that the story could be true, that perhaps, to his extremely good fortune, there had been a blank cartridge in the revolver when it became his turn to be executed.

Brigadier Wilson would not accept that explanation. He

thought Basu was lying. Worse, Basu's name suggested that he was probably related to Indian National Army leader Subhash Chandra Bose (Basu and Bose mean the same thing in Bengali), honored by Indians as a great revolutionary and patriot and regarded by the British as a dangerous traitor (see Appendix 4).

Basu, Wilson surmised, was in league with the Japanese through Subhash Chandra Bose, and actually may have been a party to the massacre of British and loyal Indian officers. He recommended to the higher authorities that the case be investigated by the intelligence branch, and that Basu be court-martialed.

Basu was subsequently moved to Fort William in Calcutta. Further interrogation, including that of all of Basu's relatives in Calcutta, did not elicit any further or different information.

After about three weeks of detention in Fort William, Basu suddenly lost his voice. A neurological examination did not reveal any cause, and Basu apparently was not doing it on purpose. What seemed to be happening was that his subconscious had simply told his body's speech mechanism in chemical words, "No use talking, nobody listens to you anyway." Basu's loss of speech was misconstrued and his detention lasted until after the end of the war.

In August 1945 the investigating authorities came to the conclusion that Basu was innocent. The day this was announced, his speech came back. He did not have to give any further explanations. He was reinstated, and soon after was posted to the army hospital in Pune, where I was already working.

The Crushing Burden of Memory

I was glad to see Basu, but it was clear that he was a completely changed man. Because of the difficult times and the great stress he had gone through, he had become very depressed. He was also forgetful, very introverted, and avoided social functions and get-togethers. It was very difficult to convince him that all of it—the war, his ordeal at the hands of the Japanese, his imprisonment—was really all over. The Japanese had been defeated and were no longer there. Soon the British left India for good. But Basu still suffered.

It seemed impossible for him to forget the inhuman behavior of the Japanese toward the innocent doctors, who were treating Japanese casualties the same way they treated wounded Indian and British soldiers. He had suffered from three kinds of pain, and all of them still lingered: the pain caused by the assault on his colleagues and his own near death; the pain inflicted on him during confinement in Fort William in Calcutta; and perhaps worst of all, the pain he felt when his loyalty was called into question.

Basu had firmly believed the Japanese were making fools of the Indian people by using the Indian National Army (INA) for their own purposes. Now, with the war over, he was discovering a great deal of information to support his beliefs. An increasing body of documentary evidence was coming out, as well as personal testimony by witnesses and participants, which was embarrassing Japan into retracting earlier denials about its atrocities during the world war.

As far as the Japanese were concerned, the INA *was* only a mask to deceive the ignorant Indian masses. No doubt the Indian nationalists who founded the National Army believed they were doing a great service to their country. By opposing the British and fighting on the side of the Japanese, they felt they would hasten the end of British rule over India. But it is a fact that when the Japanese took Indians as prisoners, they either lined them up and shot them in cold blood, as they did to all of Basu's colleagues in the field hospital, or they turned them over to the Indian National Army authorities. There, instead of fighting the invading Japanese, they would fight against their own people, their own kith and kin.

The Japanese were intent on destroying the Allied forces, including all British nationals, and in their eyes, Indians were British nationals. Strengthening the ranks of the Indian National Army was not aimed at helping liberate India from the British rulers, but a strategy designed to help their own imperialistic ambitions. In pursuing their goal of dominating all of Asia, the Japanese ran over Burma and parts of India, including Manipur and Nagaland. They were not defeated here; they withdrew during the middle and later part of 1944, about the time Basu's doctor colleagues were shot dead, because their lines of communication had become too long and difficult to maintain.

It also came to light that Japanese doctors used healthy prisoners of war to practice surgical techniques, and then killed them with intravenous anesthesia drugs.

Most of the Japanese who had done these things did not recognize their acts as crimes, because for them it was "justice" to kill, especially the Chinese and other Asians. It was all for the Emperor. Their minds had been conditioned to believe that the Emperor was God on this earth, that they as a people had also descended from heaven, and that all their homicides and sacrificial suicides were done in service to the Emperor. Fortunately, some of the participants in the crimes revealed many facts to investigating officers after the war, goaded by their conscience and their concern that the true history of the war might die with them.

It was difficult for me to believe all these terrible things, especially after I met and interacted with the Japanese people years after the war. I straightaway got the impression that they are the most disciplined people on earth. Having been to Tokyo and Kyoto, I was convinced the Japanese are a fine people in every respect. But you cannot ignore historical facts. And in August 1993, Japan's Prime Minister, Morihiro Hosokawa, finally acknowledged his nation's wartime aggression and atrocities.

After the Germans surrendered to the Allies, the Japanese resistance continued. On the fateful day of August 6, 1945 the Allies dropped an atomic bomb on Hiroshima, destroying the city and killing 140,000 people. Three days later another atomic bomb was detonated, about 504 yards above the city of Nagasaki. It devastated the entire city. More than 70,000 innocent people were killed in the flames, radiation, and blast. The bombs reduced both Hiroshima and Nagasaki to a radioactive moonscape. Was this the act of man? The man God created in His own image?

The Japanese surrendered six days after the Nagasaki bombing, on August 15, 1945. This brought an end to the Second World War, but then the cold war, the underground war, the war of fear between men and men, began. This was worse in many ways. Now, with the cold war over, there are still enough nuclear weapons in Russia and the United States to destroy the earth. Who has ever won a war? But man goes on killing man.

No Regrets for the Past, No Fear of the Future, Live in the Present

Thoughts similar to these disturbed Basu's mind, and he continued to suffer from acts of violence and torture in his mind. Although the physical experience of them had ended long ago, the imaginary experience continued, complete with vivid visualizations. His memories and the accompanying fear re-sulted in frequent attacks of screaming during his sleep over the nightmarish reality in his head.

He confided in me that his dreams were strange and horrifying. Once he got lost on a frozen mountain; in another dream armed robbers ransacked his house. Another time he was being chased by Japanese soldiers. They got hold of him and shot him dead, only this time he really "died" and as the bullet pierced his heart he shrieked with pain and found his wife holding his hand and shaking him awake.

His mind refused to accept that the past was all gone, and that he should be living in the present, which could be very fulfilling. Worst of all, he never opened his mind to anyone, not even his wife or his colleagues. He had no friends. Life seemed a struggle for him. As a result of continuing imaginary threats from all sides, and chronic stress, he was always physically fatigued and mentally disoriented when looking after sick patients.

I tried to impress upon Basu that if we experienced some

fearful event in our life at an earlier stage, we ought not go on projecting that fear into our day-to-day life. We have to free ourselves from the past, set it aside and live only in the present. Deepak Chopra wrote about this in his first book, *Creating Health*. He said:

> No one has discovered a means of altering the past. Once a thing has occurred, there is no way to change it . . . time has carried it off beyond anyone's efforts to make improvements. Dwelling on past mistakes or injuries is unproductive. It is also harmful, because it releases into your system all kinds of toxic substances that raise blood pressure and strain the heart . . . Recognize past mistakes for what they are, learn from them, and leave them in their permanent home, the past.

If only Basu could let go of these painful past experiences, open his mind and let them spill out, talk about them, leave them behind. But he could not. "If you bring forth what is inside you," said Jesus in The Gospel of Thomas, "what you bring forth will save you. If you don't bring forth what is inside you, what you don't bring forth will destroy you."

Then one night he went to sleep; his wife was by his side. In the morning he was gone. What dream did he have that night? Or perhaps he had none; no one knew. He was a good soul who fell victim to circumstances. His heart just stopped one night without giving warning. Whoever gives up in the game of life is just swept away.

Basu's mind was caught up with pain over the past and anxiety about the future. But the more one vacillates between the past and the future, the more restless the mind becomes. When you are driving on the highway, you occasionally look at the traffic behind you in the car mirror, but you don't dwell on it. Your attention is primarily on the traffic to your left, your right, and just in front. Past experiences may guide you a bit, but to

The Courage to Live

A vivid contrast to Basu's tragic life after the war and an inspiration to anyone who has undergone suffering and difficulties, is the story of Viktor Frankl. A Jewish psychiatrist in Austria in the 1930s, Frankl was imprisoned in a Nazi concentration camp during the Second World War. Subjected to unspeakably horrible privation and torture, he somehow managed to be one of the few to survive. After the war, having lost both his parents, his wife, and his brother, he nevertheless rebuilt his life. He went on to become a world-renowned doctor and the founder of an important new school of psychotherapy. How did he manage to put the past behind him?

"We who lived in the concentration camps," Frankl wrote, "can remember the men who walked through the huts comforting others, giving away their last piece of bread. They may have been few in number, but they offer sufficient proof that everything can be taken away from a man but one thing: this last of human freedoms—to choose one's attitude in any given set of circumstances, to choose one's own way."

The way these men bore their suffering, Frankl said, "was a genuine inner achievement. It is this spiritual freedom—which cannot be taken away—that makes life meaningful and purposeful."

It is perhaps the great theme of this book that we are all free to create our own life. We are free to choose health, to choose happiness and well-being.

Most of us have not been faced with the cruel and harsh circumstances that Dr. Frankl had to face. For us it should be far easier to put our past sufferings behind us and create a meaningful life. Even in the most extreme of circumstances, we have that freedom. How much more so in ordinary life.

"We must never forget," Frankl wrote in his book, *Man's Search for Meaning*, "that we may find meaning in life even when confronted with a hopeless situation, when facing a fate that cannot be changed. For what then matters is to bear witness to the uniquely human potential at its best, which is *to transform a personal tragedy into a triumph* . . . When we are no longer able to change a situation—just think of an incurable disease such as inoperable cancer—we are challenged to change ourselves."

function in a meaningful way and use your potential, you have to live fully in the present moment.

> *Unborn tomorrow and dead yesterday—why fret about them, if today be sweet.*
>
> —OMAR KHAYYAM

In Deepak Chopra's novel, *The Return of Merlin*, the great secret of Merlin the Wizard is that to be truly alive now, you have to be dead to the past. To be alive now is to have life-centered, present-moment awareness. If you have your attention on what *is* and see its fullness in every moment, you will discover the dance of the divine in every leaf and petal, in every blade of grass and rushing stream, in every breath of every living thing. Then you are truly alive, truly living in the present *the most precious moment of your life*.

20

With Contentment Comes Peace to the Soul

As a result of contentment, one gains supreme happiness.
—PATANJALI, YOGA SUTRAS, 2:42

Indra, the king of the gods, wanted to experience what it would be like to live the life of a pig. So he transformed himself into the form of a pig and wallowed in the mire. He had a she-pig, a litter of baby pigs, and was happy with his lot.

Some of the gods saw this and went to him. "What are you doing here, in this state?" they asked. "You are king of the gods and you rule all the gods in heaven."

"Never mind," said Indra. "I am all right here. I do not care for heaven so long as I have this sow and these little pigs."

The gods were at their wits' end. How were they going to break his attachment to his new life, and bring him back? They decided to slay all the pigs, but when they started to do that, rather than desiring to leave he began to weep and mourn. Realizing that they would have to take even more drastic action, they ripped his pig body open. Then he emerged from it and began to laugh, realizing what a hideous dream he had dreamt: He, the king of the gods, had become a pig, and thought that a pig's life was fine to live! He had even begun to think the life of a pig was all there was, that there was nothing beyond it to look forward to.

One of the lessons of this story (which was related by Swami Vivekananda) is that there is a difference between being contented and being lazy and overpowered by tamas. Being contented is not the same thing as being complacent. Unfortunately, the power of tamas in some people is so great that they don't want to make any effort to change their lives. But for human beings, the life of a pig can never bring genuine contentment.

For us, contentment comes from evolving, from unfolding our full human potential. The story tells us that inside our material, animal body is the spiritual aspect of our being. True contentment comes from setting that free.

Contentment does not mean we stop working, or that we have no further goals. It is an attitude of mind, a way of seeing things. A contented person is an optimist. Looking at the lower part of a glass with milk in it, he says "The glass is half full." He has a feeling of gratitude for what the glass contains. He is happy and works happily, knowing that the glass can also become completely full.

Contentment doesn't mean you don't work for more; rather, you work in a joyful way that in itself increases your immunity against disease. A contented person tends to be healthy, because being contented is a good strategy for coping with stress. If you feel at peace, things won't easily bother you.

A man who is not contented is a pessimist. He looks at the upper part of the glass and says, "This glass is half empty." He loses heart, and his immune system buckles and gets weakened.

The contented person says, "If it is my lot to crawl, I will crawl, contentedly; if to fly, I will fly, with alacrity. But as long as I can avoid it, I will never be unhappy."

The key phrase here is "If it is my lot." So long as there is nothing you can do about it, if you have to crawl, you might as well accept it. That doesn't mean you are not at the same time trying to fly. When you become able to fly, fly gladly and joyfully. "He who is content with whatever he gets is wise," the Gita tells us.

> Contentment comes when you stop complaining and start performing.
>
> —OSCAR WILDE

Whenever we live in the depths of the present moment, without regretting the past or worrying about the future, we cease to feel anxious and we feel happy. That is contentment.

A person who repeatedly ruminates over past glory, or the one who spends his time dreaming of a utopian future, can never be contented, and can never achieve anything in life. It is only

Words of Wisdom About Contentment

You are contented only when you have quietude of mind. Undisturbed calmness of mind is attained by cultivating friendliness towards the happy, compassion for the unhappy, delight in the virtuous, and indifference toward the wicked.

—*Patanjali, Yoga Sutras*

There is no one luckier than he who thinks himself so.

—*Old German Proverb*

I am always content with what happens, for I know that what God chooses is better than what I choose.

—*Epictetus*

Contentment is the Philosopher's Stone, that turns all it touches to gold.

—*Benjamin Franklin*

Contentment can never make you idle. It is a sattvic (pure) virtue that propels man towards God. It gives strength of mind and peace.

—*Sivananda*

those who free themselves from the clutches of both past and future who will be happy and be able to fly higher in life.

Don't be caught up worrying about whether or not you will harvest the fruits of your action; engage in action with all the best of your creativity and intelligence. Fear of not receiving the fruits of our action stems from the desire for the fruits. Let the desire and the fear fall away and you will experience contentment.

21

Share Your Wealth—Both Material and Spiritual

A man's true wealth hereafter is the good he does in this world to his fellow man.

—MOHAMMED

He is poor who is dissatisfied; he is rich who is contented with what he has; and he is richer who is generous with what he has.

—JAMES ALLEN

In all abundance there is lack.

—HIPPOCRATES

When I was in Hyderabad in 1944 I heard a lot of stories about Usman Ali, the Nizam, or ruler, of Hyderabad. He lived in his old palace, King Kothi, and was reputed to be the richest man in the world. Despite his enormous wealth, the Nizam was known to be a greedy man and a terrible miser. We heard that he had not had his favorite cap washed or dry cleaned for years, lest it get spoiled; he didn't want to have to buy a new one. Whenever visitors went to King Kothi, after they left the Nizam would collect the half-smoked cigarette butts from the ashtrays and keep them for himself so he wouldn't have to buy cigarettes.

The shopkeepers in Hyderabad, especially the owners of jewelry shops, would put their shutters down when word went round that the Nizam's womenfolk were heading toward the market, because no one was ever paid for items these women "purchased." If a nobleman knew that His Highness was likely to visit his house, he would pick up all the most valuable items in his living room and hide them. Even then, if the Nizam made a comment about the beauty of a chandelier in the sitting room, it was packed and sent on its way to King Kothi before His Highness even left the house.

Once, when the Nizam and his son were inspecting his personal mint, where gold, silver, and copper currency was being produced, they scooped up some coins for a closer look. His son let a few slip through his fingers, dropping them on the floor. A person standing by asked him why he did not pick up the coins, and he replied, "The Nizam's son does not pick up coins." The Nizam bent to the floor, took up the coins, and said, "But the Nizam does."

I heard that once two noblemen visited the Nizam, bringing precious gifts. While they were talking, the topic of charity came up. One noble declared that giving charity to the poor is an offering to God. He drew a small circle on the ground and said, "At the end of every month, I throw all the month's profits up in the air. Whatever falls in the circle is for charity; whatever falls outside the circle is for me."

The second noble drew a very large circle and said, "Everything I save at the end of the month I throw into the air. Whatever falls inside the circle is for me, and whatever falls outside is for charity for the poor and downtrodden."

It was now Nizam Usman Ali's turn. The richest man in the world didn't hesitate. "Well," he said, "I don't think the poor deserve any charity. So I don't waste my time drawing circles on the ground, I deal directly with God. I throw the money into the air religiously twice a month and say, 'O God, accept whatever you want.' Then whatever falls to the ground is for me."

All Wealth Belongs to the Universe

There is nothing wrong in acquiring riches. One should earn wealth by fair and honest means, and enjoy it. But we must also remember that all wealth belongs to the universe. If you have it, consider yourself a trustee of it and share it with others. It is yours for only a short time. You have borrowed it, and some day you will have to give it all back.

This advice, which comes to us from the wise in ages past, applies to both material and spiritual riches. If you have it, it has been given to you because of your hard work, or you have earned it by your karma in this life or a previous life or lives. Why not create more good karma for the future by being generous with what you have?

Greed and the hoarding of wealth are a waste of time. One of America's richest men, Joseph Hirschorn, once said that no matter how wealthy you are, "you can eat only three meals a day. I tried eating four and I got sick. You can't sleep in more than one bed at night. I may have twenty suits, but I can wear only one at a time."

Deep down, the greedy person is usually fearful and insecure; he thinks he will gain security by acquiring a lot of wealth and worldly objects. He does not realize that although wealth can provide some temporary material security, it can disappear at any time. In the end, an insecure man is left holding onto an uncertain object, like a drowning man holding onto another drowning man. Wealth does not give you true freedom.

Surinder was quite a successful businessman. One afternoon he was on a picnic with his family on the banks of the Yamuna. Swimming close to the riverbank, he saw something shining in the rays of the sun on top of a piece of timber in the middle of the river. It looked to be something precious.

Surinder was not a good swimmer, but without a moment's hesitation he began swimming toward the shining object, and got hold of it. To his amazement, the packet contained gold and jewels. His pleasure knew no bounds. All this treasure was now his.

He started swimming back toward the riverbank where his wife was sitting and watching, worrying about him as she knew his swimming capabilities. As he neared the bank, he got caught up in a whirlpool and in the struggle to save himself from the fast currents, he lost his grip on the treasure in his hand. The packet quickly went downstream and disappeared.

Surinder reached the riverbank with great difficulty, quite a distance from the place where his wife and children were sitting. His wife was greatly relieved, and ran down to him, thanking God that he was alive and intact. But Surinder starting crying aloud about the treasure he had lost.

This story symbolizes how quickly material wealth can come and go; we can't rely on it. We never know what is going to happen tomorrow, next week, next year. Most of us spend a great deal of time lamenting things we never had and never will have. That is why sages always say that the real wealth is spiritual, the inner strength, integrity, and purity that we develop by our own efforts, that goes with us whether we have material riches or not. As Sathya Sai Baba says, "The riches you should strive to amass are not fields or factories, bungalows or bank balances, but wisdom, and experience of oneness with the grandeur of the universe and the force that runs it without a hitch." Prosperity without wisdom can be a curse.

On the other hand, this does not mean it is wrong to be wealthy. The ancient sages said that the two main causes of poverty are wrong thinking and inaction: lack of sattva, and dominance of tamas. One should be prosperous, earning riches by right action, without being greedy.

You are really rich when your desires are less than your assets. Our needs are limited, but greed and desire have no limit. You can fulfill your needs, but never your greed. Physical needs such as food and shelter can be taken care of, but the desires of the ego can never be satisfied. You should take from the universe what you require, not try to get everything you might want. Trying to extinguish the desire for riches by acquiring more and more is like trying to put out a fire by pouring oil on it. The more you acquire, the more you want. See that your needs are taken care of, count your blessings, and be as happy and free as the birds.

You don't have to renounce anything, only free yourself from imaginary needs and imaginary bonds. You need only one bed to sleep in, but you are not satisfied with even a nine-bedroom house; you want a guest house, a farmhouse, a house in the health resort. You are not satisfied with the car you drive; even though it gets you where you need to go in comfort and safety, you want a bigger one, a second or third one. But you don't need these things; it is your ego that drives you to desire them. What you do need is to renounce that ego, because of which you identify with your body and your possessions. You cannot renounce anything else anyway: nothing but your ego belongs to you.

There is nothing wrong with having desires. Desires are an essential part of life. But don't get stuck on worldly objects. If I am too much attached to worldly things, I measure myself according to what I have—money, power, house, car, etc.—and not what I am.

Great men were never measured by their worldly possessions. As Henry Ward Beecher wrote, "No man can tell whether he is rich or poor by turning to his ledger. It is the heart that makes a man rich. He is rich according to what he is, not according to what he has." Mahatma Gandhi, for example, was great not for what he had, but because of what he was. Gandhi worked all his life not for any worldly possessions or pleasures, but for a cause he believed in. I know we can't all be like him, but if we have even a fraction of his being, we will have peace, happiness, and fulfillment.

True Wealth

Riches are of many kinds. Material wealth is only one kind, and it is the least substantial. There is also wealth of knowledge, and of love, family, friendship. There is richness of beauty and appreciation of beauty. Many people say, "Health is wealth." A rich man may be comfortably unhappy, suffering from family discord, poor health, and a hard heart intent on acquiring more and more, while a poor man may be uncomfortably happy, content with what he has, blessed with friends, a good family, and honest work.

But the truest wealth is spiritual wealth. No one can ever take away your inner goodness and integrity, your purity of mind and sense of service, or the awareness of the divine reality you have gained through meditation. As Sivananda said, "The imperishable, inexhaustible wealth is spiritual wealth. No thief can plunder this. He who has this wealth is the richest man . . . even if he is clad in rags." In the Bible, Jesus says almost the same thing:

> Lay not up for yourselves treasures on earth, where moth and rust consume and where thieves break in and steal, but lay up for yourselves treasures in heaven, where neither moth nor rust consumes and where thieves do not break in and steal. For where your treasure is, there will your heart be also.

Share Your Wealth

Bikku, a beggar by profession, got ready for the day's work rather early one morning. It was an auspicious day, and he had high hopes for it. He had heard that the king was passing through their town. Accordingly, he made his clothes seem even more ragged and disheveled than usual, so that he looked like a true specimen of misery. His plan was to stand along the king's route and not move aside until he received handsome alms in charity.

In the palace, as the king was getting ready for the festive procession, his minister came to him. "Your majesty," the minister said, "be prepared to have your carriage blocked by beggars, as there are very many of them in the town."

The king was not at all perturbed. Instead, he said to the minister, "I want to know how they beg, and how they feel when they are begging."

The minister said, "How can you do that while sitting in the royal carriage?"

"Then," said the king, "I will dress up like a beggar and stand near the crossroads and pretend I am waiting for the king."

The king put aside all his fine clothing and jewels, and had himself dressed in rags. He went into town and walked toward the crossroads. When he saw Bikku, he stood before him and held out his hand for alms.

Bikku, waiting for the king, had no idea that the royal person was actually standing in front of him asking for charity. He was accustomed to asking and receiving alms; he never thought he would be faced with the need to give something to somebody else.

Bikku had two handfuls of corn with him. In disgust, he put a hand into his pocket and picked up a handful of it. But before he took his hand out of the pocket, he had a second thought and dropped everything back except a single seed of corn. He dropped that single kernel into the begging bowl of the king and walked away.

The rest of the day's collection was not bad, but Bikku was dissatisfied. He had expected a lot that day, and was disappointed because the king never appeared. When he returned to his tiny home, he put the fruit of his day's work—a few coins, some rice, and some grain—on a cloth before his wife, who began sorting through it. "You've brought home a lot today," she said with an approving smile. But Bikku did not appreciate her smile. She suddenly shrieked with joy. "Look, a piece of gold!"

Sure enough, Bikku saw a shining piece of gold in the palm of her hand. He was wonderstruck, as he instantly realized that the "corn" of gold was exactly the shape and size of the kernel of corn he had given so reluctantly that morning to the beggar. Now he was all remorse and regrets—not because he had cheated the beggar, but because of his meager reward. He remembered that he had been on the verge of giving a handful of corn, and the thought pierced his heart that if he had been generous with what he had, he would now be a wealthy man!

The lesson Bikku learned is that giving leads to receiving. It is a law of nature that we get back what we put forth. "As you sow, so shall you reap," the Bible says. This is the law of karma which we talked about in Chapter 5. But those who give, who are generous, who share their wealth (whatever it may be) know something even greater: giving *itself* is real riches. By giving you receive a lot more, a hundredfold, in the form of inner satisfaction, happiness, and peace.

Once you give a gift to someone, forget about it. Whenever you give something away, consider it a gift, and don't expect that in some way you will be compensated for it. It is not easy for many of us to give a gift silently, without recognition and having no sense of self-glorification or pride.

Giving away a few coins when you have millions—and even doing that little bit with the feeling that "I am the giver"—is not charity, it is miserliness. On the other hand, if you share your possessions, spiritual or material, especially if you don't have abundance, it generates cosmic love and has been defined by the sages as "love in action."

> The rich would have to eat money, but luckily the poor provide food.
>
> —RUSSIAN PROVERB

One of the most beautiful qualities in a person is generosity. Everyone appreciates it. "The perfection of generosity," a Buddhist text states, "is the absence of selfishly motivated action, and its replacement by the warmth of giving," whether one gives material goods to alleviate worldly needs, comfort and safety, knowledge, or spiritual guidance. Giving away something which will be of use to somebody, out of what little you have, especially if it is something you also require or may require later, is a true act of sharing. "Without generosity," the Buddhist text continues, "there is only poverty, dejection, and a cramped mental attitude."

The intention behind your giving is the most important thing. The intention should be to create happiness for the giver and the receiver. The return is directly proportional to the giving when it is unconditional and from the heart.

Putting the law of giving into practice is actually very simple, says Deepak Chopra. If you want joy, give joy to others. If you want love, learn to give love. If you want attention and appreciation, learn to give attention and appreciation. If you want material affluence, help others to become affluent. If you want to be blessed with all good things in life, learn to silently bless everyone with all good things in life.

The highest kind of giving is a life based on service to others, which we have talked about in Chapter 15. This is a life fully in accordance with Dharma, radiating compassion. We can all live such a life to some extent; there are always opportunities to serve others. A blessed few base their entire life on giving, as shown by the example of Mother Teresa.

Gather wealth but by fair means and without hurting others. Enjoy it without being vain and boasting about it. Remember everything belongs to the universe and you should share your wealth—material and spiritual—with others. Neither give indiscriminately nor for showing off. Be generous but not wasteful. Never be greedy.

> Continuing to fill a pail after
> It is full, water will be wasted
> Continuing to grind an axe after it
> Is sharp will wear it away
>
> Excess of light blinds the eye
> Excess of sound deafens the ear
> Excess of condiments deadens the taste
> He who possesses moderation is
> Lasting and enduring.
> Too much is always a curse
> Most of all in wealth.
>
> —LAO-TSE

Some Thoughts on Wealth

He is the richest who is content with the least.

—Socrates

Without a rich heart, wealth is an ugly beggar.

—Ralph Waldo Emerson

That country is the richest which nourishes the greatest number of noble and happy human beings.

—John Ruskin

A rich man is nothing but a poor man with money.

—W. C. Fields

Morals today are corrupted by our worship of riches.

—Cicero (ca. 50 B.C.)

This, then, is held to be the duty of the man of wealth: First, to set an example of modest, unostentatious living, shunning display or extravagance; to provide moderately for the legitimate wants of those dependent upon him; and after doing so to consider all surplus revenues which come to him simply as trust funds, which he is called upon to administer, and strictly bound as a matter of duty to administer in the manner which, in his judgment, is best calculated to produce the most beneficial results for the community—the man of wealth thus becoming the mere agent and trustee for his poorer brethren . . . The man who dies leaving behind him millions in available wealth, which was his to administer during life, will pass away "unwept, unhonored, and unsung."

—ANDREW CARNEGIE

22

If You Are Happy You Are Healthy

Laughter is both a tranquilizer and an equalizer.

—MAHATMA GANDHI

During the Second World War, Winston Churchill was holding an emergency cabinet meeting to discuss a particularly knotty problem. No one could find a solution and Churchill appeared very morose and upset. Suddenly Lady Astor spoke up rather loudly.

"The way you behave, if you were my husband I would put poison in your coffee."

"Madam," Churchill replied, "if I were your husband, I would drink it."

Everyone laughed and the tension was broken. Within the next few minutes, they found an answer to their problem.

Humor can be a powerful ally in difficult situations when problems seem overwhelming and solutions are not in sight. Start every meeting with laughter and you will have a successful meeting. A laugh breaks the ice, warms the atmosphere, and makes people more receptive to you and what you have to say. As the humorist Victor Borge commented, "Laughter is the shortest distance between two people."

You must know how to laugh, how to create laughter, and

how to find humor in all situations, even the most absurd or serious. Don't be one of those solemn, ponderous folks who plow through life with a stony grimness.

Laughter Is Your Best Medicine

People generally believe that if you are healthy you will be happy, but there is an old saying in India that may be more to the point: If you are happy, you are healthy. We have all heard that "Laughter is the best medicine," and it is very true. Humor and laughter are increasingly recognized as sound countermeasures to the effects of stress. If you have ever laughed until your sides hurt and your eyes were watering, you have had the experience of tension being washed out of your system.

Laughter can even help you regain lost health. The value of humor in physical healing came into prominence when Norman Cousins, former editor of the American literary magazine, *Saturday Review*, published *Anatomy of an Illness*. In this book he relates how he cured himself of what his doctors had pronounced an incurable illness, by prescribing himself daily doses of laughter. He watched hours of films and videotapes of old comedy movies, and described how after a good laugh he felt less pain in his body. Cousins challenged mainstream medicine to understand the mechanism of what he had accomplished. Scientists took up the challenge and now have at least the early stages of an answer.

Research has shown that our feelings, whether positive or negative, are converted into neuropeptides or messenger molecules, which eventually influence every cell in our bodies toward health or illness. When we laugh, for example, our positive emotions and feelings are converted into chemicals that can prevent and heal disease. Blood tests reveal that endorphins are produced which act as a painkiller, and our immunity increases.

"Laughter," said Norman Cousins, "is inner jogging." Indeed, laughter is almost like an exercise. It increases the rate and depth of breathing, and exercises the abdominal muscles. Laughter creates a coordinated rhythmic movement of the muscles of the chest, abdomen, and face, which massage the respiratory and abdominal organs, including the intestines. This improves circulation and increases the secretion of various enzymes that are good for digestion. After laughing there is a decrease in physical tension and stress, and a feeling of peace and relaxation sets in.

How to Use Laughter to Create Health

As I mentioned briefly in Chapter 2, research has confirmed the effectiveness of using physical techniques to improve your mood. This shouldn't be too surprising, as we have spoken quite a bit about effects in the opposite direction. Mind and body are an interconnected whole. Just as happy moods translate into happy molecules that build a healthy body, we can reverse the process and work from the side of the body to create a happier mood. Let me give you an example.

A rarely seen but very effective yoga practice is intentional group laughter. This artificially induced laughter, according to psychotherapist Annette Goodheart, is interpreted by the body as real, and as a result the brain releases healing neuropeptides. Once you get yourself to start laughing in this way, you can continue laughing naturally and without restraint. This relieves the mind and body of exhaustion and tension and brings a feeling of well-being. The brain induces a flow of "happy" molecules, which flood all our fifty trillion cells, combating stress and strengthening our hormonal system and our immunity.

This yoga practice explains research that shows that even when you don't feel happy, smiling can elevate your mood. Smiling artificially—or even manipulating people's facial expressions by pushing their eyebrows and lips to create the equivalent of a smile—can lead to a release of positive neuropeptides. If this process is repeated a number of times, it can raise immunity and help to heal disease.

Our bodily movements and postures influence our feelings

and emotions, just as our emotions and moods affect our body's movements and functions. So if you want to feel good and create a positive influence on your health and circumstances, you can choose to do so. By smiling at someone, you can begin to turn a difficult situation in your favor. Making other people laugh helps them become healthier while at the same time it helps you live longer. A smile on your face opens your heart to happiness and health.

When you feel happy, you smile; smile and you will feel happy. So even if you don't feel like it, smile—soon you will feel better. Smiling is easier than frowning, anyway. It takes forty-four muscles to frown, and only thirteen to smile.

You can initiate a smile by holding a pencil between your teeth. It may quickly blossom into laughter. On the other hand, if you hold a pencil between your lips, you start a frown, with a subsequent flow of negative neuropeptides flowing through your body, lowering your immunity against disease.

Laugh with Others, Not at Them

Humor and laughter are essential human activities. But in classical Indian tradition, humor is divided into two types. One is when one laughs at others. The other kind, which is considered superior, is when one laughs at oneself.

Laughing at others is considered vulgar and unseemly. Taking delight in the drawbacks or physical handicaps or frailties of fellow human beings is mean and harmful, both for the person who is mocked as well as for the one who laughs. Persons of a superior type make people laugh at themselves or at circumstances.

Genuine humor is never at anyone else's expense. Never be hostile in your humor, or use ridicule to create a laugh. Never laugh *at* people, laugh *with* them. This will give you inner peace and create a feeling of fellowship and brotherhood.

Being happy is healthy. But laughter, and the little pleasures of life, cannot be equated with true happiness. Material gain and sense pleasures, though surely an important part of life, are transient and cannot be counted on for happiness.

If you think about an experience of great joy, Deepak Chopra suggests in his book, *Perfect Health*—the birth of a child, the sight of a glorious sunset or an alpine lake at dawn—and then carry your feeling to its farthest shore, you arrive at a new state called "pure joy." This pure joy is the fundamental quality of life. In Sanskrit it is called *ananda*, which is usually translated as bliss.

With the growing popularity of Eastern teachings, people have come to use the word bliss to express many kinds of positive emotions. But ananda, the bliss that is described in the Vedic literature, resides at the quantum level in its pure form, and bubbles to the surface only under the right conditions. You cannot see or touch the thousands of processes in the brain and body that need to be coordinated in order to create bliss, but nevertheless it is a real experience.

According to ancient Indian sages, all joy stems from this pure joy, ananda, bliss. It is the bright light we do not see directly, but only by reflection in smaller joys. These lesser lights could not exist without the greater one. Even in Western society, where money, physical beauty, and success are generally equated with happiness, everyone has unexpected moments when life seems absolutely perfect and full of joy. If you could live in this state
of pure joy all the time, you would have the practical essence of perfect health.

Laughter is Contagious

Laughter is natural to man. Human beings start giggling and laughing at a very young age. Mother kissing her baby's tummy unleashes a torrent of excited giggles.

Scientists say that as children we laugh 400 times a day, but as adults only 10 to 15 times.

Laughter is contagious. Once laughter begins in a group of

people, it can spread as a chain reaction, breaking tension and increasing fellowship. There is a story about a monk who would stand in a marketplace and just begin laughing. People would at first wonder, "What is wrong with this monk?" But gradually everybody would join in. When asked if he had anything more to say, the monk would reply, "Nothing more is required after one

The Value of Laughter

Humor is not a trick, not jokes. Humor is a presence in the world—like grace—and shines on everybody.
—*Garrison Keillor*

What soap is to the body, laughter is to the soul.
—*Yiddish Proverb*

Time spent laughing is time spent with the gods.
—*Japanese Proverb*

If you cannot laugh at yourself, do not laugh at others.
—*Julie Sneyd*

Laughter is a universal bond that draws all men together.
—*Nathan Ausubel*

Laughter lifts us over high ridges and lights up dark valleys in a way that makes life so much easier. It is a priceless gem, a gift of release and healing direct from Heaven.
—*Alan Cohen*

23

The Healing Power of Music and the Arts

All songs are a part of Him, who wears a form of sound.
—VISHNU PURANA

The dancing foot, the sound of the tinkling bells,
The songs that are sung and the varying steps,
The form assumed by our Dancing Gurupara—
Find out these within yourself;
Then shall your fetters fall away.

—TIRUMULAR, TIRUKUTTU DARSHANA
(VISION OF THE SACRED DANCE)

One summer vacation in the early 1940s, while I was still a medical student, I went with three friends to Pahalgam, a beautiful health resort in the hills in Kashmir. We had a modest tented accommodation (there were not many hotels then) on the hill right next to the river.

Lying on the green grass, we felt as if we were in the lap of nature, gazing at the blue sky and watching white clouds float by. We watched the sun rise and set every day. It was exhilarating and refreshing to hear the murmuring of the river by day and night, as the crystal clear waters rolled downstream over the rocks, stones, and pebbles in its bed. The sound produced a wonderful, soothing effect.

In the mornings the songs of the chirping birds and the wind rustling through the leaves added to the musical murmuring of the river. It was nature at its best. The whole universe seemed to be full of music, which induced a feeling of tremendous well-being.

The Rhythms of Life

The effect of music on all living organisms—plants, animals, and humans—has been mentioned in many ancient texts, including the Vedas, the Bible, and the writings of Confucius, Plato, and Aristotle. It is said that at a time of drought, music played by great legendary musicians such as Tansen could bring rain to the withered and thirsty land. And when Lord Krishna played his flute, not only were the gopis (the cowherd girls) affected, but the cows were also moved by the sound of the music and yielded more milk!

Music influences all of life. That is because, as modern physics has shown, all life, all of nature including man, is composed of waves of energy. We are composed of energy vibrations or frequencies, and we live and move in a world of frequencies that constantly interact with one another. These frequencies and rhythms, whether the sounds of nature, musical instruments, or language, directly affect the waves and frequencies of other beings.

Numerous experiments have been performed in which music has been played to plants. Scientists working at an agricultural research institution in northern India demonstrated that when stalks of wheat were played classical sitar music, they grew bigger and stronger. In another study, Mozart's "Eine Kleine Nachtmusik," played to nocturnal plants, produced healthier specimens.

Scientists in Singapore randomly divided chickens into two groupings over half a mile apart. Music was played to one group most of the time, while the other group heard none. The hens in the "music" group seemed to dance to the rhythm of the music, wagging their tails. They became healthier as compared with the control group, and yielded more eggs.

Music and Medicine

The response of human beings to music is complex and fascinating. Not just feelings and emotions are influenced, but the very cells of our bodies. When we hear martial music, for example, catecholamines flood the body. Pulse rate goes up and muscle strength increases. The system goes into "alert," ready for battle.

On the other hand, soothing melodies release endorphins and induce a feeling of well-being. Blood pressure normalizes and the pulse rate slows as the person relaxes. The heart's functioning improves as irregularities and missing beats self-correct.

This has practical applications, not just for our own personal well-being. A study published in the *Journal of the American Medical Association (JAMA)* in 1994 states that neurosurgeons are likely to do a better job at the operating table with a little background music playing. The surgeons had lower blood pressure and pulse rates, and performed better with less stress. When the surgeon chose the music himself, it had an even more positive effect.

This study adds to the growing body of scientific evidence that music allays stress and can heal. As the American composer Stephen Halpern writes, "Properly chosen sounds can help bring you into a greater degree of physical and psychological harmony and balance."

The philosopher Nietzsche wrote, "without music, life would be a mistake." Over a century later, researcher Karen Allen of the State University of New York at Buffalo commented, "Our data prompts us to wonder if without music, surgery would be a mistake."

At the Yale University Medical School, Kay Gardner composes music that can avert pain and reduce the need for anesthesia during surgery. Various hospitals in the United States now regularly use music to help in the cure of various diseases. The progress of certain chronic illnesses, for example, seems to slow down with music therapy.

Mr. Faraggi, Professor of Music at the prestigious Ecole Normale de Musique in Paris, composes special music for babies. It comes as no surprise that music calms babies; mothers throughout the world sing lullabies to soothe their children to sleep. But Professor Faraggi says it can do much more. He has invented special "instruments" that babies can play by striking. "They enjoy the experience so much that they cry when their mothers come to take them home," he says. The music-making babies are healthier and grow faster as compared with other babies their age, the professor states.

Although all good music can be healing, it is said that the ancient classical music of India, known as Gandharva Veda, has exceptional power to heal and restore balance. According to the theory behind it, specific Gandharva ragas are appropriate for certain times of the day. They correspond directly with the rhythms of nature and embody the most fundamental vibrations that pulsate through the universe at every moment. By reconnecting us to nature, of which we are an integral part, this music can quickly create balance in our mind and body.

These principles are spoken of in ayurveda, the ancient Indian system of natural medicine, where it is said that imbalances in the body can be corrected by particular ragas of Gandharva Veda, resulting in better health and even the healing of disease.

Scientists hypothesize that the music employed in the mantras of Vedic chanting, the sustained single note drone in the calls of the muezzins, the wails of dervishes, as well as the music of other ancient cultures, has helped heal people through the ages by producing harmony in the rhythms of the heart, breath, and brainwaves. The music helps the cyclical functions of these aspects of the human physiology, all of which follow a wave pattern. When the body's rhythms become disturbed, resulting in ill health, they can become rebalanced by the harmonious rhythms and melodies of the music.

The highest development of this science of sound occurs in the ancient Vedic literature of India.

The Vedas and the Science of Sound

Oftentimes Vedic texts are considered only in terms of the meanings they convey. Yet it is well known that extreme care has been taken to preserve the precise rhythms and pronunciations of the texts for literally thousands of years. Why is this so?

To understand, we have to remind ourselves that verbal language is not the only way of communicating. Preverbal "language"—in the form of sound and vibration—exists throughout nature. Sound patterns convey information, but without "words" as we know them. Whales, for example, can literally talk to each other through the medium of sound over hundreds of miles.

The whole universe is alive with this preverbal language. At a later stage of evolution and development of the human nervous system, verbal language appears. This is just a more sophisticated version of the information and energy waves pervading all of nature, but an extremely powerful new form: it has given rise to a whole new world, the world of civilization, culture, religion, literature, and spirituality.

Words are symbols that express emotions, intentions, and desires. Words have incalculable power, constantly creating and changing the drama of our existence. Wrong words can be the harbinger of misery, war, and death. The right words can bring peace, harmony, laughter, happiness, and health. But words, before they have meaning, are sounds, vibrations.

This science of sound was perfected in the ancient Vedic literature. The Vedic rishis were said to be able to comprehend, in their settled, meditative consciousness, what is now being discovered by modern physics: that all natural forms and phenomena have wavelike properties. What appears to be solid on the surface, on a deeper level is really energy in the form of waves and frequencies. Vedic chanting is said to consist of those basic underlying sounds which uphold all of nature.

These frequencies and vibrations can be understood as *sound* or *music*, since sound has to do with wave properties. Indeed, the Vedic literature that is traditionally accorded the highest respect is known as *shruti*, or "that which is heard."

The Vedic tradition, including ayurveda and Gandharva Veda, makes practical use of this science of sound to promote healing. Like all of nature, our body consists of energy fields which at the surface level appear as the solid material aspects of the physiology. These energy patterns on the deeper levels are really like sounds: they are wave patterns, vibrations, frequencies. To promote health, sounds can be used which correspond to the particular vibrational quality of a part of the physiology in need of healing.

For example, in a patient with angina, the brain, working through messenger molecules that stimulate muscle cells in the middle layers of the blood vessels, sends specific signals which constrict the arteries, resulting in the angina pain. Betablockers, a group of drugs, help to an extent by inhibiting the action of these chemical messengers. But if one goes directly to the thinking process and corrects the impulses sent out by the brain, simply through the use of specific sound patterns (such as Gandharva ragas, mantras, or primordial sounds), treatment is more effective and far gentler.

Listening to chants of Vedic mantras helps to promote both healing in specific areas and to enhance general health and immunity. These healing Vedic mantras can be found on audio tape. The most effective way to listen to them is to sit (or lie down) quietly with eyes closed and let the mind flow with the chanting.

> The wise who recite the sacred primordial sound of Aum and who merge its harmony into the waking, sleeping, and dreaming states of consciousness become steady. They tremble no more. They find the peace of

the supreme spirit, where there is no dissolution nor
death and where there is no fear.

—PRASANA UPANISHAD

Today musicians are composing music containing animal sounds,
the songs of whales, the chirping of birds, the murmuring of
rivers and streams, the ebb and flow of ocean waves, the sighing
of wind in the leaves. These sounds are soothing and healing, and
they remind us that we are interconnected with everything in
nature through vibrations and the sounds of music.

This being true, we should all take some time every day for
quiet listening to beautiful music, chanting, and the music of
nature, not just for our pleasure but for health and healing.

The Spiritual Power of Indian Dance

Our grandchildren, Priya and Mallika, daughters of Sanjiv and
Deepak, studied Bharat Natyam in Boston. When Priya stayed
with us in the summer of 1989, spending her days volunteering
at Amar Jyoti (see Chapter 16), she took intensive dance training
every evening, and at the end of the summer gave a performance
before a fairly large audience in Delhi. She danced continuously
for two hours, and her performance was praised by art critics in
the national press. I found two of the six pieces she performed
particularly moving.

The first was the *Rasa Leela* or dance of Krishna and the
Gopis (milkmaids). Leela means the Creator's play or drama of
creation. Rasa means dance. As they play, blissful musical sound
is produced from the tinkling of the bells and the gopis'
ornaments and bangles. The dance is preceded by a "hide and
seek" between Krishna and the gopis. The musician George
Harrison said of the dance, "Krishna is God, the source of all
that is, was, or ever will be. Everybody is looking for him. Some
don't realize that they are, but they are." This search for God—
and the bliss of finding Him—is the essence of the Rasa Leela.

As God is unbounded, unlimited, He has many names:

Rama, Allah, Jehovah, Self, Consciousness, The Supreme. As a single drop of water has the same qualities as an ocean of water, so our consciousness has the same qualities as God's consciousness. But through our identification and attachment with the material aspect of life (the physical body, sense pleasures, material possessions, etc.) our true transcendental consciousness has been polluted, and like a dirty mirror is unable to reflect a pure image.

Through many lives our association with the temporary has grown stronger. The impermanent body, a bag of bones and flesh, is mistaken for the true Self. And we have accepted this temporary condition as final.

But God consciousness can be revived in all living souls. For as Krishna says in the Bhagavad Gita, "Steady in the Self, being freed from all material contamination, the yogi achieves the highest stage of happiness, in touch with supreme consciousness." Through meditation and devotion, you can attain perception of God. You can actually see God, hear Him, and play with Him. It might sound crazy but He is actually there with you.

The spiritual significance of the Rasa Leela, the eternal dance, is that Krishna, the Supreme Personality of the Divine, is already and always present as the "supersoul" in the bodies of the gopis, as well as their husbands and all other beings. He dwells in the heart of all beings and is the guide of all, directing individual souls to act while remaining a witness.

The drops of the ocean are the same as the ocean. The gopis represent the drops: the prakriti, the creation, and all beings; Krishna represents the ocean, the Purusha or supreme consciousness. The beautiful dance and music of Krishna's Rasa Leela depict the relationship between the ocean and its drops, the hide and seek of the Supreme and its expressions. The subtleties and nuances of this eternal dance are displayed in the dancing physique, the movements, gestures, and facial expressions of the dancer. This is what Priya did so successfully in her solo Bharat Natyam performance.

Shiva's dance, the second of Priya's dances I would like to

talk about, depicts the experience of Self-realization, the dawn of knowledge of the Self and the end of spiritual ignorance. Shiva represents one of the three fundamental powers of nature manifest in the world. Brahma is the god of creation, Vishnu is the preserver, and Shiva the god of destruction. These three powers exist all the time in this universe.

The trident that Shiva carries (in traditional statues and paintings as well as in the dance) symbolizes the three gunas, sattva, rajas, and tamas, which underlie the material universe. When a person transcends the gunas, he attains Self-realization. The throwing away of the trident during the dance thus symbolizes victory over the three gunas and the ecstatic experience of the bliss of the Self.

The traditional dance posture (seen in so many representations of Shiva Nataraja, the dancing Shiva) with one leg lifted and the other on a dwarf, signifies that a man of perfection deals with the world below yet has attained knowledge of the higher Self as well. The dwarf demon being crushed under his feet represents man's ego being conquered. The glory of man is in conquering his lower nature and becoming master of his desires, senses, and ego. This too is depicted in the dance.

Shiva Nataraja represents the absolute Reality. The drum in his hand indicates the phenomenon of creation, as vibrations of sound are, as we discussed earlier in this chapter, said to be responsible for the process of creation. The flame in Shiva's other hand denotes destruction. The dance then represents the continuous process of creation and destruction which maintains the universe.

Night follows day, the plant follows the seed and the seed follows the plant. Birth and death follow each other. The perpetual process of creation and destruction goes on.

Nataraja maintains a silent, blissful countenance, representing the supreme tranquility of the Self experienced within, while at the same time he is untiringly engaged with great agility in his eternal dance. This is to demonstrate how a man should be in the world: engaged all the time in worldly activities, but with quietude and peace in his heart. This, as Swami Vivekananda remarked, is the same teaching that stands out luminously on every page of the Bhagavad Gita: intense activity, in the midst of which there should be eternal calm.

As the noted philosopher and art historian Ananda K. Coomaraswamy wrote of Shiva Nataraja in his book, *The Dance of Shiva*:

> The Supreme Intelligence dances in the soul . . . for the purpose of removing our sins. By these means our Father scatters the darkness of illusion (maya), burns the thread of causality (karma), stamps down evil, showers Grace, and lovingly plunges the soul in the ocean of Bliss (Ananda). They never see rebirths, who behold this mystic dance.

This is the profound spiritual message these beautiful traditional dances wordlessly speak to our hearts.

PART FOUR

SECRETS OF LONGEVITY AND HEALTHY AGING

24

Secrets of Longevity and Healthy Aging

To be seventy years young is sometimes far more cheerful and hopeful than to be forty years old.

OLIVER WENDELL HOLMES

Would you like to live another fifteen, twenty, or twenty-five years? Would you like to live to be one hundred?

Younger people rarely hesitate to answer in the affirmative, but if you are sixty-five, seventy-five, or older, you may very well reply, "It depends." If you can remain active and independent, in relatively good health, the answer is almost certainly "Yes." But no one looks forward to a life of weakening powers, pain, and increasing dependence. As Alexis Carrel wrote in *Man the Unknown*, "Longevity is only desirable if it increases the duration of youth. The lengthening of the senescent period would be a calamity."

The good news is that many of the commonly observed effects of aging are far from inevitable. Scientific research has identified numerous ways we can live an active, healthy, enjoyable, and productive life well into our seventies, eighties, and even beyond.

"Aging is like a long horse race," says Professor Patrick Rabbit, Britain's foremost expert on cognitive aging. "At the beginning, all the horses are bunched together, but towards the end there is a big difference between the leaders and the trailers."

Two healthy twenty-year-olds are likely to look almost identical if you compare their hearts, livers, skin, eyesight, and so on. But after middle age no two people have aged the same way, and two seventy-year olds will almost certainly present dramatically different profiles. One may suffer from arthritis, the other may have heart disease. One may have hearing or vision problems, the other may not.

Chronological age is only one measure of the aging process. There are many seventy-year olds who show little or no decline. Nelson Mandela took the reins of the government of South Africa at the age of seventy-seven, after nearly three decades in prison. Such people may be in the minority, but they are more than a few. And others can learn to become like them. In one well-known experiment, a group of people in their eighties proved superior in learning computer skills to a group of twenty-year olds.

If I may use myself as an example, it is now twenty-eight years since I took early retirement from my profession as an army doctor. At that time, I made a firm decision that I would never stop working. I will ultimately go "with my boots on," which in army language means that I plan to work till the very end.

I am now in my late seventies. I work full time, often fourteen to sixteen hours per day in the hospital as a consulting cardiologist. I engage myself in academic activities, conferences, continuing medical education programs for doctors, and in addition spend a lot of time on public awareness programs, teaching prevention of heart disease. I enjoy my work, and I am sure it keeps me young.

I am not the only older person who is this active, productive, and happy in my later years. But many are not, and it is becoming a serious problem.

Growing Old Today

According to the Proceedings of the International Salzburg Seminar (Session 357) on "Aging Populations—The Challenge of Society," held on June 12–14, 1998, the percentage of the population aged over 65 is 13 percent in the USA and 16 percent in the UK. The number of people in India over sixty years old has risen past fifty million and is growing so fast that by the turn of the century there will be seventy-five million. Yet things have never been so bad for the elderly in India as they are at the present moment. In a country with a great tradition of reverence for the aged, people are increasingly indifferent to them.

For many centuries, older people were traditionally considered a valuable asset to the family and community. Their wisdom was respected, their guidance and blessings sought. But values and priorities have changed. The extended family system has collapsed, the generation gap has widened, rapid urbanization has created a shortage of living space and many economic problems. Once respectful attitudes have begun to disappear. And with changes in the social structure, the world of the old has become depressing. Many feel neglected, unwanted, lonely, and uncared for. Fear of facing an emergency is always on the minds of even those who are financially well off.

After retirement the old folks in our society are often thrown into the "scrap heap," as it were. A day comes when the once active worker and earner becomes inactive, a passive receiver. Former colleagues and relatives, even sons and daughters, have no time to talk to them.

In such a climate, senior citizens have only one viable alternative: to take more responsibility for themselves and seriously participate in improving their own lives. They should take good care of their health, be sure to get sufficient exercise, spend as much time as they can in activity that is useful to their family or community, and be as independent psychologically and financially as they are able.

Elderly persons should find no time to feel bored. They can run the house, tend the garden, play with the grandchildren, and make themselves socially useful. They should, with alertness and openness to new ideas, be ready to adjust to other members of the family, and to appreciate their children and grandchildren. The peace of mind achieved by these attitudes and behaviors helps to prevent heart disease and other illnesses. This is the way to add life to years as well as years to life.

While it may be necessary that governmental support continue, and voluntary agencies also contribute to the setting up of daycare centers, self-help groups, and old-age homes, the goal should be to foster as much independence and self-reliance as possible. People need to continue working, feeling useful, and keeping mentally and physically fit. Retirement does not have to mean living on a pension and reminiscing about the past. It is not the time to "call it a day." Rather, it should be a time to continue working in whatever way you can, earning whatever you can, and feeling good about yourself and what you are doing.

This approach will largely prevent the need for institutionalization and hospitalization, and it will lower the cost of health care for everyone. The way to accomplish this is to educate people of all ages in ways to maintain health and vitality and prevent disease. This will be best for each person as he or she grows older, and best for the country as a whole.

Holding Back the Years

Elderly people are commonly afflicted with chronic diseases, including coronary artery disease and heart attacks, the leading cause of death in persons over sixty-five years of age. Doctors used to believe that it was too late for this group of people to benefit much from what we call "coronary risk factor modification"—making changes in their lives to reduce the risk of heart disease. Recent data contradicts this pessimistic view. With the proper lifestyle changes, older people may look younger and feel younger than their chronological age, and can look forward to an extended active life.

What kind of changes are required? Primarily, reducing or eliminating factors that are *known* to increase the risk of heart disease. For example, physical inactivity is common among elderly people. Smoking and chewing tobacco, and a diet high in fatty food, are not uncommon. All of these are known to be risk factors for heart disease, and they are all habits, lifestyle patterns we can control. Modification of these factors can reduce illness and death in *all* groups, not only the elderly. Among people who take this challenge seriously and modify their lifestyles, more and more are reaching older age with better health.

It is a common observation in my practice that two patients with similar risk factors and similar health problems may make their recovery in quite dissimilar ways. Their cardiac evaluations may initially reveal similar heart functions and "effort tolerance," but their eventual recovery and return to work and normal life may be widely different.

Duni Chand was a business executive in his early fifties who suffered a sudden heart attack. His cardiac evaluation and long-term prognosis were excellent. Despite the assurance that he had only had a minor, uncomplicated attack and was making an excellent recovery, he simply could not get over the mental shock of "having a heart attack." Neither psychotherapy nor physiotherapy helped him during his rehabilitation period. He was somehow convinced that he could no longer lead an active, productive life, and he gave up all efforts in that direction. He started suffering from depression and felt he was growing old rather fast. As a matter of fact, he soon began looking much older than his age, and asked for early retirement from his job.

Then there was Shyam Sunder, about the same age and holding a comparable position, who suffered a rather similar heart attack. Although his long-term prognosis wasn't quite as good as Duni Chand's, he returned to work after two months and told me, "I like my job better than ever before. It may seem surprising but it is true that I work fewer hours now but achieve more. I'm no longer rushing for the deadline; somehow I just seem to plan things better. I'm more productive, and I enjoy life. I find time to relax and look around; I have time to stand and stare. I never knew the world was so beautiful." Speaking of his wife, Shyam Sunder told me appreciatively, "Earlier I never took the time to see her lips enrich the smile her eyes began."

Many years ago, Mr. Kapil Bhatia, aged fifty-three, was admitted to our hospital with a massive heart attack. Things were very different then. We had no intensive coronary care unit, and no monitoring system. He was simply cared for in a private room in the hospital.

Though Mr. Bhatia had a number of complicating factors, including mild diabetes and a habit of moderate smoking, he made a fairly good recovery. But soon after going home, depression overwhelmed him. "If something should happen to me," he thought, "what will happen to my wife and my only child, an unmarried girl?" He also felt that his career was over.

After a few days, he took hold of himself. He stopped smoking, began a regular exercise program, and went on a low-fat, sugar-free, vegetarian diet. He started smiling and laughing, both at work and off work. And he never looked back. His career took off, and he eventually held top positions in the country, including serving as chairman and consultant for a large number of companies and governmental organizations.

His daughter married and migrated to the USA. Not long afterward, his wife died of a brain tumor. He lived alone now, but kept very busy performing social services. His old age, after that massive heart attack, was the most productive part of his life. I would see him pass our house every morning on his long walk, up till two days before he died at the age of ninety-three.

These typical case histories illustrate the point that I am emphasizing throughout this book: to a large extent, your life is in your own hands. You can do with it what you want. The choice is yours. It is never too late to set your life on track for better health and greater happiness.

Studies reveal that retired men who are inactive die earlier than their age-matched counterparts who continue to work in one way or another after their official retirement. The death often occurs due to the effects of high blood pressure or a stroke. A number die of heart attacks, seemingly because they have nothing better to do. Varying degrees of cerebral atrophy, a condition that can lead to loss of memory or even convulsions, has been seen by the CAT scan.

All this can happen to elderly people who do not continue to use their brains in a productive way. People who could be wise counselors for their family and community become unwanted, useless old fools and a liability to their families. "The tragedy of old age," says Robert Butler in his book, *Why Survive*, "is not that each one of us must grow old and die, but that the process of doing so has been made unnecessarily painful, humiliating, and isolating through insensitivity and ignorance."

The rising trend of degenerative diseases among the elderly in our society can be significantly retarded if elderly people learn to stay occupied. I am not advocating activity solely for the sake of keeping busy. For many people, the retirement years provide an opportunity to begin doing work they didn't have time or freedom to do when they held down a full-time job or were busy raising a family. It may be some activity that is personally rewarding, such as taking up art or devoting time to spiritual study or practice. Often it may be work of great service and benefit to society that goes beyond just making an income.

Various studies have shown that if you enjoy your work and work for joy, it has a positive effect on your health and aging. To me, old age is always fifteen years older than I am.

BERNARD BARUCH (ON HIS EIGHTY-FIFTH BIRTHDAY)

K. Warner Shate, an expert in cognitive aging at Pennsylvania State University, says that the brain's continued good functioning into the late years is helped by good education, a stimulating and challenging lifestyle, and being married to an intelligent and supporting spouse. People who retain their wits to a ripe old age are likely to have good family ties, read challenging material, and are fond of travel and also of walking.

Among other measures to help the aged I would include:

* *Revive the extended family system:* Although times have changed, I believe that everyone would be served if we revived the tradition of the extended family system. It may look a little different from how it looked in the past, but the value would be tremendous. The elderly could live with their children and grandchildren with increased dignity, and at the same time could be useful to them.

Living together in mutual understanding can enhance emotional and spiritual well-being for both the elderly and the younger generation. Think of the joy grandparents can derive just from being with their grandchildren, not to speak of the joy of watching and helping them grow. And think how beneficial it is for young children to have the attention of devoted elders who love them and wish to share the wisdom gained over a long life.

In Japan more than 40 percent of the people still live in extended families, with at least three generations residing together in a single, often very small dwelling. On the whole, these families live happily together. I often think this may be a key reason the Japanese enjoy the highest life expectancy in the world, currently eighty-six for women and seventy-seven for men. (This compares to an average life expectancy of seventy-eight and a half for women and seventy-three for men in the UK; seventy-nine for women and seventy-two for men in the US; and just short of sixty for women and sixty for men in India.)

The Japanese also have the highest percentage of people over the age of sixty-five, 16 percent of the population as compared to only 6.8 percent over the age of sixty in India. In 1991, Japan had 3,625 people over the age of one hundred, while India in the same year, despite a vastly larger population, had only 150 centenarians. The figure for Japan in 1996 had increased to 7,400. (In the USA there are 40,000 centenarians; in the UK 6,000. These numbers are estimated to rise dramatically with the continued aging of the "baby boomer" generation.)

Be around young people: I know a man of seventy-two, very active physically and mentally, who refuses to be in the company of people his age. "Leave these old fellows to themselves" is his refrain. "Let us go and have fun," he tells one or another of his younger friends who play tennis with him every single day. He feels young psychologically and that is the secret of his healthy, active, and happy life. As Oliver Wendell Holmes wrote, "To be seventy years young is sometimes far more cheerful and hopeful than to be forty years old."

About three years ago a journalist came to me and said he wanted to ask only one question.

"Go ahead," I replied.

"What is the definition of old age?"

"I will let you know when I get there," I replied. I am not sure how long he will have to wait for the answer.

Have the right attitude: Deepak Chopra writes of peasants in the Bulgarian mountains who are famous for their longevity. Numerous centenarians there live an active life, including swimming and riding in the snow-clad mountains. What is responsible for their long lives? Apparently it is not their diet, nor the climate, nor any such factor, but their *expectations* and the expectations of their culture about what old age is supposed to mean.

The collective mindset of these people is that as you grow older, you get better. Growing older means growing wiser, and wisdom is highly prized. Thus, as you age, you get more responsibility and receive more respect. The most "glamorous" individual in that society is not the young man or woman just starting out, but the person with a long history. This positive collective perception of aging gets translated into a biological expression in the body: long life.

If we expect to live a long, healthy, creative life, the chances are good that we will achieve it. If we believe we have to retire from active life at sixty and that everything will go downhill from there, that we will quickly fall apart physically and mentally and lead a miserable life in a home for the aged—chances are that is what we will create for ourselves. Our attitude is extremely important.

Accept the facts of life: Along with its joys and satisfactions, life brings all of us many hardships and disappointments, and we have to be prepared to face them with strength and flexibility. As the ancient Buddhist text, *Anguttara Nikaya*, teaches:

> Old age will come upon me some day and I cannot avoid it.
>
> Disease can come upon me some day and I cannot avoid it.
>
> Death is bound to come upon me some day and I cannot avoid it.
>
> All things that I hold dear are subject to change, decay, and separation and I cannot avoid it.

Old age, sickness, loss, and death are simply part of life. No matter how much we might resist or desire things to be otherwise, they cannot be avoided. So it is better for us if we accept them. By not accepting, we create problems for ourselves.

In advanced old age, our bodily energy gradually ebbs away and we start fading. Can you find a flower that never fades? Yet before it fades it is dancing in the winds, and playing with the butterflies. It unfolds from the bud and keeps on changing, until finally the petals fall off. But all this time it has been spreading fragrance all around. Why not look at your own life that way?

If you are afraid of old age or death, you are actively promoting both these states. Nothing makes people age faster than fear. But fear of disease, old age, and death won't haunt us if we realize that birth and death are normal events in the continuum of life. Death is not a full stop, it is only a comma. As so many sages have told us since times immemorial, death of the body is not the end of life. Every *body* dies, but truly speaking no one ever dies; life goes on. Life is eternal.

As the Bhagavad Gita teaches about the true Self:

> He is never born, nor does he ever die; nor once having been, does he cease to be. Unborn, eternal, everlasting, ancient, he is not slain when the body is slain.

Ancient wisdom teaches that, in addition to the eternal continuity of consciousness, the individual soul comes back time and again, taking on new bodies in its quest for ultimate fulfillment. In Chapter 5 I touched on the concept of rebirth and how it helps to explain many phenomena, but I would like to discuss it a bit more deeply now.

Many people believe that after death, if you have done a lot of good things, you go to some kind of "heaven." There, it seems, you don't have to do anything; everything is done for you. You have the choicest foods to eat, streams of wine are flowing, you walk on roads paved with gold, enter your luxurious bejeweled bedroom through gates studded with pearls. Since you have no daily work to do, you have to kill boredom by watching dancing girls and winged fairies, and drinking wine.

On the other hand, if you have done bad things on earth, you go to "hell." Some people believe that you go to hell forever. But how can it be? God is all compassion. Would a loving God send people to hell to suffer forever? It doesn't make sense. The concept of hell also depends on which part of the world you live in. If you lived in northern India, hell means a place where you will be thrown into tanks of boiling hot oil, as you did not like the hot weather of your homeland. However, if you lived in frigid Tibet, hell means a place where you will be frozen in mounds of ice and surrounded everywhere by ice and snow.

I don't believe there are any such places. Heaven and hell are states of mind. If you are happy and in bliss, you are in heaven. That is what Jesus meant when he said the Kingdom of Heaven is within you. You can attain heaven—on earth—by performing right and good actions, in accordance with the dictates of your conscience.

When a person dies, what passes away is the gross outer

body. The subtle body, which includes the mind (which thinks), the intellect (which discriminates and decides) and the ego (which is responsible for the sense of "I" and "mine") separates itself from the outer gross body, and soon finds itself in a new home. This is ancient knowledge. In the same sequence of verses from the Bhagavad Gita that I quoted above, Krishna tells Arjuna:

> As a man casting off worn-out garments takes other new ones, so the dweller in the body casting off worn-out bodies takes others that are new . . . Even if you think of him as constantly taking birth and constantly dying, you should not grieve . . . Certain indeed is death for the born and certain is birth for the dead; therefore over the inevitable you should not grieve.

The subtle body holds all the impressions of the soul, not only from this one life, but from all lives past. After the death of the gross body, the subtle body, with all its impressions and inclinations, its memories and unfulfilled desires, takes a new birth in accordance with the laws of karma. No one tells it where to go. Nor are there any judges, prosecutors, or defense counsels to pass judgment. In actuality, you direct yourself, since it is your own accumulated karma, and your own unfulfilled wants and desires, which determine your next birth.

A bullet, says Swami Chinmayananda, can travel only in the direction in which the gun is fired. Once the bullet has left the gun, neither the gun nor the bullet can control the flight pattern. Like that, the subtle body travels in the direction decided by the sum total of our thoughts and actions, the karma of our entire lifespan. We find a suitable body for another dwelling to live in for another limited time.

These impressions, tendencies, and potentialities, which exist in our subconscious, are known as samskaras. Automatically, we choose a birth that can help us fulfill our desires, or help us realize the Truth by rising above these desires to experience the Reality.

Why, then, are we afraid of death, if it is only a process of going from one body to another? The reason is that we identify ourselves with the body and we are attached to it. We feel, "I am the body," when the truth is that we are only the *dweller* in the body, and a temporary resident at that. It is quite similar to the relationship of a bird with its nest.

The nest is safe so long as the bird lives in it, while it is feeding and raising its young ones. It continues to look after the nest during this period, but as soon as the purpose is fulfilled and the little ones have grown up and flown away, the bird also flies away to another place, never thinking of its old nest. In due time, it builds or finds another nest. Without the bird to care for it, the old nest disintegrates and goes back to the elements it was made of—fragments of grass and twigs fly off in every direction.

Very similarly, the subtle body leaves behind the physical body, which must perish. But "I" have not perished; I am not the body, and I am still there, ready to continue my journey toward total awakening to my eternal Self.

Because death is nothing to fear, and because fear itself hastens the process of aging and deterioration, it is imperative that we live every moment of our lives without bothering much about old age and death. With acceptance rather than fear of these inevitable phases of life, we have quietude of mind under all circumstances, favorable or unfavorable.

The evening before my granddaughter Priya's graduation, I went for a walk with her through a little forest near their home outside Boston. I don't recall how the topic came up, but I told her, "I have had a very good innings, a happy life. When I leave this world I will do so with a sense of joy and peace in my heart, and with the satisfaction that I am leaving behind in this world such wonderful children and grandchildren. There may be silence for a while when I leave this world, but all my children should understand and celebrate the occasion."

Priya was silent for a minute or so and then said lovingly, "I know you have raised two fine sons. You are proud of them and rightly so. No, I won't celebrate the occasion, but I can assure you, I won't cry."

Deepak Chopra says in *Ageless Body, Timeless Mind* that when we see ourselves in terms of timeless, deathless Being, rather than in terms of our ever-changing body, each of the fifty trillion cells in the body awakens to a new existence. True immortality can be experienced here and now in this very body. It comes about when we are aware of Being, the Self, with everything we think or do.

Research studies at the University of California at Davis, Duke University, and elsewhere are casting doubt on the notion that there is a biologically fixed lifespan for humans. The idea that there is a limit to a person's life, which we inherit from our parents, is overly simple. For instance, if a person is fortunate enough to make it to old age, a slowing of biological changes may occur, increasing the chance to enjoy more good years. With all the advances in preventive medicine and the knowledge of what constitutes a healthy lifestyle, once you make it to eighty your chances of reaching ninety or beyond and leading a useful, healthy life may actually increase.

Many, many people in our country will reach old age in years to come, with better health and a chance for greater usefulness and fulfillment. More and more of our elderly are vitally interested in making the kinds of lifestyle changes we have talked about, changes which will lead to a fuller life. Medical professionals and other leaders of society should work hard to make health education and preventive care strategies widely available, so that we can quickly improve the quality of life for our aging population.

But no matter what programs are available or what knowledge is disseminated, the "bottom line" belongs to each one of us. Our attitude toward life and aging, and our day-to-day behaviors—what we eat, whether or not we smoke, making the time to exercise or to meditate—these decisions, which structure our bodies and our minds, rest with each person.

Old age cannot interfere with our lives if we have devotion, discipline, and love for the Lord. As a sage of the ancient Rig Veda sings:

> God made the rivers to flow. They feel no weariness, they cease not from flowing. They fly swiftly like the birds in the air. May the stream of life flow into the river of righteousness. Loosen the bonds of sin that bind me. Let not the thread of my song be cut while I sing and let not my work end before its fulfillment.
>
> —RIG VEDA, 11:28

Or in the words of Swami Chinmayananda (see Appendix 5), a modern sage:

> I feel blessed that God has chosen me
> As one of his instruments,
> That I am in God's hands
> And God can use me as He likes.
> I have joy in being made
> Joy in being used
> Joy in being broken and
> Joy in being thrown away
> After my mission is fulfilled.
> If I am still alive it means my mission is not complete.

If you have this attitude, you can prolong the duration of youth, and die young in old age.

Epilogue

Ancient Wisdom—The Magic Mantra for Healthy Living

It is mentioned in the ancient text Bhagavatam (ca. 3000 B.C.) that only two kinds of person are free from stress: an utter fool and a realized soul who has transcended his mind and is in the world, yet not in the world. For the primitive man, stress was usually of an acute nature, but when the ferocious beast walked away and man did not have to fight, chemicals like adrenaline, secreted during the period of stress, were washed away in the normal course of running for food.

Episodes of acute stress still exist today. You may not have to face a beast these days (although you may sometimes encounter a tiger-man or a scorpion-man). Even crossing the street one sometimes has to run to avoid being hit by an oncoming bus. But it is usually the little hassles of life which pose a threat to your well-being, happiness, health, and progress in life.

Our memory, which has developed over a long period of time, troubles us. Recall of unpleasant events is stressful, and one starts feeling that one is living in a hostile world. Unless the increased adrenaline, which is poured into our blood with each real or imaginary episode of stress, is utilized and washed out, it can wear a person down. Your immunity buckles and you can suffer from the cumulative ill effects: fatigue, exhaustion, agitation, hostility, which in turn can lead to high blood pressure, heart attacks, cancer, and whatnot.

It has been shown that our mental attitude is the most crucial determinant of our state of health, productivity, and creativity. We have to suffer from the ill effects of increased adrenaline levels in our system, or find ways and means to utilize these chemicals to our advantage. Instead of grumbling and protesting, we have to realize that we cannot afford to throw away this extra energy. We need it. Rather than allow this stress-caused energy to cause agitation, we can harness it to generate the zeal, determination, and perseverance which can help us reach our goal.

As you climb higher on the ladder of success, more responsibilities do not have to mean more stress. They may bring you more opportunities, better solutions, and better performance. But for that, you need a calm mind. Dependence on alcohol, smoking, and tranquilizers is no solution. Temporarily you have a "chemical high" but as you get addicted to these toxins, the initial calm you might have felt is replaced by fatigue, exhaustion, irritability, anxiety, depression, and lurking grief. All these factors have been found to be responsible for failure in business and more than half the patients of cancer and heart attack have no other known risk factor.

Stressors in the modern world are many and varied. All over the world people are having to deal with occasional acute stress such as an emergency landing, being present in a hijacked airplane, a fire in a highrise building, a bomb blast by terrorists. On a more day-to-day level, one must learn to ignore or live with small stressors, such as traffic jams, misplaced documents, waiting in the doctor's waiting room or the immigration or customs line at a busy airport.

There is no point in getting stressed if your grown son comes home late at night, or your daughter-in-law is fond of cocktail parties. You want your son to become a doctor and he wants to become a freelance journalist. Your wife threatens that she is going to divorce you; you take it seriously even though you know she doesn't really mean it. You worry that your husband is getting friendly with his secretary although you know in your heart of hearts that he has always been and continues to be faithful to you. You are jealous of your competitor, who you think is doing well because he has political influence.

Most of these things get sorted out if you have patience; hasten slowly in life and do not rush to conclusions. Discuss things but never argue to prove your point. Be yourself; never pretend you are someone else. If you truly know yourself, you will not look to others for approval.

From the early days of human history, music and dancing have been an instinctive part of our life and living. Music was loved by all in various cultures. In Greek and Roman mythology its origin was traced to the gods in heaven. Orpheus was a legendary Greek poet and musician whose music was so enchanting that not only the humans and animals but also the rocks and trees followed him.

Similarly, it is said that the power of the melodies coming from Lord Krishna's flute was so magical that it not only enchanted the gopis, but also the cows and the rest of the animal kingdom. Everyone rushed to the spot where the music was coming from. The magic of it softened even the hardest of rocks.

In India, the sages of ancient times stated that music comes from Brahman, the supersoul, the supreme consciousness, the source of all creation. As such it is an expression of bliss. It frees us from stress and bondage and shows us the way to reach God. According to ancient scriptures, before the creation of life the entire space of the universe was filled with energy, and then with the divine sound, Om (a-u-m). One of the four Vedas, Sama Veda, deals with music, singing, and dancing. Later Gandharva Veda came into being; it deals with especially soothing music which allays the stress of life and heals.

Music has a profound effect on every bit of what goes to make a human being—the soul, the emotions, the mind, and each of our body's cells. It elevates you to great heights and raises your immunity. With its help you can conquer stress, heal yourself, and heal the world.

Regular exercise, such as swimming and walking, also

diffuses stress, increases physical proficiency, and makes your mind more alert.

Laughter, which is internal jogging, is very healing. Laughter occurs naturally when people are comfortable with each other, when they are open and free. It enhances the sense of social bonding. Deep inside, when you feel you are interconnected, you share moments of grief and happiness with your fellow beings and spontaneously manage stress in day-to-day life much better.

The way you speak matters a lot in life. The words you speak should be kind words, right words at the right time. As the Bhagavad Gita says:

> Spoken words that cause no excitement, words that are
> good, pleasant, beautiful, and true. All this and the study
> of scriptures contributes to the austerity and harmony of
> speech. (17:15)

Anger, jealousy, hatred, lack of contentment, selfishness, guilt, pride, ego, lingering desires, greed, resentment, despair, self-condemnation, not having the ability to forgive are all impurities of mind. Only humans entertain such feelings. Fear is the basis of all these impurities of the mind, which in due course punish us.

> He who considers wealth a good thing
>   can never bear to give up his income.
> He who considers eminence a good thing
>   can never bear to give up his fame.
> He who has a taste of power
>   can never bear to hand over authority to others.
> Holding tight to these things
>   such men shiver with fear.
> And should they let them go
>   they would pine in sorrow.
> They never stop for a moment of reflection
>   never cease to gaze with greedy eyes.
> These are the men punished by Heaven.
>
> —CHUANG TZU, 14

Degeneration of human values is responsible for stress, corruption, strife, and unrest in the world. This has led to a decline in culture. People have become very selfish. Power and money are the great aims of life, and the means used to achieve these ends don't seem to matter.

> There is no crime greater than lingering desires
> There is no disaster greater than not being contented
> And no misfortune greater than being covetous.
>
> —TAO TE CHING

We have to learn to respect basic human values, which are common to all religions and all cultures. Only then can we have peace in our hearts and in the world we live in. The fragrance of a man of virtue goes all over.

> The perfume of flowers goes not against the wind, not even the perfume of sandalwood, of rose bay or of jasmine, but the perfume of virtue travels against the wind and reaches unto the end of the world.
>
> —DHAMMAPADA, 54

Our ancient scriptures are full of wisdom. The value system reflected by this wisdom has a direct and an indirect relevance to the study of management in industry and the business world of today. We should take advantage of the vast treasures of wisdom left behind by the thinkers and philosophers of the past thousands of years. If we follow a holistic approach in management where discipline, devotion, and attention to the details of the work in hand are considered more important than the fruits of our actions, we will achieve much more in life without stress or frustration. Ancient wisdom and values are already being considered as the "magic mantra" for conquering stress by many management experts in the corporate sector.

Now that we have journeyed together through this book, I am sure you will agree with me that this is not a book of religion or morals. But our scriptures are full of wisdom that can be applied well to our lives today. Only a bit of it has been highlighted.

Commenting on Karma Yoga as expounded in Bhagavad Gita, Swami Vivekananda said, "While performing actions, your actions (karma) should not be influenced by fear of hell or temptation of enjoyment in heaven. You should work for work's sake, do your duty for duty's sake, and love for love's sake, and you will live in peace in this life and the life hereafter."

Thousands of thoughts pass through the mind every day. The majority of them are purposeless old thoughts which agitate the mind. In meditation, the mind quiets down. There is only focused awareness of the moment. You learn to have no regret of the past or fear of the future, only enjoyment of the present moment. The thought pattern changes; buoyancy and love prevail in your entire being.

Usually our experience of the world is an experience of our limitations. Astronauts report that when looking back on earth from outer space they experience a new awareness, a strangely mystical experience of altered consciousness. It only demonstrates that the view of the world we live in is dictated by how we have learned and have been conditioned to perceive the outer world and how we perceive our inner world. Change the perception and we change the world we perceive.

During meditation the mind is directed to pay attention to the incoming and outgoing breath as we breathe in and out with slow, rhythmic breathing. But it is not just air we breathe, it is prana, the vital force of life. It is a divine force, cosmic prana, the breath of the cosmos. When breathing quietly and consciously like this, you are in harmony with the vibrating cosmos. When a rishi or master is in meditation, it is not for himself but for the whole universe. Through regular meditation, you become one with the Self, the Supreme Consciousness, and that guides and influences your life.

The corporate world has, of late, increasingly turned to meditation in its quest for stress management, greater creativity and productivity, and improved interpersonal relations. The reason for this great interest lies in the large amount of research that shows that with regular meditation the blood pressure can be reduced in hypertensive subjects, the heart slows, and external pressures don't seem to bother you as much. Anxiety and depression are reduced. The brainwaves, as seen in the EEG, show coherence between the left and right brain; you become more intuitive and creative. Life takes on greater meaning and purpose.

With continued regular meditation, you experience the Self, the Buddha in you. As Deepak Chopra says in his book, *Seven Spiritual Laws of Success*, the Self is the field of pure potentiality, the field of infinite correlation and infinite organizing power, the ultimate ground of creation. That is our real nature. Once you reach this, you find that everything is inseparably connected with everything else. You enjoy Unity Consciousness, in which "You see the Self in all beings and all beings in the Self." You discover the joy of the life throb of ages and the unbounded potential for creativity.

The doctrine of Dharma has always existed in the world. It has never perished. Some people have followed it scrupulously, knowingly or unknowingly, because it is part of them. The rest of us have to be reminded about its existence. The path of Dharma lies in front of you. You may have gone off it for the time being; you only have to take a few steps to the right or the left and you are on it once again. And as Juan Mascaro says in the introduction to his translation of the Dhammapada:

> We should know that the path of Dharma is the path of righteousness, the path of life which, as a matter of fact, we have to make with our own footsteps and our own actions. It is the path which leads to supreme Truth. It is the path of light, the path of love, the path of liberation and freedom, the path of the Creator himself, the path of God. Even if we do not reach the end of the journey when on this path, the joys of the pilgrimage are ours.

Once you are on the right path, fear of disease, aging, and death won't haunt you, especially if you have good fellow travelers.

Trouble arises only when we forget our real nature and behave worse than beasts. We humans believe that beasts are not capable of the nobler emotions and feelings, and cannot know what Dharma is. But what would the beasts have to say if they could talk?

A lion cub saw an army marching through the forest, and ran back to its cave to tell its mother about the movement of hundreds of soldiers with arms. The lioness replied, "They are going on a spree to slaughter their own species, other humans, their own kith and kin. They will do this in the name of religion or language, or to justify expansion of their territory. It may be that they don't want to share the water of the river which flows through their state into the neighboring state. They want to justify that the river belongs to them. Tomorrow they may claim the sun and the moon to be their property. They don't realize it is God who makes the rivers flow and the sun and moon to shine. Everyone and everything in the world belongs to the universe. We must share it while we are here. May God forgive these humans, my child, for they know not what they do."

During the journey on the path of Dharma, one is bound to face stress caused by obstacles and hurdles. As the progress towards our goal depends on our mental attitude and emotions, which are not always easy to handle, we must have inner calm to surmount them. It is here that our ancient wisdom comes to our rescue.

You are traveling in a plane and the weather suddenly becomes bad. Thunder and lightning are all around you, a strong wind is blowing in the opposite direction, slowing your speed so that it may appear you are not moving forward. And your flight is bumpy, with the plane jumping up and down and in all directions. A deep silence comes over the passengers as they look out at the dark storm clouds. The pilot is clever: instead of changing direction, he pulls the plane up to a higher altitude. There, everything is quiet. The speed is good, the turbulence gone, and the passengers are smiling again.

Similarly, when there are obstacles and hurdles in your path of Dharma, you have to raise your spirits and continue your journey. The obstacles will be surmounted when you fly higher, and you won't be overcome by the hurdles.

I am the outcome of my thoughts and deeds. If I cannot do everything, at least I can do something. Let me curb my pride, my passion, anger, or greed. This will enable me to be on the path of Dharma. I may not achieve salvation but I will lead a stress-free life.

From a higher level of consciousness, you can love un-conditionally and serve more effectively. There is no room for anger, bitterness, or hostility. Your actions are without attach-ment to results. You realize success and achievement are desirable, but not the only purpose of life. You gain inner harmony, joy, and peace. You have the opportunity to love, serve, and give, and thus fulfill the purpose of being here on this planet.

Our mission in life of treading the path of Dharma will succeed if we have courage and perseverance, which always come with devotion to and faith in God, the supreme Reality. A sense of frustration should never overcome you. The path of Dharma lies in front of you. It is yours for the asking. In the words of an ancient Irish blessing:

> May the road rise to meet you
> May the wind be always at your back
> And the warm sun shine on your face
> May the rains fall soft on your fields
> And may God hold you in the palm of His hand.

Appendices

Appendix 1: Religion, Scriptures, and the Concept of Various Gods in India

Sanatan Dharma is the religion of ancient India. Sanatan means ancient (since the beginning of time) and Dharma means the path of righteousness. This is the path we create with our thoughts and actions (Karma). For it we have to know the purpose of being here in this universe.

Some ancient injunctions are common to all religions, inherent in humans everywhere, including the remotest corners of the world unaffected by so-called modern civilizations, and there has never been any real difference of opinion on the definition of Truth. Satya (Truth) and Dharma are the two most important elements of the Vedic way of life. Dharma is a very broad concept governing both the life of man as an individual and the entire cosmos. The entire creation, both insentient and sentient, is bound by Dharma. Speaking the truth and showing reverence to our parents are two of the basic tenets of Dharma, as well as knowing the purpose of the great gift of life that humans are blessed with. The knowledge and wisdom we have from the ancient sages can guide us towards leading a life of love and fulfillment.

> Great streams of divine words flow out
> From the minds of sages, like rapids
> Rushing down a slope
> Surging with the high waves of wisdom
> They beat through all obstacles.
>
> RIG VEDA 4.58

The sages of ancient India believed that the Vedas—the books of knowledge—were created from the breath of God. The Vedas contain invocations, prayers in poetic form, that are very relevant to our day-to-day life, explaining all that is needed for a peaceful and happy existence in this world, and for ultimate salvation.

> Vast is the ocean of sacred words in the Vedas which
> Enlightens the universe with divine vision.
>
> RIG VEDA 1.1.12

The Upanishads, of which the Bhagvat Gita is considered to be one, were later appended to the Vedas in order to explain the philosophy of the truths expounded in them. The stories, legends, and myths contained in the Upanishads and other scriptures, such as the Puranas, are really only illustrations of the moral and spiritual truths, the philosophy of life and living, contained in the hymns and verses of the Vedas. Humanity is the most highly evolved species in creation on this planet, and the Vedic texts are precious gifts to mankind to remind us of our divine nature and our enlightenment.

> Life is the perennial search for Truth.
> The restless swan, the human soul, is on
> The journey infinite to find the Truth
> For thousands of years he is flying
> With his wings outstretched and
> The will to reach and the will to
> Reach the unscaled heights of heaven
> Higher and ever higher and ever higher
> The restless swan is on a journey infinite.
> He has all the blessings of the almighty God;
> His piercing eyes perceive all the universe
> Below, yet he knows no rest, no peace
> And keeps flying higher and ever higher
> The restless swan is on the journey infinite.
>
> RIG VEDA 10:8:18

The verses of the Vedas and the Upanishads stand unique in their age-old charm, and they will continue to cast their spell over humanity for all time to come.

Neither the Vedas nor the Upanishads mentioned the term "Hindu religion." The word "Hindu" came into being when the Aryans came to India. All those who crossed the mighty river Sindu in the northwest of undivided India were termed "Sindus." They were later called "Hindus," and much later "Indus," then "Indians." The word "Hindu" therefore originally only referred to those living in that part of the subcontinent. Christianity and Islam came along later and people who followed Sanatan Dharma are now wrongly supposed to belong to the "Hindu religion."

In the ancient times, the powers of the physical world were worshipped, including the Sun, the Moon, Heaven and Earth, Wind, Rain, Fire, the sacred rivers, and a number of gods who presided over the workings of Nature. This kind of polytheism was practiced not only in India but also in Greece, Rome and among many other ancient civilizations. The Roman gods supposedly assured the development of higher psychological functions: Minerva was the goddess of learning and wisdom, the arts and crafts; Apollo, the sun god, got the portfolios of poetry and prophecy; Hephaestus, the fire god and divine smith, got the portfolio of labor.

Similarly, the Indian mythological gods and goddesses, such as Lakshmi, Durga, and Siva all have their own roles. Lakshmi is the goddess of wealth, both material and spiritual; Durga is the eighteen-armed goddess who rides astride a lion and is worshipped as the destroyer of demons and all evils. Siva is one of the three aspects of the same divine Being—He is the destroyer. The other two aspects are Brahma and Vishnu, the creator and the preserver.

Some people in India still worship the gods as separate entities, but the majority understand that they are symbols or expressions of the One—the one and only God—and the vast majority of Indians worship Him only. The gods—or God—have to be invoked by inner sacrifice and called to us through the specific powers of mantras; we have to destroy the opposing forces, the powers of darkness, which conceal the light of wisdom from us.

Appendix 2: Sir Mohammed Iqbal

Iqbal has been acclaimed as the greatest Asian poet of the early twentieth century. He was the National Poet of erstwhile undivided India, and possessed great vision and insight into nature, human life, and human potential. His poems have a universal appeal.

He started writing poetry while he was a young man at college. He went on to study for a Masters in Philosophy at Cambridge University, and was later called to the Bar in London. He was awarded a Doctorate in Philosophy by Munich University in Germany, and was knighted by the British Government for his outstanding contribution to literature. And so Iqbal was now Sir Mohammed Iqbal.

I first read the poem mentioned on page 82 while I was at school. The poem was written in Urdu, which is one of the national language of India. Some of the Urdu words have very subtle meanings and it is difficult to find the English equivalents. Here is my own translation:

> There are many planets and galaxies
> Beyond the stars we can see.
> If you love God's creation
> You have to learn how to perceive its beauty and mystery.
> Your life is not the only one whose
> Fragrance can ride on the morning breeze.
> There are hundreds of others around you
> Whose fragrance can spread all around, even go against
>   the wind.
> You are a free bird, flying is your nature;
> Fly higher, higher, ever higher;
> There are skies, and skies beyond skies to explore.
> At one time I thought I was alone

Even though I was amongst many.
Now I realize we share each other's
Secrets and I was never alone or separate from you.

Appendix 3: Postures suitable for meditation

It is important to realize that in meditation the posture has to be one that is firm and in which the body feels at ease. An old Chinese Buddhist text says that "If the body is at ease, the Tao will prosper." You can even achieve this while sitting on a chair during meditation. However, you may wish to try the lotus or the sukham postures.

In the famous lotus posture (which some people find difficult), both feet are upturned on the thighs, the right foot on the left thigh, the left foot on the right, each as high up the thigh as possible. The knees should be kept down firmly against the floor. The hands should be rested along the knees, or clasped loosely in the lap.

The sukham posture is a half-lotus posture (sukham means comfortable). The right leg is bent at the knee and the right heel is pulled in against the perineum. The left leg is then bent and pulled back so that the left heel is against the pubic bone. Both

Lotus Posture   Sukham Posture
                                 (Posture of Comfort)

knees are kept down against the floor. The hands are positioned as they are in the lotus posture.

Both of these postures can be very comfortable for prolonged meditation.

Appendix 4: Subhash Chandra Bose

The Indian National Congress was led by Mahatma Gandhi, who had a policy of non-violence. Subhash Chandra Bose joined the party but did not agree with Mahatma Gandhi's pacifist approach. In 1942, at the height of World War II, Bose disappeared from India and resurfaced in Germany. He was reported to be an admirer of Hitler, who was fighting the deadliest war in history for personal glory and was also busy killing millions of innocent people in concentration camps and gas chambers. Bose met Adolf Hitler, and offered to launch his own Indian National Army (INA), enlisting Indian prisoners to fight the Allies.

The scheme did not materialize and Bose was sent to Tokyo in a submarine, where he met with the Japanese authorities before going on to Bangkok via Penanag. Bose had already announced the formation of the Indian National Army (INA) while he was in Germany, but he formally set it up while he was in Bangkok. Many of the Indian Army officers, such as Shah Nawaz, G. S. Dhillon, and P. K. Sehgal who were interred in Japanese jails as prisoners of war, joined the INA as generals and brigadiers. Bose donned a uniform and designated himself "Supreme Commander" of the INA. The Japanese used him and his name as propaganda against the Allied Forces.

To the British, Bose was a traitor and they did not believe that he or the INA could make any difference to the outcome of the war. When it came to an end in August 1945, Shah Nawaz, G. S. Dhillon, P. K. Sehgal, and many others were imprisoned and brought back to India, where they were court-martialed for treason under the Indian Army Act. As the war ended, the Japanese authorities announced that Subhash Chandra Bose had died in an air crash. A large sector of the Indian population did not believe the story and for them his "death" remains a mystery to this day.

Appendix 5: Swami Chinmayananda

Swami Chinmayananda was a modern sage (see page 288). He established the Chinmaya Mission in India and many other countries in the world, with a view to spreading the message of the Vedas and the Upanishads. There is a big center in New Delhi known as the "Chinmaya Center for World Understanding."

Eleven years or so ago, he came to Delhi from Bombay to conduct a week's seminar course. However, he was very unwell.

After a thorough clinical examination and some investigations, such as echocardiography, I told him, "Swami ji, your heart's function is impaired—you cannot be working for fifteen to sixteen hours a day dictating, counseling, giving interviews, taking lectures, conducting seminars, and what not. You need rest; you can work only for two to three hours a day."

"Okay," said Swami ji, "I have never disobeyed my doctor, I will work only for two hours. He will do the rest of the work for me." And then he recited the verse given on page 291: "I feel that God has chosen me / As one of His . . ."

Swami ji kept on working for fifteen to sixteen hours a day after that, for another eight years, until he left his mortal coil.

Glossary

Arjuna The mighty armed hero of the great epic *Mahabharta*. It was to him that Lord Krishna imparted the teachings of the Bhagavad Gita.

Ashtavakra A sage at the age of twelve years. The name literally means bent in eight places—as he was. The dialogue between him and Rajrishi Janaka forms the text of the ancient Ashtavakra Gita.

Bhagavad Gita The great ancient scripture of India. The dialogue between Arjuna and Krishna represents an exchange between an embodied soul and the Super Soul, the Supreme Consciousness, Krishna, who reveals the knowledge of life and living, and the path of Dharma. The Bhagavad Gita is a book of perennial wisdom, suggesting solutions for the constant conflicts played out in the battlefield of the human mind.

Bhagvatam Shrimad A popular devotional ancient Indian scripture containing legends, stories, and the teachings of various divinities—composed by Vyasa.

Bharat Natyam Literally "dance of India." The theme of a particular mythological story is displayed by the dancing physique and the subtle movements of the limbs, eyes, gestures, and facial expressions.

Bhikshu Bhiku A mendicant, a monk.

Brahman Derived from the root "Brh," which means to grow. It means bigger than the big, meaning the biggest or the infinite. Biggest when not associated with an object, it indicates the limitless. Brahman, the higher Self, the Supreme Consciousness.

Buddha Comes from the root "Budh," to be awake, to be conscious of, to know. Gautama became Buddha after enlightenment.

Chetna Consciousness, awareness, the field of supreme energy that illumines, pervades all beings and all things, running the show of the entire cosmos.

Dharma The Sanskrit word *Dharma* is derived from the Pali word

Dhamma, which comes from the Sanskrit root "Dhr," meaning to support— a spiritual law of righteousness.

Ego (Ahmkara)   Limited "I" awareness; identification with mind and body, self-image. The sense of doership or ownership.

Ganges (Ganga)   The sacred river that flows from the Himalayas through North India to the Bay of Bengal in the Indian Ocean.

Gopis   The milkmaids, childhood companions, and devotees of Krishna. They represent the world at large, whereas Krishna represents Consciousness. Gopis are revered as the embodiment of the ideal state of ecstatic devotion to God.

Gunas   Triangle of forces or qualities (satwa, rajas, tamas) opposed yet complementary. Satwa—purity and tranquility; rajas—passion and action; tamas—resistance and inertia.

Janaka   Saintly King of Mithila in ancient India, he was a sage and seeker of Truth.

Japa   Recitation of a mantra or the name of the Lord.

Jivanmukta   He who has realized the Truth of the oneness of the Self and Brahman as well as oneness with the whole universe. He is in the world but not of the world.

Karma   Physical, mental, or verbal action; the law of cause and effect. Also applies to the results of such actions in a previous life, this life, or a life hereafter—the law of Karma explains the apparent injustice in the world.

Krishna   Mythological God in human form, representing Consciousness/Super Soul. His teachings are contained in sacred texts—the Bhagvatam, the Mahabharata, and the Bhagavad Gita.

Kundalini   Coiled-up divine cosmic energy in the human body. When awakened by intense mediation, it leads to inner purification, increasing creativity, and performances.

Lila   Divine play of God, the dance of creation.

Maharishi   A great sage.

Mantra   A sacred word or sound invested with the power to transform and protect the one who recites it.

Meditation   An unbroken flow of thought towards the object of attention.

Namaz   A special type of prayer offered by Muslims, taught by Allah and the Holy Prophet. The body and mind has to be clean of impurities. Namaz must be offered five times a day at particular periods of time—praising the Prophet and Allah, and invoking His mercy and compassion for all.

Prana   Vital force of the body. Its origin is from the cosmos; it sustains life.

Pranayama   Breathing exercise by which the prana's entry into the body is regulated.

Prakriti   Elemental undifferentiated stuff of mind and matter; the energy by which all phenomena are projected. It is not the ultimate Reality. It is the power or effect of Brahman—Reality, in the same sense that heat is the effect of fire.

Purusha   Literally godhead that lives within the body. It is that same thing as Atman (word used in the Upanishads) or self; pure consciousness.

Ramayana   Literally the story of Rama, the eldest son of King Dashratha. It is the oldest mythological epic about life and the exploits of Rama, the apostle of virtue. It was written by the sage Volmiki.

Rishi   A seer of Truth, a sage.

Samadhi   Absence of thought waves; complete absorption or identification with the object of meditation.

Turiya   The transcendental state, the fourth state of consciousness beyond the waking, deep sleeping and dreaming state in which the true nature of Reality is directly perceived.

Upanishads   Literally "sitting at the feet of the Master." Spiritual treatises containing teaching that is both universal and eternal—112 Upanishads were written in Sanskrit 3,000 years ago; thirteen principal Upanishads have been translated into English.

Veda   Literally "knowledge"; or science of manifest or unmanifest creation.

Yoga   Union with the transcendent, which is the aim of various yoga practices including meditation, pranayama, and yogasnas involving special exercises termed Hatha Yoga.

Yoga Vasishtha   The ancient text on non-dual philosophy of life in which the seer Vasishtha instructs Lord Rama. The theme of the text is that the world is created by your mind.

Bibliography

Borysenko, Joan, *Guilt Is the Teacher, Love Is the Lesson*, New York: Warner Books, 1990.

Bracho, Frank, "Food Habits of the Pre-Columbian Peoples," *The Journal of Alternative and Complementary Medicine*, Washington, I, 2 1995.

Brown, Kerry, ed., *The Essential Teachings of Hinduism: Daily Readings from the Sacred Texts*, London: Arrow Books, 1988.

Budhananda, Swami, Teachings of Buddha in *Anguttara Nikaya* in *The Mind and its Control*, Pithoragarh: Pithoragarh Press, 1991.

Chinmayananda, Swami, *Ashtavakra Gita*, Bombay: Chinmaya Mission Trust, 1979.

——*The Holy Gita*, Bombay: Chinmaya Mission Trust, 1978.

Chopra, Deepak, M.D., *Return of the Rishi: A Doctor's Search for the Ultimate Healer*, Boston: Houghton Mifflin, 1988.

——*Creating Health*, Boston: Houghton Mifflin, 1987.

——*Quantum Healing, Exploring the Frontiers of Mind-Body Medicine*, New York: Bantam Books, 1989.

——*Perfect Health, The Complete Mind-Body Guide*, New York: Harmony Books, 1990.

——*Ageless Body, Timeless Mind, The Quantum Alternative to Growing Old*, New York: Harmony Books, 1993.

——*The Seven Spiritual Laws of Success: A Practical Guide to the Fulfillment of Your Dreams*, San Rafael, CA: Amber-Allen and New World Library, 1993.

Chopra, Gautama, *Child of the Dawn—A Magical Journey of Awakening*, San Rafael, CA: Amber-Allen, 1996.

Dossey, Larry, M.D., *Meaning and medicine, Lessons from a Doctor's Tales of Breakthrough and Healing*, New York: Bantam Books, 1991.

Douillard, John, *Body, Mind and Sport, The Mind-Body Guide to Life Long Fitness and Your Personal Best*, New York, Harmony Books, 1994.

Dyer, W. Wayne, *Real Magic, Creating Miracles in Everyday Life*, New York: Harper Collins, 1992.

Edelman, Marian Wright, *The Measures of Our Success, A Letter to My Children and Yours*, New York: Harper Collins, 1992.

Forem, Jack, *Transcendental Meditation, Mahrishi Mahesh Yogi and the Science of Creative Intelligence*, New York: E.P. Dutton & Co., 1974.

Frances, Moore Lappe, *Diet for a Small Planet*, New York: Ballantine Books, 1992.

Gibran, Kahlil, *The Prophet*, n.p.: One World Publications Edition, 1995.

Engel, George L., "Sudden and Rapid Death During Psychological Stress," *Annals of Internal Medicine*, 74, 771–82.

Mahesh Yogi, Maharishi, *Science of Being and Art of Living*, New York: Signet, 1968.

——*On the Bhagavad Gita, A New Translation and Commentary*, London: Penguin Books, 1967.

Mascaro, Juan, trans., *The Upanishads*, London: Penguin Books, 1979.

McClelland, David C., "Motivation and Immune Function in Health and Disease," Paper presented at the meeting of the Society of Behavioral Medicine, New Orleans, March 1985.

Mitchell, Stephen, ed., *The Enlightened Mind, An Anthology of Sacred Prose*, New York: Harper Perennial, 1991.

Nikhilananda, Swami, *Hinduism, Its Meaning for the Liberation of the Spirit*, Madras: Sri Ramakrishna Math, 1968.

Nisargadatta Maharaj, Sri, *I Am That*, Durham NC: ACOM Press, 1987.

Oates, Robert M., *Celebrating the Dawn, Maharishi Mahesh Yogi and the TM Technique*, New York: G.P. Putnam's Sons, 1976.

Ornish, Dean, *Reversing Heart Disease*, New York: Random House, 1990.

Parthasarthy, A., *The Vedanta Treatise*, Bombay: Vedanta Life Institute, 1984.

Pert, C. B., Hill, J. M., and Zipser, B., "Neurochemical Basis of Emotional Behavior," *Handbook of Neuropsychology*, Amsterdam: Elsevier, 1989.

Prabhavananda, Swami, *Patanjali's Yoga Sutras*, Translated with a new commentary by Swami Prabhavananda and Christopher Isherwood, Madras: Sri Ramakrishna Math Printing Press, 1991.

Radhakrishnan, S., *Bhagavad Gita*, Bombay: Blackie & Son, 1982.

Robbins, John, *Diet for A New World*, New York: Avon Books, 1992.

Russell, Peter, *Brain Book*, New York: Penguin Books, 1979.

Siegal, S. Bernie, *Peace, Love & Healing*, London: Arrow Books, 1991.

Sivananda, Swami, *Ten Upanishads*, Tehri Garwal: The Divine Life Society, 1973.

Srinivasan, M., "Occult Chemistry Re-evaluated: Pre-emptying the Discovery of Isotopes, of Quarks and Sub-quarks," *The Hindu*, October 30 and November 6, 1994.

Toben, Bob and Wolf, Fred Alan, *Toward An Explanation of the Unexplainable*, New York: Bantam Books, 1987.

Venkatesananda, Swami, *The Concise Yoga Vasistha*, New York: State University of New York Press, 1984.

Vivekananda, Swami, *Karma Yoga—The Yoga of Action*, Pithoragarh: Advaita Ashram, 1995.

Yogananda, Paramhansa, *Man's Eternal Quest and Other Talks*, Los Angeles: Oxford and IBN Publication, 1975.

Index